The Battle of Crecy
A Campaign in Context

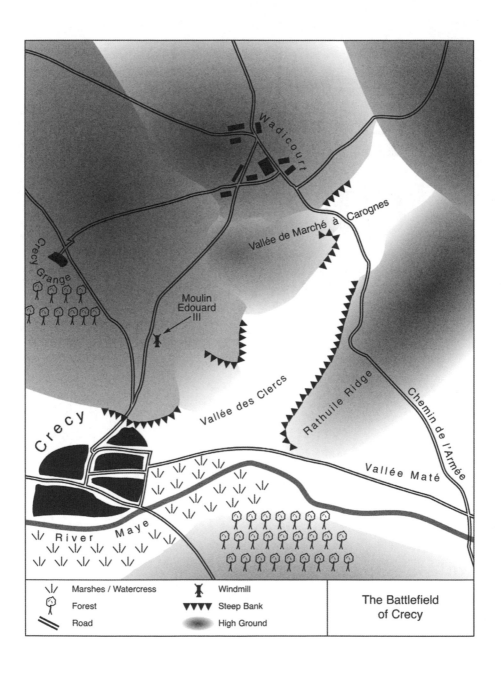

Wadicourt

Vallée de Marché à Carognes

Crecy Grange

Moulin Edouard III

Vallée des Clercs

Rathuile Ridge

Chemin de l'Armée

Crecy

Vallée Maté

River Maye

	Marshes / Watercress		Windmill		The Battlefield
	Forest		Steep Bank		of Crecy
	Road		High Ground		

THE BATTLE OF CRECY

A CAMPAIGN IN CONTEXT

by

Rupert Matthews

SPELLMOUNT

British Library Cataloguing in Publication Data:
A catalogue record for this book is available
from the British Library

Copyright © Rupert Matthews 2007
Illustrations and maps by the author.
Photographs from the author's collection
unless otherwise indicated

ISBN 1-86227-369-3

ISBN 978-1-86227-369-6

First published in the UK in 2007 by
Spellmount Limited
The Mill, Brimscombe Port
Stroud, Gloucestershire GL5 2QG

Tel: 01453 883300
Fax: 01453 883233
Website: www.spellmount.com

1 3 5 7 9 8 6 4 2

Printed in Great Britain by
Oaklands Book Services
Stonehouse, Gloucestershire GL10 3RQ

Contents

List of Maps

Acknowledgements

I would like to thank two re-enactment groups. The Medieval Combat Society, which can be contacted via their website www.themcs. org, and the Company of St Barbara, which likewise has a website www.co-of-stbarbara.co.uk. I would also like to thank Kelly Ostler for her support and assistance on my visits to the places mentioned in this book – and especially for her excellent mapreading skills when finding the more obscure locations along unmarked French country lanes.

Front jacket image: © The British Library. An illustration of the battle from Froissart's *Grandes Chroniques de France*, folio 152v. Towards the end of the battle, 'Sir John of Hainault … said to the [French] king "Sir, depart hence, for it is time, do not lose yourself wilfully, if you suffer loss at this time, you shall recover it another season." And so he took the king's horse by the bridle and led him away perforce.'

Preface

The Battle of Crecy changed everything. Society, warfare, international relations: nothing was ever the same again. Before the Crecy campaign began, France was recognised as having the greatest, most powerful and most modern army in all Christendom. England was thought of as a prosperous but relatively backward kingdom lying somewhere in the sea off the European coast. But six hours of bloodshed, slaughter and heroism beyond imagining changed all that. The pride of France was humbled, her army destroyed and her king sent as a wounded fugitive fleeing through the foggy night.

But it was not only the mighty French army that was smashed at Crecy. Future generations would look back on the dramatic events of that summer's day as the beginning of the end for the knight in armour. It would be some decades before the glittering figure of the armoured horseman vanished from the battlefields of Europe, but the seeds of his destruction were sown at Crecy.

It was the massed archery of the English that laid low the armoured knights who had ruled the battlefield supreme for generations. And with his place as master of the battlefield went the claim to social superiority that the knight held across Europe. If he could no longer keep his lands and dependents safe from attack, what was the point of his existence? It was a question that took many years to answer.

Despite what is often thought, there was nothing new about either the bows or the arrows used at Crecy. Indeed, in some ways, by 1346 the English or Welsh longbow was an old-fashioned weapon. But, as we shall see, this time it was used in a novel and frighteningly effective way.

The humble social position of the archers made the longbow's effectiveness all the more shocking and surprising to contemporaries. These men had no noble blood in their veins, still less any pretensions to wealth or sophistication. Yet they dominated the battlefield at Crecy, and would continue to do so for generations to come.

The shock of the new can be overstated. The archers were not uneducated, illiterate peasants slaughtering noblemen. They were, by and large, drawn from the ranks of fairly prosperous farmers and woodsmen who could afford the cost of the gear needed to go on campaign. And the men they killed so effectively were not only the very rich. Some knights had little more land and wealth than did a successful farmer.

Nonetheless, the events at Crecy sent shockwaves across Europe. The charge of the heavily armoured knights had been defeated in open battle. Moreover, the dead numbered among them some of the most skilled and famous soliders in all Christendom. One king was killed, another injured and two more turned in flight. Men could hardly believe it when they heard the news.

The story of the Hundred Years War between England and France, of which the Crecy Campaign is but a part, is relatively well known. The events were dramatic, exciting and far-reaching in their importance, so they were diligently recorded at the time and have been much explored by historians since. Of all the incidents in these wars, which stretched over several generations, few were as dramatic as the Crecy Campaign, the subject of this book. The Crecy Campaign has been rather overshadowed in more recent years by the Agincourt campaign – largely because William Shakespeare made it a feature of his play *Henry V*, and because it has featured in two great movies made of the play. But to contemporaries, the Agincourt campaign lacked the shock and horror of Crecy. At Agincourt the slaughter was neither as great nor as unexpected.

Those modern books that deal with the Hundred Years War tend to concentrate on the political side of the conflict. Battles and campaigns, though they are often dealt with in some detail, are seen as background to, and results of, the intrigues and machinations of the rulers and nobles who fill the pages of these writings.

For a military historian, this can all be rather frustrating. The reasons for battles and who won them are given clearly enough, but only very rarely is there any discussion about how the battles were fought. We read almost nothing about weapons, tactics or logistics. But how were the armies kept supplied with food? How did a French knight expect to fight his battles? What made the archers so special on the battlefield?

In a way this neglect is fair enough. The most widely available account of the Crecy Campaign – both in the fourteenth century and today – is that given in the *Chronicles* of Jean Froissart. And Froissart did not put pen to paper for the fun of it. He was producing a book designed to please his patrons and to impress the book-buying public, which in his day was a very restricted group of wealthy men. Froissart was writing for a readership made up largely of knights and noblemen. He simply did not need to tell his readers much that we, reading today, want to know. He did not need to set down detail on the weapons of the time, for his readers would have seen them for themselves. He did not need to explain how troops formed up for battle, as his readers would already have known.

The effects of this assumption of knowledge on the part of the reader can, in places, be unfortunate and lead to some serious misunderstandings. Froissart writes at length about individual acts of bravery by named knights, squires and noblemen. He does so not because these affected the outcome of a battle or campaign to any great extent, but because this was what his readers wanted to read. The chances were that they either knew the men concerned, had seen them in action at a tournament or at least knew somebody who had. Froissart does mention that archers, hobilars and other humble soldiers were present, but does not give very much detail about them. These men did not buy his book and could not give him valuable patronage.

Unfortunately, it can be difficult to peek behind the chivalric chronicles of Froissart and his like to see what was going on in reality. It is not that the contemporary writers were being untruthful or dishonest, merely that they were writing with assumptions and knowledge that we do not possess.

Imagine a modern writer producing an account of the Allied invasion of Normandy on D-Day, 6 June 1944. He would not need to explain what a tank was, nor an aircraft. He would not need to explain that Hitler was dictator of Germany nor that Churchill was Prime Minister of Britain. All this he could assume his readers would already know. He could just get on with telling the story of what happened. But for a reader in the twenty-seventh century, unfamiliar with the situation in the mid-twenieth century, all this and much more would need to be explained for events to make sense.

If that writer were to be writing an article to appear on the website run by one of the regiments that had taken part in the landings, it is inevitable that he would make much about that regiment's actions. He would name the regimental commander, its junior officers and any man that won a medal or otherwise distinguished himself that day. The readership of the article would want to learn all this detail, and could be assumed to know pretty much what the bigger picture had been. Other regiments would get more cursory treatment, not because they were less important to the outcome of the battle but because the readership would not be so interested in them.

This is how we must approach the contemporary sources for the Crecy campaign. They are, by and large, accurate. But they are partial. Each gives only a part of the truth, or even a version of it.

This book is an attempt to explain to the general reader the reality of warfare in the year 1346. It seeks to give a plausible recreation of the tactics used in the Crecy Campaign and to put them into the context of the time. It explains what the weapons were like and how they were used in action. It describes the usual tactics of the different military units involved and how these would have impacted on each other in battle. I have walked the battlefields of the campaign on foot and have handled replica weapons at some length. I have then used this information to put together an account of the campaign itself.

I would especially like to thank two re-enactment groups. Their help and support has been invaluable – though any errors which remain in this book are mine, not theirs. I should have listened more carefully. The Medieval Combat Society was particularly helpful to me in understanding the technical abilities of both archers and men-at-arms at this period. I would recommend anyone interested in this subject to visit their website www.themcs.org, and to attend one of their public demonstrations held at various events during the summer in Britain. Also of great assistance was the Company of St Barbara, who own and operate a magnificent replica fourteenth-century bombard, as well as assorted medieval firearms of various dates and sizes. Again, I would recommend that anyone with an interest in early firearms should visit their informative website www.co-of-stbarbara.co.uk and try to attend one of their firing demonstrations. I would also like to thank Kelly Ostler for her support and assistance on my visits to the places mentioned in this book – and especially for her excellent mapreading skills when finding the more obscure locations down unsignposted French country lanes.

It is usual for an historian to explain something of the way in which he has treated his sources. Footnotes are the usual academic way of doing this, but I find that the constant flicking back and forth can spoil the flow of a work for a reader. Instead, I have mentioned my sources in the body of the work and how I have interpreted them. But I have done so only when dealing with a contentious issue or when I felt it necessary for one reason or another. I shall make some more general points here.

The first and for many the main source for the history of the wars of this period are the *Chronicles of England, France and Spain* written by Jean Froissart. This book is well written, packed with exciting stories and very informative. It is also very long.

Froissart was born in Valenciennes, now in France but then part of the independent County of Hainault, in 1335. He was well educated and by the age of twenty-three was a minor cleric looking for a job. In 1361 he came to London armed with an introduction to England's Queen Philippa – who was not only wife to King Edward III of England, but also a native of Hainault. Crucially Froissart also had a book he had written about the Battle of Poitiers, which had taken place in 1356. The book was an immediate success with Queen Philippa, who gave him a post in her household and asked him to write a history of the conflict that we now know as the Hundred Years War, but which was then barely thirty years old.

Froissart's great work was interrupted by his being sent on numerous diplomatic missions by Queen Philippa and her son, Edward of Woodstock, the Black Prince. In 1369 Queen Philippa died and Froissart was once more out of work. He returned to Valenciennes, but his great work was by this stage well advanced. He had travelled widely and had spoken to many of the men who had seen events at first hand. Many of these men and their friends knew that Froissart was compiling a history, and they began to ask him for copies. Froissart had found a way to make a living.

Froissart spent the rest of his life producing copies of his *Chronicles*, though soon most copies were being written out laboriously by a team of clerks he employed. All this time Froissart continued to correspond with the men who had taken part in various events, adding to the detail and accuracy of his work.

Of the many dozens of copies churned out by Froissart and his clerks, there are three basic versions, known as redactions. The First Redaction was produced in about 1373. This is the shortest of the three and draws most heavily on English sources. By the time the Second Redaction had been produced in 1383, Froissart had been in contact with several men whose fathers had been in the French army at Crecy and who wanted their side of the story to be included. He had also met and spent much time talking to Sir John Chandos, who had been a very young and junior English knight at Crecy but by the time Froissart met him was one of the most famous warriors in Europe. The Third Redaction was produced in 1400, though the differences between this and the earlier works are concerned chiefly with the later years of the war and have little to do with Crecy. Froissart died in 1410.

Although Froissart does not mention it, he uses for the basic outline of events in the years before 1350 another chronicle, that of Jean le Bel. Le Bel was born into the minor nobility of Hainault at Liege in 1290, entering the clergy in 1313. He wrote his *Chronicle* in about 1355 at the request of John of Hainault, who was happy to give Le Bel the benefit of his considerable experience. We shall meet John of Hainault later in this book as a close companion of King Philip of France.

Le Bel drew on fewer sources than did Froissart, and those that he did use were more from the French side than the English. Like Froissart, Le Bel was writing for an aristocratic audience and so devotes more time to knights and chivalry than to archers and common soldiers. He intended his work to be read aloud, so he includes some almost poetic sequences, though the beauty of these is generally lost in translation from medieval Picard French into modern English.

Geoffrey le Baker came from Swinbrook in Oxfordshire and wrote a chronicle in about 1357 for his patron Sir Thomas More, a local land-owner and MP. Le Baker seems to have drawn largely on written sources, some of which survive and some of which do not. His work is useful as it gives some very basic accounts of events and exploits that appear in much embroidered and more elaborate form in Froissart. This chronicle was produced by and for the knightly class, rather than for noblemen. It is less elaborate than the works of Froissart and Le Bel and is more concerned with the main events and why they happened than with chivalrous exploits by noblemen.

The anonymous writer known as the Bourgeois of Valenciennes wrote a work called *Récits* in about 1370, a work of local history. In it he devotes a few pages to the Crecy campaign. He details the exploits of a local knight named Oliver de Ghistels who was with the English army at Crecy, and goes into some detail about the organisation of the English army. Crucially he gives details about the tactical deployment of the archers, which we shall deal with in Chapter 4.

Another local history of great interest is the history of Florence written by the Italian Giovanni Villani. This work includes an account of Crecy that seems to be drawn from discussions with one or more of the Italian crossbowmen who served with the French army and who returned to Italy soon after the battle. This account clearly comes from a professional soldier and goes into some detail about tactics, weapons and manoeuvres. As we shall see, Villani presents a rather different picture of the battle from that which can be deduced from other sources, but this probably has as much to do with the viewpoint of the Italian crossbowmen as anything else.

The French chronicles offer far less detail about the battle itself or the campaign. They are concerned with the political events that surrounded the military action and with the men who died. The *Grand Chroniques de France*, for instance, were written at the royal court for the royal court and about the royal court. Their only contribution to recreating the events of the Crecy Campaign is the section that bemoans the fact that so many French noblemen were killed by 'men of no value': the archers.

That said, some French chronicles do add some details of interest. The *St Omer Chronicle* gives a list of the more senior figures among the French dead. The *Chronique de Flandre* goes into some detail about the English position and dispositions at the battle which seem to be drawn from the memory or writings of a herald who was present at the battle on the French side. It is almost as if the herald is recounting the view he had from the French side of the valley of the banners of knights that he recognised and where they stood in the English army.

Other chronicles and accounts written after the event generally repeat the information from the more important sources, though here and there they seem to include information passed on by an eyewitness that is not included elsewhere.

Of great use, though they must be interpreted with care, are the sources that were written down in the year 1346 itself. Four members of the organisational staff of the English army wrote letters home that have survived. Bartholomew Burghersh wrote letters on 17 July and 29 July. Michael Northburgh, who was particularly close to King Edward, wrote on 27 July and on 4 September. The Chancellor of St Paul's wrote on 17 July and Richard Wynkeley wrote on 2 September.

All these men were at Crecy and were close to King Edward throughout the campaign. Unfortunately, none of them were military men so
they were not in the forefront of battle. They may have been in the baggage camp when the fighting took place, but that does at least put them
very close to the action and able to talk to men as they came back to
rest after conflict. Their accounts are all lucid and fascinating, but sadly
short.

King Edward III himself wrote a letter home on 3 September. This is
very much an official letter written in a rush. It announces the victory of
Crecy and emphasises the extent of the achievement, but says little about
the actual fighting. The messenger was expected to carry such details
verbally and to answer questions as they arose.

We also have a document that is generally known as the *Acta Bellicosa*,
or *Acts of War*. This has survived in only one manuscript, which unfortunately is damaged. It reads very much like a campaign diary kept by a
senior knight who served in the Advance Guard of the English army and
was close to the Black Prince. The *Acta Bellicosa* is detailed and – whenever
it can be checked against another source – accurate. Sadly, the sole surviving copy breaks off just before the battle of Crecy itself.

Finally, there is the fascinating bureaucratic record known as the *Kitchen
Journal*. This is the account book kept by the head of King Edward's
household kitchen throughout the campaign. It lists all moneys spent
by the kitchen while away from England. Crucially, it includes the place
where the accounts were drawn up each evening – in other words the
place where King Edward camped. It is therefore possible to trace the
movements of the English army with great accuracy. In passing, the
accounts also give an indication of how well the king (and therefore, one
must assume, the army), was dining. Some days the table groaned under
the weight of plundered roast ox and grilled sheep. Other days only a few
bowls of porridge and vegetables were on offer.

It must be assumed that similar contemporary French letters and documents existed, but most of the royal archives were lost during the French
Revolution and nothing relevant to the Crecy campaign survives.

There are many deductions that I have made in this book based on the
material in the sources. Some of these I explain in detail where I think this
is necessary, and others I do not. No doubt some readers and scholars
will disagree with me, but for better or worse, this is my interpretation
of events. It is based on what I believe to be sound logic, on an understanding of how war was organised and fought in that age and on my
understanding of how men thought back then – which was often very
different from how men think today.

I have done my best to produce a readable and yet well-researched
account of a military campaign that took place almost 600 years ago.
Reader, it is over to you.

Cast of Characters

While names such as King Edward III and the Black Prince will be familiar to modern readers, some of the characters that will be met in this book will be rather less well known. A few will be obscure even to specialists of the period. To aid the reader in making sense of the sometimes convoluted relationships between the people, I give a Cast of Characters.

Agace, Gobin	French peasant from Oiseville who gave the English information regarding the ford at Blanchtaque.
d'Alencon, Count	Charles Valois. Younger brother of King Philip VI and commander of the French rear guard at Crecy.
Amadeus VI	Count of Savoy and ally of France. He sent a force of his men to serve with Philip in the Crecy campaign.
d'Annequin, Godfrey	French nobleman. During the Crecy campaign he held the city of Béthune for King Philip.
d'Artois, Robert	1) Exiled French nobleman serving King Edward III from 1336. 2) His father, commander of the French army at the Battle of Courtrai in 1302.
Attewoode, Sir Edward	English knight from Staffordshire. During the Crecy campaign he served in the king's division.

Arundel, Earl of	Richard Fitzalan. English nobleman and administrator. He served in the rear guard during the Crecy campaign.
Aubert, Etienne	Cardinal Bishop of Ostia. Sent by the Pope to try to broker a peace between Edward and Philip during the Crecy campaign.
d'Aubigny, Olivier	French nobleman. He served on King Philip's staff during the Crecy campaign.
Aubyn, Robert	English gunner. Edward's royal artillator who both produced gunpowder and handled guns on campaign.
d'Aufremont, Lord	French nobleman from near Amiens.
Babbaveria	Italian mercenary naval commander who fought on the French side at the Battle of Sluys.
le Baker, Geoffrey	Clergyman from Oxfordshire who wrote a chronicle in 1357 of recent English history, including Crecy.
Balliol, Edward	Scottish nobleman and claimant to the Scottish throne who was supported by Edward III.
Basset, Sir Ralph	English knight who administered the Duchy of Aquitaine on behalf of King Edward II of England.
de la Baume, Galois	French nobleman. In the Crecy campaign he was in overall command of the infantry in the French army.
Béhuchet, Sir Nicholas	French admiral. Joint commander of the French fleet at the Battle of Sluys.
le Bel, Jean	A clergyman from Liege who wrote a chronicle in about 1355 that included a lengthy section on Crecy.

Bertrand, Robert	Lord of Bricquebec. French nobleman from Normandy who led the initial French resistance to the English invasion, and who had a family feud with Godfrey de Harcourt.
Benedict XII	Pope 1334–42. Dedicated to reform of the Church, Benedict chose not to be involved in international politics and did little to halt the growing enmity between England and France.
Black Prince	See Edward, the Black Prince. Strictly speaking this nickname is anachronistic as it was given to Edward later in his life by the French and did not enter common English usage until the sixteenth century. It is, however, how he is generally known today. In 1346 he was usually called Edward of Woodstock, from his birthplace.
de Blois, Charles	Claimant to the Duchy of Brittany. His claim was supported by Philip VI, his uncle.
de Blois, Louis	French nobleman and brother to Charles de Blois.
Bohemia, King John of	See John, King of Bohemia.
de Boys, Viscount John	French nobleman. During the Crecy campaign King Philip gave him the task of guarding the bridge over the Seine at Pont de l'Arche.
Burghersh, Bartholomew	Tutor to the Black Prince who accompanied his teenage charge on campaign.
Ceccano, Annibale	Cardinal Archbishop of Naples. Sent by the Pope to try to broker a peace between Edward and Philip during the Crecy campaign.

Chandos, Sir John	English knight on the Crecy campaign. He later became one of the most respected military commanders in Europe.
Charles IV	King of the Romans 1346–55, later Holy Roman Emperor 1355–78. Son of King John of Bohemia he served with the French army during the Crecy campaign.
Charles IV	King of France 1322–1328. Last king of the Capet Dynasty, his death without a male heir plunged France into a dispute over the succession.
Clement VI	Pope 1342–52. A learned theologian. Clement VI was born Pierre d'Egleton and the English suspected that he favoured his native France during negotiations that he brokered between the two kingdoms.
de Clisson, Olivier	French nobleman executed for treason by Philip VI in 1343.
Cobham, Sir Reginald	English soldier and diplomat. One of the experienced knights put to assist the Black Prince during the Crecy campaign.
Collard-en-Ver	French minor nobleman. He was tasked by King Philip with defending Abbeville during the Crecy campaign.
Colville, Sir Thomas	English knight from Bukdensike, Yorkshire, who served on the Crecy campaign, probably in the rear guard.
Coupland, John	English esquire who captured King David of Scotland at the Battle of Neville's Cross.
de Courant, Pierre	French Governor of Amiens in 1337.
Dagworth, Sir Thomas	English knight. He commanded English forces in Brittany in 1346.

CAST OF CHARACTERS

Daniel, Sir Thomas — English knight. He served in the rear division during the Crecy campaign.

Daunay, Sir John — English knight on the Crecy campaign.

David II — King of Scotland 1329–71, son of Robert the Bruce. His claim to the throne was disputed by Edward Balliol.

Derby, Earl of — Later Earl of Lancaster. English soldier and nobleman who commanded English forces in Aquitaine in 1346.

Despencer, Sir Hugh — English knight serving in the rear division during the Crecy campaign, son of another Hugh Despencer who had been executed for treason during the reign of Edward II.

Doria, Ottone — Genoese nobleman. Commander of mercenary soldiers who served King Philip VI in 1346.

Douglas, Sir William — Scottish knight. A senior commander of the Scots army at the Battle of Neville's Cross.

Durham, Bishop of — Thomas Hatfield. Senior English cleric and administrator. Formal commander of the English rearguard during the Crecy Campaign.

Edward II — King of England 1307–27. Father of King Edward III.

Edward III — King of England, son of King Edward II and father to the Black Prince.

Edward, the Black Prince — Eldest son and heir of King Edward III of England. He commanded the English advance guard in the Crecy campaign.

Eleanor of Aquitaine — Duchess of Aquitaine 1137–1204. Her marriage to King Henry II of England

	brought Aquitaine to the English crown and so began centuries of conflict with the French crown.
d'Estracelles, Jacques	French knight. Standard bearer to the Count d'Alencon at Crecy.
d'Eu, Count	1) Raoul II de Brienne, Constable of France who died in 1344 due to an tournament injury. 2) His son Raoul III de Brienne, also Constable of France, who held Caen against the English in 1346.
du Fay, Sir Godemar	Burgundian soldier of fortune serving King Philip of France during the Crecy campaign.
Ferrers, Sir Robert	English knight. Serving in Edward's division during the Crecy campaign, Ferrers had the rank of knight banneret.
FitzSimon, Sir Richard	English knight. In the Crecy campaign he served as the Black Prince's standard bearer.
Froissart, Jean	Professional writer who produced a chronicle that covered the histories of France, England and Spain during much of the fourteenth century.
Geoffrey of Maldon	English monk and noted theologian. He acted as a messenger for King Edward in 1346.
Ghistels, Sir Olivier	Flemish knight serving with King Edward in the Crecy campaign. His recollections formed the main source for Crecy used by the chronicler known as the Bourgeois of Valenciennes.
Grimaldi, Carlo	Lord of Monaco. Mercenary commander of naval and land forces who served King Philip VI in 1346.

de Harcourt, Godfrey | Exiled French nobleman from Normandy who served in the English army in 1346 with the official title of Marshal. He had a family feud with Robert Bertrand.

de Harcourt, John | French nobleman, brother of Godfrey. He served with King Philip in the Crecy campaign.

Hastings, Sir Hugh | English soldier. In 1346 he commanded a small English force supporting the Flemish rebels in Flanders.

Henry II | King of England 1154–1189. His marriage to Eleanor of Aquitaine brought that duchy under the control of the English crown.

de la Heuse, William | Chivalrous French knight fighting against the English in Brittany in 1346.

Holland, Richard | Constable of Nottingham Castle who helped Edward III overthrow Roger Mortimer.

Holland, Sir Thomas | English soldier and diplomat. One of the experienced knights put to assist the Black Prince during the Crecy campaign. Later Earl of Kent.

Huntingdon, Earl of | William Clinton. English noblemen. He began the Crecy campaign, but returned to England after the capture of Caen suffering from sickness.

Hurley, William | English carpenter. During the Crecy campaign he commanded the carpenters that accompanied the English army.

Isabel | Queen of England 1308–1358. Sister of King Charles IV of France. Wife of Edward II, whom she had murdered, and mother of Edward III, who imprisoned her for her crime.

Isabelle	Prioress of Poissy and sister to King Philip VI.
de l'Isle, Bertrand	French Count, joint commander of French forces in Aquitaine in 1345.
James	King of Majorca. Ally of France, he served with King Philip VI in 1346.
Jeanne	Countess of Hainault. Mother of Queen Philippa and grand-daughter of King Philip III of France.
Joan	"The Fair Maid of Kent". Heiress to the Earldom of Kent and a famous beauty. She married first Sir Thomas Holland and later the Black Prince.
John	King of Bohemia 1311–46. King John was born into the Ducal family of Luxembourg, acquiring the Bohemian crown through marriage. He was one of the foremost soldiers of his generation and a widely respected tournament champion and paragon of chivalry. He is variously known as John of Luxembourg, from his place of birth, or Blind John, on account of his failing eyesight.
John XXII	Pope 1316–34. A competent administrator who overhauled the papal court and sought to broker peace between England and France.
John, Count of Hainault	The ruler of the independent County of Hainault and ally of France. He served on the personal staff of King Philip of France during the Crecy campaign.
John, Duke of Normandy	Eldest son of Philip VI and later King John II of France. He commanded French forces in Aquitaine in 1346.
Lancaster, Earl of.	See Derby, Earl of.

Lorraine, Raoul Duke of	French nobleman who served in the Crecy campaign.
Louis IV	Holy Roman Emperor 1328–47. At first an ally of Edward III, later neutral he was embroiled in legal disputes with the papacy that absorbed most of his time. Sometimes known as Ludwig IV.
Louis VII	King of France 1137–80. His divorce of Eleanor of Aquitaine in 1152 allowed her to marry King Henry II of England.
Louis, Count of Vaud	Nobleman from Savoy who led that country's men in French service during the Crecy campaign.
Mar, Donald, Earl of	Scottish nobleman and Regent for King David II during his minority.
Marsh, Sir Richard	English knight on the Crecy campaign.
Mauny, Walter	Knight from Hainault who supported Jeanne de Montfort and later served King Edward III.
le Moine, Henri	French nobleman. He served on King Philip's staff during the Crecy campaign.
de Montfort, Jeanne	Wife of John de Montfort, she led his supporters while he was imprisoned by Philip VI.
de Montfort, John	Claimant to the Duchy of Brittany. His claim was supported by Edward III.
de Montmorency, Charles	Marshal of France. He served alongside King Philip in the Crecy campaign.
de Montpezat, Bernard	Nobleman in Aquitaine whose actions created the initial spark that led to war between England and France.

Mortimer, Roger	1) Earl of March. Lover of Queen Isabel. He arranged the murder of King Edward II and was executed by King Edward III. 2) His son. In 1346 he was knighted by Edward III but was as yet untried in battle and loyalty.
de Nanteuil, Sir Jean	Grand Prior of the Knights of St John in France.
Neville, Sir Ralph	English knight. Commander of the English army at the Battle of Neville's Cross.
Northburgh, Michael	A clergyman and senior administrator within the English Royal Household.
Northampton, Earl of	William Bohun. English soldier and nobleman who served as Constable of the English army in 1346.
Norwich, Sir Thomas	English knight. In the Crecy campaign he served with the Black Prince's division.
de Noyers, Sir Miles	French knight. In 1346 he was personal standard bearer to King Philip VI, carrying the sacred Oriflamme flag.
Pembroke, Earl of	Lawrence Hastings. English soldier, second in command of English forces in Aquitaine 1345.
Percy, Sir Henry	English knight. A member of the rich and powerful northern family that included the Earls of Northumberland.
Philip VI	King of France 1328–50. Formerly Count of Valois and founder of the Valois Dynasty.
Philippa of Hainault	Queen of England, wife of King Edward III and mother of Edward, the Black Prince.

de Poitiers, Louis	French Count, joint commander of French forces in Aquitaine in 1345.
Quiréret, Sir Hugh	French admiral. Joint commander of the French fleet at the Battle of Sluys.
de Renesse, John	Commander of the Dutch army at the Battle of Courtrai in 1302.
de Revel, Lord	French nobleman from near Amiens.
St Albans, Richard	English carpenter. During the Crecy campaign he was deputy to William Hurley.
de Saint-Pierre, Eustache	A leading citizen of Calais.
de St Pol, Count	French nobleman tasked by King Philip with defending the port of St Valery during the Crecy campaign.
de St Venant, Robert	Marshal of France. He served alongside King Philip in the Crecy campaign.
Salisbury, Earl of	William Montacute. Aged just 16, Salisbury served with his uncle in the King's division in the Crecy Campaign.
de Senzeille, Thierry	Hainault nobleman, standard bearer to Count John of Hainault.
Simon	Count of Salm. Ally of France who served with King Philip in the Crecy campaign.
Sir Robert Stewart	Scottish knight. A senior commander of the Scots army at the Battle of Neville's Cross.
Stafford, Sir Richard	English soldier. One of the experienced knights put to assist the Black Prince during the Crecy campaign.
Stratford, John	Archbishop of Canterbury 1333–48. Senior government official during the early years of Edward III's reign.

Suffolk, Earl of	Robert Ufford. English nobleman and close friend of Edward III. He served with the English rearguard in the Crecy campaign.
Swynbourne, Sir Adam	English soldier. In the Crecy Campaign he served as Deputy Constable to the Earl of Northampton.
Talbot, Sir Richard	English knight. Personal steward to King Edward in 1346.
Talbot, Sir Thomas	English knight. He served in the King's division during the Crecy campaign.
Tancarville, Count of	Jean de Melun. French nobleman and senior government official.
Tyrel, John	Lord of Poix. French nobleman serving with King Philip during the Crecy campaign.
Ughtred, Sir Thomas	English soldier. One of the experienced knights put to assist the Black Prince during the Crecy campaign, he also held the position of Deputy Marshal.
Valenciennes, Bourgeois of	Anonymous writer of a local history of Valenciennes which was completed about 1370.
de Vienne, Sir John	French nobleman. In 1346 he commanded the garrison of Calais for King Philip.
Villani, Giovanni	Historian who produced a history of Florence in 1357. The work includes details of Crecy apparently drawn from the Italian mercenaries who fought on the French side.
Warwick, Earl of	Thomas Beauchamp. English soldier and nobleman who served as one of the Marshals of the English army in 1346.

William	Count of Hainault, father of Queen Philippa. He died in 1345.
William	Count of Namur. Ally of France who served with King Philip in the Crecy campaign.
Wynkeley, Richard	A clerk within the English Royal Household, apparently responsible for drafting official letters for King Edward III.

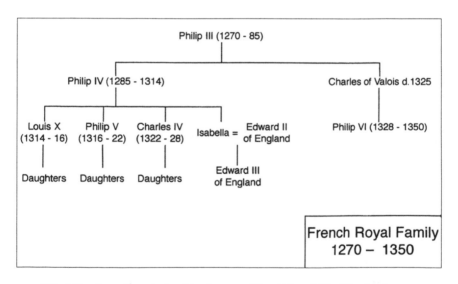

This table shows the relationships between King Edward III of England and the French royal family. Note the deaths in short succession of three French kings without male heirs. It was this unexpected series of events that plunged France into a dynastic dispute with England.

I

The Hundred Years War

The Battle of Crecy was the first major land battle in the long, drawn-out series of wars that are today collectively known as the Hundred Years War. But lengthy and complex as the war was to prove to be, it was itself only part of a longer struggle between the ruling dynasties of England and France which was already generations old by the time the armies met at Crecy.

The trouble had begun in 1152 when Eleanor, Duchess of Aquitaine, had divorced King Louis VII of France and married instead King Henry II of England. It was not so much lovelorn jealousy that caused ill feeling as the fact that Eleanor took with her the Duchy of Aquitaine. Eleanor's family had ruled this vast and enormously wealthy Duchy for centuries. It had originally been an independent state, and although the Dukes of Aquitaine had acknowledged French overlordship for some generations, the area was not fully integrated into the French kingdom.

There were several long-running disputes between France and Aquitaine about jurisdiction, fealty, loyalty, taxation and other matters. These had led to frequent conferences, numerous agreements and occasional wars. When Eleanor died and Aquitaine passed to her descendants, the kings of England, the situation changed radically. The Duke of Aquitaine could now draw on the resources of England in his long-running disputes with the King of France. And a whole host of new disputes quickly arose that had much to do with the feudal intricacies of the political landscape of the time. Feudal obligations were both personal and official. When a duke promised fealty to a king he was accepting a personal relationship as much as a political one. Now that the Duke of Aquitaine was also King of England the problem arose of the nature of the relationship with the King of France.

Sorting out what taxes and revenues were due from Aquitaine to France was complex enough, never mind trying to establish whether or not promises made by the Duke of Aquitaine also bound the King of England, who was, of course, the same person. The lords of Aquitaine would

1

The obverse (left) and reverse (right) of a silver halfpenny minted between 1327 and 1335. Edward III was the first monarch to mint halfpennies as specific coins in any numbers, the coin having first been introduced in the final years of his father's reign. Prior to this date halfpennies had been produced by the simple expedient of cutting a penny in half along the line of the cross on the reverse. It was the rising demand for cash wages paid to agricultural and unskilled labourers that led to the increased demand for low-denomination coins at this time.

support their Duke in one course of action, the barons of England would urge their king to follow another. And if the kings of France and England went to war, where did that leave Aquitaine? Should the forces of the duchy muster to support their duke or their king?

In the two centuries that followed the marriage of Duchess Eleanor to King Henry there had been many disputes between the monarchs of England and France over Aquitaine. Mostly these were solved by diplomatic compromise, though fighting did break out on occasion. Even when warfare did erupt, it was rarely serious. It was in neither kingdom's interest to embark on a major war. After a few sieges and much bluster, the wars fizzled out as the diplomats again took over.

But the war that broke out in 1337 was different. This time both England and France threw themselves into the medieval equivalent of total warfare. There could be no space for compromise or discussion. This time the war was for real, and it was this that led to the Battle of Crecy. And yet when the dispute began in Aquitaine it seemed at first to be merely more of the same old bickering.

In 1323 King Charles IV of France decided to fortify a town he owned at St Sardos. He was, of course, quite entitled to do this but since St Sardos lay within Aquitaine he should have – but had not – first obtained the agreement of the Duke of Aquitaine to the size and design of the fortifications. When Sir Ralph Basset, who was running Aquitaine on behalf of King Edward II of England, learned that building work was underway he sent an immediate letter of protest to King Charles of France and asked work to stop until the matter was sorted out. Charles refused. A local lord, Bernard de Montpezat took matters into his own hands by marching to St Sardos, levelling the half-built works and killing one of Charles's men who tried to intervene.

Charles declared he was stripping Montpezat of his lands, but since those lands were held from Edward II, as Duke of Aquitaine, the dispute had now taken a more serious turn. Edward refused to accept the punishment of his vassal, Montpezat, and was in turn stripped of his lands. The envoys of Pope John XXII now stepped in and a compromise deal was patched up. Edward II handed over Aquitaine to his son, the future Edward III, who agreed to pay a fine of £60,000, while Charles agreed to rescind his punishments and accept that Edward, as Duke, could punish Montpezat as he saw fit.

In 1327 young Edward (he was only thirteen at the time) returned to England to collect the money promised to King Charles. It was at this point that the internal politics of England and France took a hand. No sooner was Edward home than his mother, Queen Isabel, and her lover, Roger Mortimer, Earl of March, organised a coup. Edward II was forced to abdicate as King of England and soon afterwards murdered.

The coup had been carried out in the name of young Edward III, but real power lay with Isabel, Mortimer and their cronies. Most people in England were glad to see the back of weak, incompetent Edward II, though few thought that he had deserved his grisly fate. The new regime moved swiftly to stifle dissent. Charles watched events from France with an interested eye, for Isabel was his sister and the new King Edward III, his nephew.

At this point, February 1328, King Charles of France suddenly died without leaving a male heir. The last few kings of the Capet dynasty had been unlucky in the matter of heirs, three of the last five kings have died without a male child. As a result there was a small number of candidates with a realistic claim to the French throne.

As the younger sister of King Charles IV and only surviving child of King Philip IV, Queen Isabel had a pretty good claim to the French throne. But in France it had become accepted – although not enshrined in law – that women could not inherit land or noble titles if a male relative was to hand. The custom had arisen as it was widely held that women were unable to lead men into the battles that were necessary to hold on to lands, enforce law and order, and safeguard family estates.

Edward, as Isabel's son, argued that he was the nearest male relative to hand and so should become King of France. Diplomatic feelers were

3

put out to France's neighbours and support found in Castile, Brabant and Gelderland. However, the leading noblemen of France, the Grands Seigneurs as they were known, had already made up their minds. They did not want the King of England also to be King of France. A lawyer was found who promulgated the novel theory that not only could a woman not inherit, but she could not pass on her claim to a child. This effectively ruled out Edward as the nearest male relative.

The next closest male relative was Philip, Count of Valois. Philip was the son of King Charles's uncle, Charles of Valois, who had died in 1325. Philip was aged thirty-five and had a good track record as both a military commander and as an administrator. He was – just as important – in France when the old king died. He wasted little time, and in May 1328 had himself crowned King Philip VI of France at Reims Cathedral, with all the pomp and ceremony that tradition demanded.

In England, Isabel and Edward refused to acknowledge Philip as King of France, but with England still embroiled in the aftermath of the coup of 1327 there was little that could be done about it. Edward was married to Philippa of Hainault. A small duchy off the northwest frontier of France, Hainault lay within the Holy Roman Empire, but to all intents and purposes was an independent state. Count William of Hainault had lent support to Queen Isabel during her coup and the marriage was by way of thanks. Edward was given the choice of which of Count William's four daughters he would marry, and chose Philippa. The noble girl was good-looking in a plump sort of way and undoubtedly intelligent. Though Edward would later stray, there is no doubt that the royal couple loved each other.

Meanwhile, Mortimer and his supporters were proving themselves to be as efficiently corrupt as Edward II had been incompetently honest. The kingdom was being systematically stripped of its wealth to enrich a small clique.

In 1330 Edward III organised a coup of his own. Although he was constantly guarded by Mortimer's men, he managed to gather around him a small group of noble teenagers. When the court was lodged in Nottingham Castle in October, Edward found that the constable, Richard Holland, was an enemy of Mortimer's. Holland agreed to show Edward's friends a secret tunnel into the castle grounds. Late on 19 October the group of teenagers slipped into the castle. Led by Edward, they marched on Mortimer's chambers. The guards were killed in a short action and Mortimer taken prisoner. He was later hauled off to the Tower of London for a swift trial and execution. Queen Isabel was packed off to a country estate where she was allowed to live in retirement. Meanwhile, Edward was King of England in fact as well as name.

It had been a bad start to the reign, but Edward was determined to put that right. Young though he was, barely eighteen when Mortimer was executed, Edward had a knack for choosing reliable and diligent subordinates. He harboured no grudges against officials who had served Mortimer, nor did he unfairly promote those who had opposed the regime. Apart from his gang of young noblemen, Edward seems to have rewarded competence rather than flattery or noble birth.

Above all, Edward was determined to be, and be seen to be, the perfect knight of chivalry. This was no mere youthful bravado, but an astute move in the affairs of state and one that would have a profound effect on the Crecy campaign. He had a head start being young, good-looking and rich. But there was more to chivalry than that.

Chivalry was, in origin, little more than a fairly brutal code of honour by which the knights of the tenth and eleventh centuries fought their wars. It had as much to do with training as with fighting and almost nothing to do with society or manners. By the early fourteenth century, when Edward set out to become the perfect knight of chivalry, it was a far more nuanced affair.

A knight was expected to be first and foremost a soldier. He had to be skilled in all the weapons of war that could be wielded either on horseback or on foot by an armoured man. Practice with weapons and with horses was a regular part of any knight's life. He was expected to be personally brave in battle – almost suicidally so by modern standards. Yet it was perfectly chivalrous to surrender if wounded or when all that could be done had been done. Likewise, it was chivalrous to accept the surrender of a knight who had fought bravely.

However, a knight was not expected merely to be a good fighter. He also had to understand the weapons and tactics used by other soldiers in an army. He was not expected to be able to build a siege catapult nor to shoot a crossbow, but he did need to know how the weapons worked and how they should be used in battle or siege. He was also expected to have a passing knowledge of logistics and supply systems. At the least he had to be able to keep himself active in the field, which required food and supplies to be procured.

But although the main activity of a knight was war, this was not his most important role. War was merely a means to an end. That end was the peace, security and prosperity of his lands, and by extension, of the people who lived there. Knights were granted an estate, generally known as a knight's fee, which they were expected to defend against bandits, criminals and enemy armies. In return the people living on the estate paid taxes in cash or in kind that allowed the knight to buy his weapons and train for war.

This forced knights to be good at administration, justice and financial affairs. A good knight had to be an astute land agent as well as an effective soldier. Any knight who let his estates fall to ruin would soon lose the ability to ride to war.

By the 1320s there was another element to chivalry: women. It may have been the growing reverence for the Virgin Mary that was sweeping

Christendom at this time, though others believe that it was the growing popularity of the romantic poems, songs and epics that were spreading out from southern France. Whatever the cause, the concepts of both romantic and platonic love were becoming increasingly important to knights. It was no longer enough to fight well and administer estates; knights were now expected to be courteous to ladies. They had to be able to recite poetry, or even better, compose it, with real meaning. Knights had to be able to praise ladies, their beauty and charm with soft words and charm of their own.

It was not enough to be able to do all these things. A knight had to demonstrate his abilities on a regular and frequent basis in as ostentatious a manner possible. If there were no wars to fight, a knight showed off his skill with weapons at a tournament. If few people took an interest in his estate's account books, he showed his wealth by wearing expensive clothes and handing out lavish presents. And if he were not actually in love with a lady, than any chance encounter could be turned into a romantic interlude by the loud declamation of a poem.

Inevitably, few knights could live up to the ideal. They key fact was, however, that they were expected to try. And nobody tried harder than King Edward III of England.

By showing off his wealth, military skills and romantic inclinations on every occasion possible, Edward was making a very definite statement about himself. He was telling his fellow rulers that he was not a man with which to trifle. He had the skills and means to defend his lands and the determination to do so to the utmost. Edward wanted everyone to know that he was no pushover.

But this ostentatious chivalry had another purpose. Under King Edward II, England had suffered badly. Edward had been a hopeless soldier whose ignominious career reached rock bottom in his defeat by the Scots at Bannockburn. He had been a petty and vindictive ruler who took unpleasant revenge on those who crossed him. He had allowed a succession of favourites to take over the running of the kingdom on his behalf, and those favourites had generally helped themselves to revenues that should have gone on the affairs of state. The fact that some of those favourites had been Edward's gay lovers had done little to make the regime any more popular.

Then, under the Mortimer regime, England had again missed out on honest and effective government. Mortimer was further disgraced by an embarrassing campaign against the Scots that failed due to incompetent management and poor supply systems.

Young Edward III wanted to mark out his rule as a definitive break from the recent, shameful past. Edward wanted and needed the support and assistance of his people; chivalry was the method that he chose. No gesture was too small or too grand for Edward. Again and again, Edward would choose the chivalrous thing to do.

The king's lead was followed by others. Nobles and knights who wished to catch the king's eye knew that the best way to do it was to act in a chivalrous manner. The Crecy campaign would see many such escapades.

Some modern commentators see chivalry as being the preserve of the rich and well born. Those who were not of the knightly class, they say, were treated with contempt and cruelty. This is to misread the situation.

It was true that only knights and lords were expected to be chivalrous, because only they held the estates that made chivalry necessary. However, those same knights were part of a much wider society. In running their estates the knights had dealings with free farmers paying rent, with serfs tied to the land, with local clergy and with tradesmen working for cash. All these people had to be dealt with in a manner that made business profitable for both sides and kept relations cordial. If anyone was in any doubt then King Edward, that self-proclaimed ideal knight of chivalry, showed the way by inviting London merchants to his banquets.

Chivalry was not a mere affectation for noblemen on the field of battle. All medieval armies had large numbers of non-noble troops among their number. As we shall see, they came from a variety of social backgrounds and fought with a variety of weapons and tactics, but none of them were knights or noblemen. These men were not expected to be chivalrous in the way that knights were. They were not prone to indulge in single combat or to hold narrow bridges alone, neither could they expect to be kept in comfortable confinement if captured. They did not carry banners decorated with their heraldic devices into battle. But that does not mean that they had no role in chivalry.

The common soldiers had a very real interest in chivalry and the men who were involved. As we shall see, it was the knights and nobles who provided the commanders of medieval armies, and in many cases did the employing of common soldiers. It was a matter of vital interest to soldiers which commanders were better, more successful and more chivalrous than others. When an archer was looking for employment for the coming campaign, he would naturally prefer to join the company of a successful knight than that of a loser. And even among the humble ranks there was more social credit given to supporting a famously chivalrous leader than one known for base behaviour.

It must also be borne in mind that medieval armies were quite small. A force of 5,000 men was considered large and only major kingdoms embarking on important campaigns would field over 10,000. Since less than 20% of these men would usually be knights, and even fewer would be in command of companies, it is clear that everyone in an army would know at least by sight all the important knights in the army. The deeds and exploits of these men were the stuff of campfire tales and gossip. And whenever a knight embarked on a chivalrous quest, the common soldiery would stop to watch. Single combats were not only great entertainment, they did much to affect morale.

A rough analogy might be the relationship between supporters of a modern football team and the players. None of the supporters actually plays any football, any more than an archer was expected to do chivalry, but the skills, antics and lives of the knights were of just as much interest to a common soldier as are those of a modern football player.

Above all, the most important thing in chivalry was to be successful and honourable. With the reins of power firmly in his hands, Edward set out to be just that. He began with the essential business of running his lands efficiently, effectively and honestly. Having appointed men to run his government well, and spending some time to make sure that they did, Edward turned to sorting out the foreign entanglements that he had inherited.

First on the agenda was France. The money promised to France after the affair at St Sardos had not yet been paid in full. More importantly, there was now a new French king who wanted Edward to swear fealty as Duke of Aquitaine. A king, moreover, whom Edward had not recognised as such. To add to the tension, Edward was also Count of Ponthieu, a small but prosperous area of northern France. Edward had inherited Ponthieu through his grandmother, exactly the same claim he had advanced for the throne of France itself. If he did fealty to Charles for Ponthieu, did that mean that Charles was accepting the principle of inheritance through women?

In the event, a diplomatic fudge and goodwill by both Edward and Philip got over the difficulties. In 1331 Edward promised to 'bear faith and loyalty to the King of France as a lord of France'. The trickier issues were simply not mentioned.

Scotland was a more difficult proposition, but it did offer the chance for the sort of military campaigning that any perfect knight should experience. The Scottish throne was in dispute at this time; Edward Balliol and David Bruce, son of Robert Bruce who had defeated Edward II at Bannockburn, both laid claim to it. The eight-year-old David was then ruling as David II, with the Earl of Mar leading a council of regents. Balliol was in England with a group of noblemen who had lost their lands to David and his supporters. Together the exiles were known as the Disinherited. Edward turned a blind eye while they prepared to invade Scotland.

In 1332 the Disinherited sailed from the Humber and landed in the Tay. On 11 August they defeated the royal Scottish army at the Battle of Dupplin Moor and soon afterwards Balliol was crowned King Edward of Scotland at Scone. He at once offered to accept Edward of England as his liege lord, formally recognise England's overlordship of Scotland and to hand over to England various border territories.

An illustration dating to a few years after Crecy shows knights exercising under the watchful eye of their king. The knights are jousting at a quintain, a training device resembling a knight mounted on an upright pole so that it could spin freely. The knight was expected to strike the shield on the quintain squarely while riding at the gallop. If the quintain was struck incorrectly the heavy bag dangling from the opposite arm of the quintain would strike the knight from behind as the quintain span.

Edward carefully avoided either accepting or rejecting Balliol's offer. He did, however, muster an army at York and march north towards the border. He arrived to find that Balliol had been expelled from Scotland by a fresh army loyal to King David, but was now laying siege to the important border fortress town of Berwick which was then held for David but had been English in the past.

Edward joined Balliol, throwing the weight of the English army behind the siege. On 19 July a Scottish army arrived to try to break the siege. It was met on Halidon Hill by Edward and Balliol, and suffered a crushing defeat. The Lowlands and Border regions capitulated to Balliol, while Edward took Berwick for England. Balliol was to find it less easy to hold Scotland than to win it, and in any case never really secured a grip north of the Tay.

Meanwhile, tensions had been rising again with France. The promised money had still not been paid in full, and French lawyers were beginning to pick holes in the deliberately vague oath sworn by Edward in 1331. In April 1334 King David of Scotland arrived in France. He was given an ostentatious ceremonial welcome by Philip, who declared David to be the true king of the northern land. As if that were not an open enough challenge to Edward, Philip added that his legal disputation with Edward over Aquitaine, Ponthieu and St Sardos would not be solved until Edward had also made peace with Philip's close friend King David.

In May 1335 a fleet commanded (at least in name) by King David attacked the Channel Islands. The invasion began well, but the defenders eventually got the upper hand. Edward believed – with reason – that the 'Scottish' fleet and army was in fact mostly French. Philip denied the charge. Those same 'Scottish' ships spent the next few months attacking and often capturing English merchant ships in the Channel. The maritime losses were galling to Edward, whose primary duty as a chivalrous king was to protect his people. They not only did damage to Edward's reputation, but also to his treasury; taxation of the wool trade with the Low Countries was a major element of royal finances.

Despite these moves, Philip had his main attentions directed elsewhere: he was preparing to launch a Crusade. The heyday of crusading was long over by the 1330s, the last Christian fortress in the Holy Land had fallen forty years earlier. But the task of defending Christendom against Islamic holy warriors was still considered to be a sacred duty for all Christian rulers. Philip had raised a special tax to pay for the Crusade, had appointed a commander to gather an army and had even got so far as mustering a fleet at Marseille.

At this critical moment Philip received a long letter from Pope Benedict XII. Influential theologian and effective administrator he may have been, but Benedict was neither a diplomat nor a leader. The crusade, he told Philip, was cancelled. He did not think the French king had gathered a force strong enough to achieve anything effective against the Muslims and did not see any point in throwing away thousands of men who might be needed to meet an Islamic invasion of mainland Europe in the near future.

Philip was furious, and felt deeply insulted by the Pope's lack of confidence. He ordered the French fleet to move from Marseille to the Channel. By the spring of 1337 Philip would be in a position to intervene on behalf of King David of Scotland in earnest. He had not forgotten the disputes over Aquitaine and Ponthieu.

When Edward received the news that Philip's fleet was in the Channel he realised that war with France was now inevitable. All that was needed was a spark to set the conflagration alight. It was Philip who found it.

In 1334 the French Count of Artois had died without a male heir. As liege lord, Philip exercised his right to choose a successor. The losing candidate, Robert d'Artois, tried raising his supporters in rebellion, but failed to gain much support and then fled. By 1336 he was in England, lending his considerable military expertise to the English forces in Scotland. Philip sent Edward a terse note demanding that Robert d'Artois be sent back to France as a prisoner to stand trial for his rebellion.

Edward had no intention of handing over such a useful soldier as d'Artois, so he prevaricated and delayed. In May 1337 Philip insisted that d'Artois be handed over immediately. Edward refused. Philip declared that Edward was a false vassal who had broken his solemn oaths of 1331. Both Ponthieu and Aquitaine were confiscated by Philip.

In Ponthieu the confiscation proceeded smoothly and quickly. Led by Pierre de Courant, the governor of Amiens, French forces marched into the small county unopposed. Ponthieu was administered largely by local officials, though Edward had filled some key posts with trusted Englishmen. The locals surrendered; the English fled. Both recognised that the coming war would be decided by forces much greater than were available in Ponthieu. There was no point dying for a small place that would have no impact on the outcome of war – or so they thought.

In Aquitaine things were very different. The land was large, rich and easy to defend. Moreover, the locals had a long tradition of semi-independence from the French crown and were hardly likely to abandon the family that had ruled them for centuries because of a minor quarrel over a man of whom they had never heard. The Aquitainians were willing and able to fight hard on behalf of Edward. The French invasion forces, led by the Constable of France the Count d'Eu, had barely crossed the border before it was halted by the need to besiege a number of strong castles that blocked the roads.

On 28 August Edward formally answered the challenge put down by Philip when Aquitaine and Ponthieu were confiscated. After repeating the accusations of French involvement with the forces of David of Scotland, Edward rejected the charge that he had broken his oath, condemned the moves to occupy Ponthieu and Aquitaine. Finally he declared war. The Hundred Years War had begun.

II

Opening Moves

On the outbreak of war few disinterested observers could have any doubt about the likely outcome. France was going to win – and win easily.

The mere size of the two kingdoms alone gave France a massive advantage. Although it is impossible to be accurate, the population of France at this time was over twenty million, that of England barely seven million. France also had a clear advantage in terms of wealth. The towns and cities of France were closely integrated into the trading networks that were becoming firmly established across the continent.

The southern cities of Lyons, Marseille and Toulouse were locked into the complex trading networks of the Mediterranean. Hundreds of merchant galleys plied the sea, trading European grain and furs for oriental spices and silks or African gold and ivory. The great trade fair of Lyons, in particular, was a thriving and bustling centre for international trade. In northern France, Paris was the largest city in Europe north of the Alps, and Rouen was not far behind.

The trading networks and access to markets encouraged a developing economic picture. The rich, light soils of the areas north of the Seine were ideal for growing grains. The farmers here had moved into bulk grain production, turning over almost all their lands to growing wheat and barley for sale in the market towns. With the cash generated the farmers could buy fruit, meat and other products that they no longer grew on their own land. Similar specialisation was taking hold elsewhere, making a more effective and efficient use of manpower.

By contrast, England was less economically advanced. Most farmers still worked mixed farms growing grain, fruit and meat. Even where soils were not particularly good for grain, wheat was still grown. This made for less efficient farming. The only specialist product of England was wool, and while this made fortunes for all concerned in the trade it represented only a fraction of England's farmland.

This man-at-arms is probably an esquire or possibly a poorer knight from a remote rural district. Either way he wears armour of a style that was becoming outdated by the time of Crecy. He wears a suit of mail armour which covers his body almost entirely. The mail shirt reaches down to his wrists, where mail-backed leather gauntlets take over to protect the hands. The mail leggings are tied to a thick belt, which is under the mail shirt. Mail has been sewn on over his boots. The head is protected by a mail coif, that reaches down to cover the neck and shoulders. This is covered by a great helm, a heavy helmet of iron that encases the entire head and has holes for breathing and for sight. Note that this knight has a banner attached to his lance. This was a typical piece of chivalrous showmanship that was expected at tournaments but which was falling out of favour on the battlefield. Likewise becoming less usual on the battlefield was the embroidered cloth housing that covers the horse. This was originally introduced to try to prevent infantry from hamstringing the horse, but by the 1340s the way it hindered the horse's movement was leading to it being discarded in battle.

Nor was it merely a matter of population and wealth. As we shall see France had a large and highly respected army. The latest weaponry, latest tactics and most efficient supply systems were recognised as being those of France. Young knights and nobles from across Europe would volunteer to serve in France to learn the arts of war. As they grew older many of these men felt a residual loyalty to the French crown and were willing to serve the French king if asked. Thus the French king was able to call upon manpower reserves even greater than France itself could provide.

Not that anybody really expected the war that had broken out in 1337 to amount to much. It was confidently expected that there would be some skirmishing, maybe a campaign or two and then a peace deal would be patched up. At first, it seemed that this was exactly what was going to happen.

Having declared war, Edward seemed to accept that he stood no chance of defeating France on his own. After sending some English troops south to bolster the defences of Aquitaine, Edward threw himself into a diplomatic mission aimed at gaining allies for the conflict with France.

Perhaps naturally, he turned first to his in-laws in Hainault. Duke William was happy to parade his men for action, having first taken a considerable sum of English silver to pay his expenses. The Duke of Brabant was likewise willing to take Edward's side and muster his forces for war, again so long as Edward was paying the bill. The Count of Flanders was less enthusiastic, despite the fact that his cities depended for their wealth on regular imports of English wool. The Count owed allegiance to King Philip and was not one to break an oath, even when the majority of his own people disliked the whole idea of rule by the French king.

Perhaps Edward's greatest diplomatic achievement was to persuade the Holy Roman Emperor Louis (or Ludwig) IV to appoint him Imperial Vicar for the lands west of the Rhine. The title gave Edward the theoretical rights to marshal the lands of the Holy Roman Empire in that area for war. In practice, as with so much about the Holy Roman Empire, it was an empty title that depended on the willingness of local rulers to obey. It did, however, give Edward a legal right to be hovering off the northern borders of France with an army.

By the summer of 1339, Edward felt ready to strike. He took an English army to Brabant, mustered the forces of his allies and marched into France. The French hurriedly harvested their crops and retreated into the fortified towns and castles that dotted the area. Edward's forces swept onward, but were unable to take the cities of Cambrai, Laon or Soissons and so inflicted little real damage.

By October Edward was camped outside St Quentin, yet another city which he was failing to capture. Suddenly, news came that King Philip was approaching with the main French army to confront the invaders. A herald rode into the camp of the English and their allies with a message from Philip. It was couched in the hackneyed diplomatic phrases of the time. Philip condemned Edward for his actions, repeated the condemnation of him as a rebellious vassal and ended by challenging him to battle at a place and time of his choosing.

Ever wanting to be seen as the perfect knight of chivalry, Edward promptly accepted the challenge and sent scouts out to select a suitable battlefield. Philip was taken aback by the eagerness of the English king to face the French army, and at once began to prevaricate. Excuses were found why the battle had to be delayed, and then delayed again. Meanwhile, Edward's allies were getting nervous. A border raid was one thing, but facing up to the royal army of France was something else entirely. Using the fact that supplies were running low, the rulers of Brabant and Brandenburg forced Edward to fall back out of France.

Philip watched the English retreat. As he had expected, the English king had backed down when faced by the prospect of a pitched battle against the full might of France. The event confirmed him and his subordinates in the belief that they had by far the best army in Christendom, and that this fact was recognised by the English. Philip must have believed that raids and pillaging of undefended country areas could be expected of the English, but successful attacks on major cities were beyond them. Still less would the English dare face up to the French king and the French army. Content that the war would grind on in desultory fashion and end in a compromise peace, Philip went home.

Edward, however, had no such intentions. He still wanted to win the war. Not only was the ignominious retreat from St Quentin rankling, but so was the fact that the French fleet had raided and burned Portsmouth and Southampton. The war, he decided, would continue.

In June 1340 Edward was sailing from England to the Low Countries with another army. His intention was, once again, to join with the forces of Hainault and nearby states by invading northern France. This time Edward was buoyed by the fact that the great cities of Flanders had expelled their Count and risen in revolt against the King of France. The well-armed militias of the cities were marching to war on the English side.

First, however, Edward had to get to the continent, and the vast French fleet was waiting for him. With 214 ships the French Admirals Sir Hugh Quiréret and Sir Nicholas Béhuchet were confident of victory when they saw just 147 English ships sail over the horizon. The French had with them four Genoese galleys commanded by the mercenary captain Babbaveria. He was not as confident as the French and suggested that they should move away from the shoal waters off Sluys where they were anchored in case the need came to manoeuvre or flee. The French admirals refused to listen, so Babbaveria moved his ships off to the flank without permission.

Seeing the enemy fleet, Edward sent a few ships carrying the ladies and noncombatants off to the north. Chivalry demanded that ladies should be kept safe, and Edward was always conscious of the need to be chivalrous. He then turned to another aspect of chivalry: the need to be victorious in war. Although he had fewer ships, Edward's fleet was packed to over-crowding with his invasion army. The French ships, by contrast, were furnished for raiding and so had fewer and less well-equipped men.

Edward waited until the tide was at full flood, about 3.00 p.m., and then attacked. With the wind full in their sails and the tide pushing them forward, the English ships approached the anchored French fleet at speed. The two fleets met with a tremendous crash. English archers deluged the French with arrows, then English men-at-arms swarmed to board the enemy vessels.

The leading French squadron was overwhelmed after some prolonged fighting. Quieret and Béhuchet were both killed, the gloating English hauling Béhuchet's body up on a rope to dangle from a masthead. Seeing the fate of their comrades, the French second squadron tried to flee. As Babbaveria had foreseen, their position so close to shoal water gave them little chance to do so. Many ships ran aground, their crews taking to boats in the hope of getting ashore. They were met by a horde of Flemish fisher-men coming the other way to join in the plundering of the French ships and more bloodshed followed as dusk closed in.

In all, some 190 French ships were captured or burned, with only the far-sighted Babbaveria getting his ships away undamaged. The next morning the Genoese captain rounded up the surviving French ships and led them away to the safety of the Seine. Inevitably, perhaps, the Genoese was accused of having fled to save his own skin, though in truth he had merely been using his professional skills to good effect. Some residual ill-feeling between the French and the Genoese lingered.

The Battle of Sluys gave the English complete control of the Channel for several years. Not only did this make raiding England more difficult for the French, but it also disrupted communications between the French and their Scottish allies. Moreover, it meant that English ships could cross back and forth carrying messages, supplies and men more easily and with greater freedom than had so far been the case.

Edward was greatly proud of his achievement. There seemed little point in winning a great victory if the fact were not celebrated in grand fashion, and Edward knew exactly how to do this.

Plans had been underway for some years to introduce a gold coinage to England. For almost a thousand years the coinage of England had been based on the silver penny, a small coin that was adequate for the day-to-day needs of a society that still traded largely by barter. However, the increase in international trade, particularly in wool, called for higher denominations of coin. Edward's grandfather, Edward I, had introduced the groat (a silver coin worth four pennies), but by 1340 this was no longer enough.

At first Edward's moneyers intended to introduce a coin copied from the gold coins of Florence: the florin. Florentine coins circulated widely across Europe and were trusted to be of a standard weight and purity of gold, being worth the equivalent of seventy-two English silver pennies, or six shillings. The English actually got so far as minting a few of these coins, but they were soon abandoned in favour of Edward's new idea: the noble.

The new gold coin was a purely English invention. Each noble was worth eighty English pennies, or six shillings and eight pence, which made it rather larger and heavier than a florin. Instead of the usual portrait of the king that occupied the obverse of all coins, Edward ordered his moneyers to put a figure of himself in full armour standing in a warship and brandishing his sword. It was a magnificent piece of propaganda. The coins were minted in large numbers and circulated widely across northern Europe. Anyone who saw one would be forcibly reminded that Edward had won the Battle of Sluys and consequently ruled the waves. The basic design remained unaltered for almost two centuries.

Unfortunately for Edward, the rest of the 1340 campaign failed to live up to the early promise of Sluys. As in 1339 the English and allied armies roamed around the borders of north-eastern France failing to capture any important towns. This time Philip did not even bother leading his army out to face the invaders. He simply sat back and let the presumptuous English wear themselves out on the mighty fortifications of the cities while running out of supplies. When autumn came, Edward once again retreated empty handed.

This time, however, the situation was much worse for Edward than it had been in 1339. The Flemish city militias had been defeated by the French in battle at St Omer. Although the defeat was not particularly serious, it sapped the enthusiasm of the Flemish for the fighting. When a dispute erupted between Brabant and the Flemings, Edward's alliance began to unravel. French diplomats had also been busy. Among others lured away from the English cause was the Holy Roman Emperor who was persuaded not to renew Edward's position as Imperial Vicar. It was as Edward led his army back out of France that he received calamitous news from England. A serious financial crisis was about to strike, making it impossible for Edward to pay his allies or repay his debts.

So when Jeanne, the dowager Countess of Hainault, asked for an audience, Edward was willing to listen. Not only was the countess Edward's mother in law, she was also a junior princess of the French royal family. She suggested a year's truce to give the diplomats time to try to find a negotiated solution. Edward agreed, and so did Philip. The truce was signed at Espléchin.

Although 1340 had been close to disastrous for Edward, there had been one event which was to prove crucial to the conduct of the war. At the time it did not seem to have been particularly important, it was only with hindsight that the importance of the event became apparent.

Before they had agreed to rebel openly against King Philip, the Flemish cities of Ghent, Bruges and Ypres had demanded that some way be found to make their actions seem legal. After some discussions among the lawyers, it was decided that Edward should revive his claim to the French throne that had been made, and then abandoned, in 1328. Consequently, Edward had formally announced that he was the rightful King of France and called upon the Count of Flanders to come to pay homage to him. The Count refused to do any such thing, declaring that Philip was King of France. This allowed the city governments to declare that they renounced their loyalty to the Count as he was a rebellious vassal of the true king, Edward. It was a neat little legal trick, and that was all anybody thought it was at the time.

Meanwhile, Edward was hurrying back to England to deal with the crisis in government finances. Embarrassingly, he had to leave the Earls of Warwick, Derby and Northampton behind in Flanders as hostages against the payment of his debts.

The problem was entirely of Edward's own making. Before leaving for the wars in 1338 he had appointed a Regency Council led by Archbishop Stratford of Canterbury supported by the Earls of Huntingdon, Lancaster and Surrey as well as several influential knights and barons from various parts of the kingdom. He also left a set of written instructions setting out the powers and responsibilities of the Regency Council. Effectively, the day-to-day business of government was to be carried out by the Regency Council with only serious matters of state referred to the king.

Among the duties given to the Council was the collection of taxes and other payments due to the Crown. This involved summoning Parliament. By this date the feudal payments and services due to the king were no longer enough to keep the government going. Additional taxes were needed on a regular basis. In theory the king could levy customs duties, poll taxes and a host of other payments by diktat, but it had become accepted custom that such special payments would be exacted only after the representatives of those who would pay them had been consulted. A minority of payments were made by the Church or the nobles, but the most lucrative taxes were levied on the merchants, knights and landowners. So levying such a tax meant summoning Parliament to discuss it. Parliaments very rarely refused to grant a tax, so long as it was within the usual bounds and was not excessive. They did, however, take the opportunity to ask the king for new laws, regulations or privileges, and the king would normally agree to at least some of these.

What Edward had not done, however, was to explain to Archbishop Stratford or anybody else the true scale of the cash payments that he had promised to make to his continental allies. Perhaps Edward had hoped to finish the war in 1339, but certainly he was quite unable to match his promises when a second full year of war demanded more payments to allies. He covered up his financial situation by borrowing heavily, principally from the Florentine banking families of the Bardi and Peruzzi, but also from German merchants and bankers. By September 1340 he was in debt to the tune of £400,000 – more than twice the annual income of the Crown.

It was when the scale of the financial debt became known back in England that the crisis began. The lords complained directly to the king that the cost of the war was excessive, while Stratford did not dare summon a Parliament to discuss taxation for fear of what might be said and voted upon.

Edward arrived in London on 1 December 1340, unannounced and with a squad of armed soldiers at his back. He sacked the Regency Council, arrested several officials from the royal treasury and tried to heap all the blame on Stratford. The Archbishop was having none of it. He hurried off to Canterbury and ostentatiously took up residence in the same chambers that had been occupied by Archbishop Thomas Becket during his dispute with Henry II two centuries earlier. That dispute had ended with the murder of the archbishop by the king's henchmen and the subsequent complete humbling of the king, while the dead prelate was made a saint.

On 29 December Stratford preached a sermon in the cathedral in which he declared that he was a latter-day Becket. He refused to answer Edward's charges of financial irregularity, but said he would happily submit all accounts for independent audit – but only to Parliament.

Finally, in April, Edward gave in and summoned Parliament. Stratford was cleared of all charges and Edward had to agree to humiliating demands that his ministers had to appear before Parliament for questioning and that the royal accounts be submitted for regular audit by the lords. In return, Parliament agreed to new taxes. But they were not enough.

Edward could not pay everyone. After some delay and debate, Edward decided to pay off all his creditors, except the Italian bankers. To them he sent only soft words promising to pay when he could. Before long, both the Bardi and Peruzzi families went bankrupt. Edward was financially solvent once more, though only just, but his reputation with foreign bankers was ruined. Never again would he be able to raise large loans abroad to finance his wars. And much as the English liked and respected their handsome, chivalrous king, they were not willing to pay for cash-hungry foreign allies.

It looked as if Edward would be forced to agree to a humiliating peace with Philip. He could no longer afford allies, while England and Aquitaine alone could not stand up to France for long. Then fate took a hand.

In April 1341 John, Duke of Brittany, died. Like Aquitaine, Brittany was a duchy which recognised the sovereignty of the King of France, but which enjoyed effective self-rule under an ancient and distinguished native dynasty. In the case of Brittany, the sense of independence from France was heightened by the fact that most Bretons spoke a Celtic language more akin to Welsh than French.

There were two claimants to the duchy. The first was John de Montfort, a young son of the dead Duke John by his third wife. Most Bretons simply assumed that young John would inherit the duchy. However, a second claim was made by Charles de Blois who was married to Jeanne, a daughter of the dead duke by his second wife. Charles had relatively little support within Brittany, but he was the nephew of King Philip of France.

Philip suddenly announced that as the feudal superior of the Duke of Brittany, he had the right to act as judge in any disputed succession. After the pretence of studying the evidence and discussing the claims, Philip announced that Charles of Blois was the rightful Duke of Brittany and had young John thrown in to prison. John's wife, the Countess Jeanne, was appalled by Philip's duplicity. She sent messages throughout Brittany demanding that the populace rally to the support of their true duke, her husband John.

The Countess Jeanne then took the fateful step that was to transform the Anglo-French war. She declared that Philip was not the true King of France, and therefore had no right to act as judge in the disputed succession. Instead, she said, Edward was the true King of France. Accordingly, she sent her representatives off to England ask Edward to decide the issue.

Edward was delighted to have an opportunity to discomfit Philip. Donning the quartered arms of England and France, Edward studied the evidence just as seriously as had Philip. He declared that John was the true Duke of Brittany.

The affair was given a further international twist by the fact that Countess Jeanne was from Flanders. Walter Mauny, a Hainault knight, led a small force of volunteers from the Low Countries to help Countess Jeanne, while Philip sent a large army led by his son, John Duke of Normandy, to support Charles of Blois. The year was well advanced by the time Edward heard of these movements, but he promised to send English help to Countess Jeanne the following year.

In 1342 the Earl of Northampton landed in Brittany with 3,000 men. Co-operating with the forces of Countess Jeanne and Walter Mauny, Northampton lifted the siege of Brest and set about driving off the scattered Breton supporters of Charles of Blois. Northampton was laying siege to Morlaix when a scout galloped into camp on 30 September with the news that Charles of Blois was approaching with an army of at least 10,000 men.

Northampton hurriedly drew his men up astride the road along which Charles was advancing. He put his men halfway up a slope with a dense wood at their backs and open country to their front. Charles had arranged his army, in conventional fashion, into three divisions of approximately equal numbers and composition. The advance guard arrived in front of Northampton's force and, by itself outnumbering the English, attacked. With a clear field of fire, the English archers inflicted heavy casualties on the advancing French, whose attack faltered.

However, after a long summer's campaigning, Northampton's men did not have enough arrows to fight a major engagement. Having driven off the first assault, they fell back into the woods. Northampton left a few archers lurking in the trees, to shoot at any Frenchmen who came close while the bulk of the English hurried away. Charles de Blois had been shocked by the rapid shooting of the archers and the heavy casualties his men had taken. The desultory shooting from the trees was enough to deter him from attacking again. Blois had lost some 200 knights and men-at-arms, as well as many others, while English casualties were negligible.

In October Edward himself landed in Brittany with reinforcements. Hearing this, King Philip mustered an army and marched to face the English. Before any serious fighting could take place, winter weather closed in. Then in January 1343 peace-making diplomats arrived from Pope Clement VI.

This new pope was a Frenchman, born Pierre, a younger son of Lord William d'Egleton. Like many younger sons he had entered the Church as a career, rising to be Bishop of Rouen before being appointed a cardinal in 1338 and travelling south to join the Papal Court at Avignon. As a former French bishop, Clement was well known to King Philip but he was also already friendly with Edward, having met him during the years when the French and English kings had been on good terms.

Clement's envoys did their work well. This time a three-year truce was agreed between Edward and Philip. It was agreed that both kings would send negotiators to Avignon so that Pope Clement himself could chair the discussions in the hope of finding a peace formula. The deal was signed at Malestroit in January 1343.

Meanwhile, an apparently unimportant local feud had erupted in Normandy. Petty though it was, the scuffle was to have profound effects and would, indirectly, lead to the Battle of Crecy.

In 1341 two lords in the Cotentin Peninsula both bid for the hand of a local heiress whose lands bordered their own. Of the two, Godfrey de Harcourt was the richer, but Robert Bertrand of Bricquebec was the better connected, his brother being Bishop William of Bayeux. During the course of the courting and marriage negotiations, hot words and insults were exchanged between the Harcourt and Bertrand families. Friends and neighbours were dragged into the dispute which became increasingly bad tempered.

In the autumn of 1342 men loyal to Harcourt attacked, looted and burned two manors belonging to the Bertrand family. Too busy preparing to march to Brittany to deal with the matter as carefully as he should have, King Philip declared that Godfrey de Harcourt was entirely in the wrong. He gave Robert Bertrand authority to draw on royal money and troops and told him to sort the matter out.

Bertrand seized his chance. Backed by royal troops, he marched to the main Harcourt castle at St Sauveur le Vicomte. The fortress was ill-prepared to face a major army and fell quickly. Godfrey de Harcourt was not at home at the time, so Bertrand contented himself with looting the place and dragging off the garrison in chains.

Outraged that the king had not given him a chance to put his side of the case, Harcourt fled to Brabant along with a small band of followers. When Bertrand heard in March 1343 where Harcourt had gone, he declared that the fugitive was a traitor who was doing a deal with Edward, the rival King of France. The three senior members of the garrison of St Sauveur le Vicomte were promptly executed and their heads spiked over the gates of the town of St Lo. Harcourt swore to exact bloody revenge on Bertrand.

While this vicious but minor dispute was running its course, the negotiators of Edward and Philip were making their way to Avignon. The initial complexities of the disagreements had by this time been made even more tortuous by disputes that had arisen during the fighting. The negotiations dragged on for months and were clearly going nowhere. Rightly or wrongly, the English ambassadors gradually began to suspect that Clement was subtly favouring the French cause.

Although the Truce of Malestroit forbade any actual fighting between the supporters of Edward and Philip, it did not prohibit diplomacy and intrigue. Philip worked hard to get the Count of Flanders back in control of Flanders. Discord within the major cities was fuelled, and although the area refused to return to allegiance of their Count, they were effectively unable to agree on any action against France.

Philip achieved better success in Aquitaine. Carefully mixing promises and threats, Philip persuaded several Aquitainian nobles to change sides. Without fighting, Philip's armies were able to advance deep into Aquitaine.

Edward was likewise busy. A small force under the Earl of Northampton and Sir Thomas Dagworth was sent to Brittany to bolster the forces of Countess Jeanne. Edward himself went to Flanders, but was unable to get any sort of unity from the Flemish cities and went home in disgust after one of his key supporters, Jacob van Artevelde, was murdered in a brawl.

Edward was not going to accept meekly the change of loyalty by Aquitainian nobles. The Earl of Derby, aided by the Hainaulter Walter Mauny, was sent to Bordeaux with a force of 500 men-at-arms and 1,500 archers to see what he could do to stabilise the situation. As it turned out, what Derby was able to do was quite spectacular.

He began by summoning a large force of Aquitainian nobles who remained loyal to Edward. Then he marched up the valley of the Dordogne to take by storm the city of Bergerac. A nearby French army appeared, and was crushed in a short but decisive action. Derby swept on to Périgeaux, taking the supposedly impregnable castle of Auberoche with ease. This brought down the main French army in the south, led by Count Louis de Poitiers and Count Bertrand de l'Isle.

Poitiers and de l'Isle reached Auberoche in mid-October when Derby was busy reducing pro-Philip castles elsewhere. The French at once laid siege to the castle. With some 12,000 men they were confident of success.

Derby knew, as the French did not, that Auberoche was almost empty of supplies. If the siege was not raised quickly, the hapless garrison within would have to surrender in a matter of days. Unfortunately, the English-Aquitainian army was scattered across a wide stretch of country. Derby sent the Earl of Pembroke off to round up the army, while he himself marched toward Auberoche with the 200 men-at-arms and 600 archers that he had to hand.

Derby marched his men hard. On 21 October the English army was roused while it was still dark and ordered to advance in silence along the wooded road towards Auberoche. Walter Mauny had been sent ahead, and as the cold light of dawn began to break he returned with the news that the French had blundered. Poitiers and de l'Isle had put their camp on meadows that lay close to the woods. Moreover, the French were asleep.

Derby hurried his men forward. His armoured men-at-arms launched a mounted charge into the French camp just as the French were being called to wake. Lacking armour and groggy from sleep, the French stood little chance against the disciplined charge of heavy cavalry. One group of Frenchmen on the far side of the camp saw what was happening. They managed to grab their weapons and mount, but without armour they were quickly shot down by the archers who were now emerging from the wood.

As surprise attacks go, Derby pulled off a magnificent example. Over 6,000 Frenchmen were killed or captured. Both Poitiers and de l'Isle were captured, the former later dying of his wounds. Pembroke arrived the next day with the main Anglo-Aquitainian army, to be met by a grinning Derby. The French advance in Aquitaine had been shattered in spectacular fashion.

When news of the fighting in Aquitaine became known to Philip and Edward it was obvious that the war would begin again in earnest the following year. The Truce of Malestroit was due to expire in January 1346, though campaigning would not be expected to start again until the spring weather came. The question that faced both Philip and Edward was what they should do.

For Philip at least, the answer was simple and twofold. First he would send a large army under the command of his son and heir, Duke John

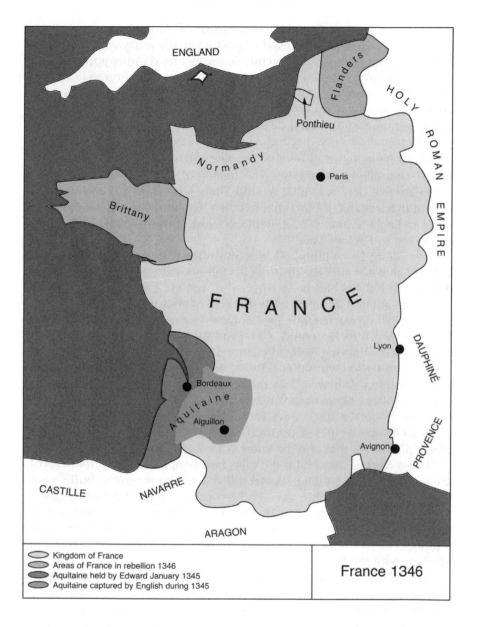

ENGLAND

Flanders

HOLY ROMAN EMPIRE

Ponthieu

Normandy

Paris

Brittany

F R A N C E

Lyon

DAUPHINÉ

Bordeaux

Aquitaine

Aiguillon

Avignon

PROVENCE

CASTILLE

NAVARRE

ARAGON

Kingdom of France
Areas of France in rebellion 1346
Aquitaine held by Edward January 1345
Aquitaine captured by English during 1345

France 1346

of Normandy, to Aquitaine. John had orders to recover lost ground and forcibly to remind those nobles who had switched allegiance to Philip that they should remain loyal to their monarch. By the end of March Duke John had some 20,000 men under arms in the upper valley of the Garonne. Most of these troops had been raised in southern France, but quite a few of the senior nobles were from Normandy. John was, after all, Duke of Normandy and it behoved his senior vassals to join him when he marched to war.

Duke John marched down the Garonne to the fortified city of Aiguillon which controlled the strategic confluence of the Garonne and Lot. If Aiguillon fell there was little to stop Duke John from advancing downstream to Bordeaux. If Bordeaux fell then Aquitaine would be almost cut off from England and so from reinforcement. It was a strategically sound move, but an obvious one.

Even before Duke John had fully mustered his army, Derby (now the Earl of Lancaster after the death of his father) had prepared Aiguillon for defence. The town had been emptied of useless civilians, fully stocked with food and had its defences thoroughly overhauled. Confident that the town could hold out for months, Lancaster organised the rest of his forces for mobile warfare. He intended to spend the summer raiding French supply lines and attacking isolated enemy garrisons.

Philip was also aware that Edward was likely to lead a force into the field in person. Whether that force would go to Brittany, Flanders or Aquitaine was unknown, nor was it clear if Edward any longer had the resources to gather allies to his cause. Philip decided to stay in Paris. He did not raise the armies of northern France to his banner; there would be plenty of time for that once he knew what Edward was doing.

One precaution that Philip did take, however, was to attempt to rectify the naval situation in the Channel. He did not have time to build a new fleet, so he decided to hire one. Philip turned to Carlo Grimaldi, Lord of Monaco, who had under his control a sizeable mercenary fleet that he hired out to whoever would pay him. On 27 December, Grimaldi signed a contract with Philip to bring 33 warships and 7,000 crossbowmen to Harfleur by April 1346.

This was not enough crossbowmen for Philip, so he also hired a leading nobleman from Genoa, Ottone Doria, to supply another 3,000 such troops. Doria's men were to march overland, arriving in Paris by March.

King Philip also contacted King James of Majorca to ask for help. King James was in no position to refuse. The state of Majorca had originally been a part of the Spanish Kingdom of Aragon and included the Balearic Islands, Roussillon, Perpignan and Montpellier. In 1276 the ruler of Majorca had declared himself independent of Aragon and the title had descended to James. Unfortunately for James, King Peter of Aragon had in 1343 denounced the declaration of independence of 1276 and attacked.

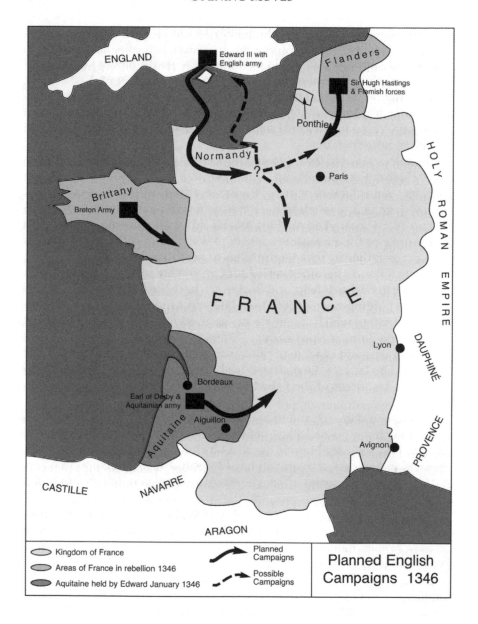

ENGLAND

Edward III with
English army

Flanders

Sir Hugh Hastings
& Flemish forces

Ponthieu

Normandy

?

Paris

Brittany

Breton Army

FRANCE

HOLY ROMAN EMPIRE

Lyon

DAUPHINÉ

Bordeaux

Earl of Derby &
Aquitainian army

Aiguillon

Aquitaine

Avignon

PROVENCE

CASTILLE

NAVARRE

ARAGON

Kingdom of France	Planned Campaigns	**Planned English Campaigns 1346**
Areas of France in rebellion 1346	Possible Campaigns	
Aquitaine held by Edward January 1346		

The Balearics and Roussillon fell quickly to the Spanish, but James held out in Montpellier.

James had appealed to Philip, who had sent south men and money to bolster James's independence. Now Philip wanted his men back. James replied that he would come in person with 500 men, leaving the bulk of his force in Montpellier to guard against an Aragonese attack. James contacted Grimaldi and asked for a lift. As we shall see, he secretly asked for rather more than that.

Looking forward to the campaigning season of 1346, Edward had rather more choices than did Philip – he also had more troubles. His main problem was a lack of money. Parliament had agreed to some taxes, but nowhere near enough to raise the money to renew the war in grand fashion. Nor was anybody willing to lend Edward much money, not with the example of the Florentine bankers to warn them off. Edward had no prospect of gathering meaningful allies to his cause with cash.

He was left with his allies in Flanders, who were too busy arguing with each other to be much help, and Brittany, where the Countess Jeanne was just about holding her own. His own lands in Aquitaine were now secure under Lancaster, who had confidently assured Edward he could hold out against Duke John of Normandy.

Edward was still capable of raising an army from England and Wales that would be large by English standards, but still fairly small in comparison to the resources of the French crown. The question was what to do with it.

Edward could go to Flanders and hope to use his army to rouse enthusiasm among his supposed allies, but the prospect was not overly attractive. Edward had seen for himself the disunity of the Flemings the previous year and in any case, the campaigns of 1339 and 1340 had convinced him that the cities and castles of north-eastern France were too strong to fall quickly.

Alternatively, Edward could go to Brittany. The arrival of a large English army could transform the situation there, turning near stalemate into a decisive French defeat. Strategically, however, Brittany was a dead end. Even if Countess Jeanne did secure freedom for her husband and her Duchy, it would have at best only a marginal impact on the Anglo-French conflict.

Aquitaine might offer better prospects. After all, the war had begun because of Aquitaine and tiny Ponthieu. If Edward could recover all his lands and secure his borders it would bolster his position for future campaigning seasons.

But Edward could not look forward with any confidence to future campaigning seasons. The English nobles and parliament had made it abundantly clear that they were getting fed up with Edward's exploits in France. Having a chivalrous king was all well and good, but having peace to trade

A fourteenth-century image of a king dining in his private apartments attended only by his family and personal servants.

prosperously was even better. Edward might care deeply about Aquitaine, and appreciate the large sums that taxes from the southern Duchy poured into his coffers, but the English were not too bothered. They were more concerned with English prosperity, English lives and English money. The war had been draining away all three. England wanted peace. The nobles and parliament had been persuaded to part with enough money to finance the war for 1346, but Edward was under no illusions. There would not be much money in the future.

Effectively, 1346 was Edward's last chance, and he knew it. When the winter weather brought an end to campaigning for the year he would almost certainly have to make peace with Philip. Given the effective stalemate that had set in, that peace would not be to Edward's advantage. No doubt he would get back Aquitaine and Ponthieu, but equally certainly he would have to hand over border fortresses and maybe accept another huge fine such as that agreed after the St Sardos affair, though that had still not been paid in full.

What Edward needed was a success that would greatly strengthen his negotiating stand come the peace talks. It did not really matter what that success was, be it military or diplomatic, but it had to be spectacular and it had to be quick. Neither Edward nor his advisors could see any prospect of achieving such a success.

It was while Edward and his nobles were considering their options, according to Froissart, that the Norman refugee Godfrey de Harcourt arrived in England. What he had to say to the English king would change the fate of nations.

III

The English Army

Although nobody realised it at the time, the army being mustered by Edward III for the campaigning season of 1346 would spark a revolution in warfare and, indirectly, cause massive upheavals to the entire social fabric of Europe. At the time, of course, all anybody was interested in was how best to defeat the French.

The commander was Edward himself, but his choice of senior officers was to have a profound influence on the way the campaign was to be fought. As convention dictated, Edward divided the army into three more-or-less self-contained divisions for supply, movement and tactical purposes.

The central division was commanded by the king himself; the advance guard was given to his eldest son, Prince Edward, who is better known as the Black Prince. The rearguard was put under the command of the Bishop of Durham and the Earl of Arundel. The Earl of Northampton, who had been brought back from Brittany the previous autumn, was appointed Constable, while the Earl of Warwick became Marshal.

The Black Prince was, if anything, even more devoted to the concept of chivalry than was King Edward himself. In 1346 he was aged just sixteen, and although everyone knew him to be tall, tough and handsome, his military abilities were entirely untested. He could sit a horse well enough and was famously dextrous with his sword, but how he would behave when brought face to face with an enemy intent on killing him, nobody knew. Nor was the boy's education over, for he took with him on campaign his tutor Bartholomew Burghersh.

No doubt King Edward wanted to give his son and heir experience of command, but he was pragmatic enough not to risk the safety of one third of his army on the decisions of an inexperienced teenager. Edward gave his son some talented and experienced knights to act as his staff and advisors. Among these were Sir Reginald Cobham, Sir Thomas Ughtred, Sir Richard Stafford and the colourful figure of Sir Thomas Holland.

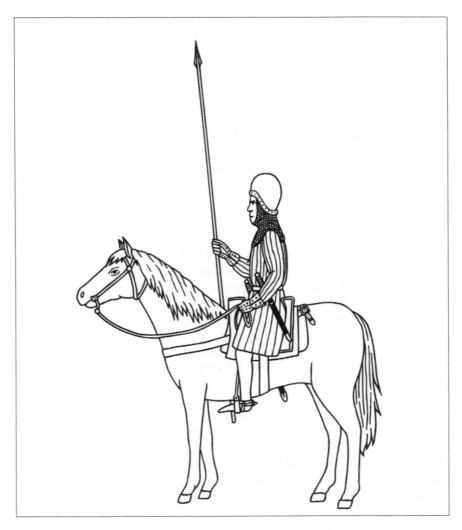

This hobilar is typical of this type of mounted infantry which the English copied from the Irish. He is mounted on a cheap riding horse which will not have been trained to cope with the noises of battle and so will have been ridden on campaign, but left behind when going into combat. A riding horse such as this would have cost around £3 in 1346. The man himself wears an iron palet helmet, a close-fitting, open-faced helmet with heavily padded lining. Mail hangs down from the sides and rear of the helmet to cover the shoulders and neck. His main body armour is a padded coat, which would have been more effective than perhaps it sounds. For weapons, he carries a short lance that could also be used on foot, and a sword paired with a dagger. The Crecy Campaign was the first time that hobilars had been seen on the continent in any numbers. The mobility of the English raiding parties and plundering expeditions took the French rather by surprise.

Sir Thomas Holland was more than twice the age of the Black Prince and one of the toughest and most respected knights in England. He had been active in the earlier campaigns against France and fought on Crusade against pagans in Prussia. He had lost an eye in battle and wore a large black eyepatch that covered not only the empty socket, but also the hideous scarring that surrounded it. Some years before the campaign began, he had become engaged to Joan, a young girl whose good looks earned her the nickname of 'The Fair Maid of Kent'. Joan was heiress to the enormously wealthy Earl of Kent and a granddaughter of Edward I.

Before the actual wedding could take place, however, the Earl of Kent changed his mind and engaged Joan to the wealthy Earl of Salisbury. The resulting legal action was still dragging on when Edward summoned both Sir Thomas and Salisbury to join him in Portsmouth in the spring of 1346. There seems to have been no ill will between the two men.

Although the Black Prince was in nominal command of the advance guard throughout the campaign, nobody was in any doubt that real power lay in the hands of the older and more experienced men that Edward had put to serve with his son.

Putting Thomas Hatfield, Bishop of Durham, in command of the rear guard might be thought an odd decision on Edward's part. But in the fourteenth century men of the cloth were not necessarily men of peace. At this date Durham was a county palatine, meaning that it ran many elements of government for itself. Most importantly, the Bishop of Durham was expected to organise his territories for defence against any Scottish invasion, so Hatfield would have brought plenty of experience in the organisational side of warfare to the army.

Durham was the Keeper of the Privy Seal in 1346. As such, he was a key figure in the national government and so almost duty bound to follow the king wherever he went. In any case, Durham's command was almost as nominal as that of the Black Prince. The rearguard had the earls of Arundel and Suffolk as joint second in command.

Richard Fitzalan, Earl of Arundel, was (after the king) probably the richest man in England. In 1346 he was aged thirty-three and had an impressive career behind him. His father had been executed on trumped-up charges during the Mortimer regime in 1328, but Edward had ensured that young Richard inherited his father's lands and titles intact. Trusted without hesitation by Edward, Arundel had been appointed Sheriff of Shropshire and chief justice of Wales, both posts that he had filled confidently and well. In 1341 scandal struck when he fell in love with the married Eleanor of Lancaster, sister to the Earl of Derby who was fighting so well in Aquitaine. Eleanor's husband died conveniently in 1344 so, after allowing a suitable time for mourning, she married Arundel in 1345.

Superb administrator though he was, Arundel had never served in a major military campaign. Presumably he was there to look after the organisational side of things.

Arundel's colleague, Robert Ufford, Earl of Suffolk was neither rich nor young. His rise to importance had begun when he joined the gang of younger men who helped Edward arrest Mortimer and end that baron's rule. In 1346 Suffolk was forty-eight years old, and at heart still a minor rural nobleman, despite his elevation to an earldom in 1337 and the acquisition of the spreading landed estates that went with the title. He retained his links to his old home and friends, and seems to have been popular with the lesser gentry.

The two key appointments were those of Marshal and Constable. As Marshal, Thomas Beauchamp, Earl of Warwick, was officially in command of the men-at-arms. It was his duty to ensure that the mounted, heavily armoured men were ready for action, in the right place and prepared to obey orders. Given that many of the men-at-arms were knights and not a few were nobles this was no easy task. Family pride and ambition were constant spurs to action for men determined to catch the king's eye, and discipline was not always a high priority. This was not such a problem for the English army as for the French, but it was a factor. Warwick had a deputy in the form of Sir Thomas Ughtred, who was placed more or less permanently alongside the Black Prince.

As Constable, William Bohun, Earl of Northampton, had a role similar to that of a modern staff officer. It was he who organised the supply of the army, selected which roads the various units would use and who advised the king on tactical matters. It was a wide-ranging and demanding role that called for administrative ability as well as martial skill. In essence, his task was to ensure that the army was able and willing to carry out the orders of the king quickly and efficiently, whatever they happened to be.

Northampton was a good choice for the role. His family had been prominent barons for more than two centuries, so he had plenty of family contacts and friendships upon which to call. His father had been a famous soldier, though he had been unable to avoid capture by the Scots at Bannockburn. He himself had fought in Scotland – where his twin brother had been killed – as well as in the abortive campaigns of 1339 and 1340. Most recently, he had been leading the English contingent in Brittany where he had performed well against the odds at Morlaix. Edward had brought him back specifically to act as Constable in the royal army for 1346.

Like Warwick, Northampton also had a deputy: Sir Adam Swynbourne. Unlike the Deputy Marshal, Swynbourne was not tied to a particular division but seems to have stayed close to Northampton.

Although both Northampton and Warwick had roles that, officially, were largely administrative, they were both active chivalrous knights. They realised that if they were noted for ostentatious chivalry, this would help them to be respected and obeyed in their official roles. As the campaign progressed, both Warwick and Northampton showed great flair for leading from the front in the most dangerous conditions.

Under these great captains were a number of lesser commanders and captains. Although all knights were entitled to carry their arms painted on their shields, only those exercising battlefield command over a unit of men were allowed to have their arms displayed on a banner. These knight bannerets, as they were known, led their men on the march and in battle. The *Acta Bellicosa* lists forty-eight of these men. Although this list may not be complete, it certainly indicates that the English army was divided into about fifty or so tactical units.

The army that Edward had brought these men together to command was, by English standards, a large one. It was certainly the largest that Edward had so far raised to fight in France. With so much at stake, Edward was clearly determined to take with him the very best fighting force possible.

Preparations had begun in October 1345 when the orders were first sent out through England to muster men and supplies. It was decided that the army would gather at Portsmouth in March and be ready to sail for France at the end of that month. As events fell out, the timetable proved to be too ambitious and the army was not ready until June.

There were, at this date, three methods of raising an army. With his international credit rating non-existent Edward was unable to hire mercenaries, even if he had wanted to do so. He was therefore thrown back on the military manpower resources of England and Wales.

The traditional method of recruiting a feudal army was by commission of array. It was a basic feudal duty that able-bodied men were liable for military service. In an emergency all adult men were expected to turn out to protect their homes from bandits or raiders, but it was recognised that serving in an army was a different matter. For a man to be useful on campaign he had to be fit, tough and have at least a reasonable skill with weapons. He also needed to turn up fully equipped with weapons, outdoor clothing, marching boots, assorted tools and other essentials for spending several weeks out of doors in all weathers. Clearly only a minority of men would be physically able to serve on a lengthy campaign, and even fewer would have the inclination.

The commission of array for a county or town instructed the local officials to find a set number of volunteers, and to persuade those men who would be staying at home to pay the money to equip those who were going. There was no set number that a county or town was expected to produce, and each time the commissions were issued the numbers varied depending on how many men the king wanted in his army. In turn, this probably depended on how many men the king could afford to pay, feed and transport on campaign.

The records of the commissions of array for the muster of 1346 have survived. These show that Devon was asked to send 60 men, Kent 280 and other counties various totals in between. In all, the counties of England were summoned to send 3,900 men. The towns had smaller totals, as few as two men from Watford or as many as forty from Lincoln. London was unique in being asked to send 200. The towns and cities between them were asked to send 1,850 men. In all, therefore, England was asked to produce an array of 5,750 men.

How many of these men actually turned up is unknown. Very few records survive to tell us, and those that do may not be typical. Norfolk, for instance, sent 129 of its 200 men and Cheshire 71 instead of 100. However, these figures may have survived simply because the officials responsible were criticised for failing to produce the men required. It is likely that around 4,600 Englishmen were recruited to the army by array.

The men from each county or town came complete with a commander, usually a local knight who was very often the official responsible for mustering the array. In theory, the contingents were divided up into units of twenty men, each of which had a junior commander called a vintenar. In practice, the subdivisions within each contingent were of irregular numbers, depending on who had turned up, and quite often on where they had come from. There seems to have been a real desire by men from adjacent villages to serve together with the consequent disruption this caused to the official groupings of twenty men.

Although the records are unclear, it seems that the counties were expected to provide infantry. Most of these men were archers. The towns, however, were generally expected to send men who rode ponies or light horses. These were not cavalry for they were not expected to fight from horseback. Instead, they were mounted infantry who fought on foot but rode to battle. This made them more mobile than their county comrades, and so they were able to undertake more wide-ranging duties when on campaign. Such mounted infantry were generally known as hobilars.

The array contingents were not allowed to carry their own banners into battle. That privilege was reserved for the knights banneret whose banners served as rallying points in the confusion of battle. However, some towns did make the effort to dress their men in uniforms of a kind. Certainly many equipped their men with clothes of a single colour, though possibly there were various shades of green, brown or red within a single contingent. The Londoners must have made a particularly inspiring sight as they marched off to war in suits made from a cloth with bold red and white stripes. The men from Cheshire all wore a distinctive hat, though sadly nobody thought to record its design.

Commissions of array were also sent to Wales. Given that the Prince of Wales, the Black Prince, was setting out on his first campaign, a special effort was made to recruit Welshmen. The Welsh arrays were organised not by county or town but by lordships. A total of over 7,000 men was demanded of Wales, though again the numbers that actually mustered were rather lower. It may be that something between 5,000 and 6,000 Welshmen arrived in Portsmouth ready to join the campaign.

Unlike the Englishmen, the Welshmen came equipped in distinctive fashion. About half the men were archers, the others spearmen. As we shall see later, these men seem to have formed up together in battle as a distinctive tactical formation.

In addition to the common soldiers raised by commissions of array, the traditional feudal system demanded that men who held land of a certain value were expected to turn up in person to serve for a set number of days. Under this feudal levy, the men had to provide for their own equipment and serve for a set number of days (usually forty) at their own expense. If they were called upon to serve for longer, the king would pay them a daily rate and supply them with food.

In theory, a man who held land producing an annual income of £40 or more should arrive equipped as a knight. A man with an income of between £20 and £40 was expected to appear at muster equipped as an esquire. As we shall see when we turn to look at actual equipment, the knights and esquires tended to be grouped together as men-at-arms. Men with an income of between £10 and £20 were expected to arrive equipped as hobilars, or mounted infantry. Although they were not expected to do so, men with incomes as low as £5 sometimes turned up equipped for war. It did their standing in county society no harm at all to be seen to be as keen for a chivalrous encounter as the richer men.

In practice this system had long since been in decline. Many landholders were old, sick or handicapped by illness or injury. For many years it had been customary for such men to send sons or younger brothers to take their place. More recently, it had become possible for these men to pay a cash sum instead of turning up and going on campaign.

It should not be thought that war was any less popular than it had been. Most knights and esquires considered it a basic duty to serve their king in battle. It was just that there were many other demands on a man's time. Much of this was produced by serving the king. As the governmental systems of England developed, so too did the burdens on county gentry. It had always been the knights and esquires who had been expected to act as the king's agents locally. Now that taxation, judicial systems and even road building was becoming better regulated, there was an increased need for knights to serve as part-time royal administrators. Going to war was becoming just one among many ways to serve the king.

By the 1340s a new system of recruiting armies was beginning to come into use: the indentured retinue. The mustering of 1346 is the first time that we have evidence for this being used on a large scale.

The key men in the new system were local gentry of warlike temperament. A local noble or knight with chivalrous reputation would announce that he was forming a retinue to serve with the king. Any local man who wanted to go to war would go along at a set date to be assessed. As with the older feudal levy, the men were expected to supply their own war gear but now they expected to be paid a daily rate from the day that they left home to go on campaign.

There was also much greater flexibility as to who could go. Quite humble families could club together to equip one of their number as an esquire, or the sons of a nobleman might volunteer to serve as knights. Anyone who could scrape together the money to pay for armour and weapons, and who was fit and able would be welcome. As a result, the retinues came to include a much wider cross-section of local society than had the old levies. In the longer run, this would provide a route for young, talented men to get on in life and make English society more interlinked from top to bottom.

Again, chivalry was important. A retinue leader who had earned a reputation as a chivalrous knight would find it easier to recruit good men than one who had not. Moreover, it must be remembered that two important elements in chivalry were success and reliability. A chivalrous knight would be successful in war only if he made sure his retinue had good equipment, nutritious food and regular pay. As ever, there was a lot more to chivalry than is often supposed.

At the time of Crecy the concept of a retinue raised in this way was relatively new. Even so, some retinues were becoming semi-permanent formations. When records survive of the names of men serving in the retinues of particular knights or nobles we see the same names cropping up year after year. The fact that these men were serving together for years at a time gave the units a cohesiveness and discipline entirely lacking in the units raised by array or levy that served for just a few months, then disbanded.

The importance for King Edward as he mustered his army for 1346 was that the new system was much more reliable than the old one. Men organising retinues could state with absolute confidence how many men, equipped with what weapons, they were going to bring with them. Moreover, Edward would know that every man who served in a retinue was there because he wanted to be and could be counted upon not to slip off home at the first opportunity. The same could be not said with any confidence of the feudal levy or the commissions of array.

When the king accepted a retinue into his service a written contract was drawn up which set down how much would be paid and when, as well as details such as where the retinue was to meet the king and how long it would be on campaign. Very often the king would pay a cash sum on signature of the contract, known as a prest, to offset the expenses of the retinue leader. Some contracts specify that the king will replace equipment lost on campaign; usually this refers to horses but sometimes to other war gear.

When the contract had been agreed, signed and sealed it was cut in half using a pair of scissors with a wavy edge, rather like modern pinking shears. This ensured that only matching copies would fit together and was a device to stop fraud on either side. The indentures caused by the cutting give these retinues their name.

Rates of pay for men serving in indentured retinues were fairly standard:

Spearman	2 pence per day
Archer	3 pence per day
Mounted archer	6 pence per day
Hobilar	6 pence per day
Esquire	1 shilling per day
Knight	2 shillings per day

The size of the retinues varied greatly, as did the proportions of the various types of soldier within them. Sir John Ravensholme, for instance, arrived for service equipped as a knight, with two esquires and three archers. By way of contrast, Sir William Kildesby brought along four knights (including himself), seventy-three esquires, sixty-eight mounted archers and eleven archers. The larger retinues, such as Kildesby's, served as a unit themselves, and their commander was made a banneret. The smaller retinues were grouped together for battlefield purposes and only one of the leaders allowed to be a banneret.

There is often a discrepancy between what the king was paying for and what the contract specified. The king might be paying for ten knights, while the contract specified twelve. This was simply a way for an aspiring knight or noble to impress the king. Paying extra taxes would impress nobody except a clerk in the exchequer, but marching to war with an extra contingent would be noticed by the king. There were also attempts to stand out from the crowd by providing superior-quality arms and armour for men in a retinue, or giving them all uniform clothing embroidered with heraldic devices.

Given that most of the contracts, or at least summaries of them, have survived it is possible to be rather more accurate about the numbers of men who arrived in retinues than it is for those who came as part of the arrays. These give totals of:

Earls	8
Knights	654
Esquires	1,821
Mounted men	2,133
Archers	138
Spearmen & others	666
Total Retinue strength	5,420

It should be noted that the 'mounted men' included both hobilars and archers who came to the muster mounted. Because both these types of soldier were paid the same daily rate there was a tendency simply to group them together without distinction.

In total, therefore, there must have been something around 15,000 combatants in the English army when it left England. There were also, of course, a number of non-combatants that went on campaign.

The most numerous of these were the government officials who had to go wherever the king went. At this period a surprisingly eclectic mix of matters were expected to be dealt with by the king in person. As the head of the government and of justice, the king was (in name at least) responsible for all government decisions and all court cases. Although by the fourteenth century most of the work was done by officials, any thorny issue was still passed to the king for his decision. This did not involve only awkward points of law, but any matter that involved one of the richer or more powerful barons – or anyone who had the contacts to get a baron to intercede on their behalf. Queries about taxation, land boundaries, inheritance disputes and many other matters had to be decided by the king, even when he was busy fighting a war. To deal with the mass of documents that this routine work would entail, Edward took thirty-six household clerks with him.

The royal kitchen was expected to feed any barons or senior knights who happened to be near the king at dinner time. For the king not to invite such men to dine with him would have been a serious breach of chivalrous protocol. Since the king's table was expected to offer the best foods and wines available and to be attended by a suitable number of uniformed servants, another twenty or so men were needed. There were also fishermen tasked with hauling fish out of any rivers the army passed, as well a couple of men to put up and take down the royal tent. There were even two musicians.

There were also a number of military specialists who were not included under the retinues or arrays, but were nonetheless necessary to a medieval army. There were twelve blacksmiths, forty carpenters and sixty miners that we know of, and no doubt there were other specialists, records of which have not survived.

Many of the retinues and array contingents brought along non-combatants who do not appear on the formal records, but are mentioned in various chronicles and letters. There were several friars and a few priests who ministered to the spiritual needs of the army. In this age when more-or-less all men were devout Christians, the business of religion was of great importance. Men expected to take part in services on a regular basis, even when in a foreign land on campaign.

There were also doctors, there to care for men who fell ill as well as for the wounded. We know that during the Battle of Crecy itself all the doctors and medical staff were gathered together in one place some distance behind the battle lines. It seems that any wounded man could avail himself of their services during battle, though they may have given priority to the men of their own unit at other times.

Medical skills were not as crude in the fourteenth century as many might think. It is true that knowledge of disease was limited in the extreme, but when it came to the more practical business of caring for wounds simple trial and error over the centuries had taught doctors a lot. It was known that fragments of clothing or weapons needed to be extracted from a wound or it might turn septic. Gaping wounds could be sewn up and then, like less severe wounds, bound up with bandages and herbal compresses of surprising effectiveness. Some herbs were known to combat infection and were used widely. Broken bones could be set and shattered limbs amputated with at least a fair degree of success. Wounded men stood a respectable chance of survival – so long as they were on the winning side.

The main fighting strength of the English army in 1346, as with any medieval army, was expected to be the men-at-arms: the knights and esquires. To understand how these men performed in battle it is necessary to look at their weapons and their armour.

The men-at-arms usually fought together and at the time little real distinction was made on campaign between knights and esquires. The key difference was social: a knight had been knighted while an esquire had not – though both were men-at-arms for military purposes. This in turn reflected the social standing within local society of the men themselves. It might be a tidy exercise for royal officials to state that men who held land worth £40 or more in annual rents should be a knight, but that did not reflect reality on the ground. Some men with rather less land became knights because their fathers had been knights and they felt their family deserved the social dignity. Other men with much greater incomes did not become knights because they sought to evade the obligations to serve the king that went with the status.

In practice, however, knights did tend to be rather richer than esquires. As a result they usually rode to war with better armour, weapons and equipment. Nevertheless, there was no clear break or distinction with regard to gear. With each man free to pick and choose his own equipment and weaponry there was a seamless gradation from the very richest with the best of everything down to the impoverished rural esquire who could barely scrape together odds and ends.

Even to the casual observer, however, there was one clear difference on the field of battle between a knight and an esquire. A knight was allowed to have his own coat of arms painted on to his shield, while an esquire was not. While the knights proudly sported an amazingly varied collection of brightly coloured heraldry painstakingly painted on their shields, the esquires favoured either plain shields, or crudely painted designs based on those of their retinue commander, county or town. Increasingly,

English soldiers favoured the Cross of St George: a red cross on a white background. Small St George badges were often sewn on to clothing by poorer soldiers and it is likely that at least some esquires painted the design on their shields. At the time of Crecy this habit was only just beginning, so the red cross would not have been as ubiquitous at this date as it was to become later.

The basic equipment expected of a man-at-arms was a horse, body armour, a helmet, a shield and a sword. There was within this a wide variety of gear to be found. The richest men wore plate armour on their bodies, legs and arms over the basic mail suit while the cunningly wrought bascinet protected the head. Poorer men might have only a mail suit and a few at this date were still wearing the heavy, cumbersome great helm that encased the entire head in metal.

The arms and equipment of the English men-at-arms was broadly similar to that of their French opponents. It was in the realm of tactics that the English were unique.

As the Earl of Derby (by 1346 Lancaster) had shown at Auberoche, a charge by men-at-arms on horseback was a terrifyingly effective tactic. When executed properly, such a charge could sweep all before it and win a battle in minutes. By this date, however, the English were specialising in foot combat, often in a defensive position.

What the English had realised was that war horses, no matter how well trained, will not charge into an apparently solid object. The success of the mounted charge depended on the target enemy troops being in open formation or disordered in some way. Given the poor discipline and general paucity of formation training of the period this was very often the case. Infantry were particularly vulnerable to a mounted charge. Not only did they have a natural lack of height, but they were usually troops raised by array and so were only part-time soldiers. The men-at-arms, by contrast, were trained for war from birth and if not professional in modern terms were certainly experienced and effective. Even if the formation was well formed, it was unlikely to remain so for long. The sight of several hundred large men in full armour riding big horses approaching at high speed is guaranteed to strike fear into any man. A great many units and even entire armies simply dissolved into panic-stricken flight as a well co-ordinated charge of knights approached – and little wonder.

To a horse, however, a dense formation of men is as solid as a stone wall. If the infantry stand shoulder to shoulder and keep their nerve, the apparently unstoppable charge will founder. At the last moment the horses of the front rank will shy away or stop. The rear ranks of horsemen will give some momentum, pushing forward those in front, but the ranks of the charging knights will become disordered and confused. The fight will then become a static one in which the men on both sides will thrust and hack at each other with their weapons. The mounted men will have the advantage of height, but those on foot will have an advantage of numbers. A man on foot occupies marginally less than a metre of frontage, one on horseback just over two. So there would be at least twice as many men on foot able to use their weapons in a given length of frontage.

To suit their new infantry tactics, the English men-at-arms had some distinctive equipment. The first of these was the great sword, probably copied from the Scottish claymore. This had a blade at least 1.1m long with a diamond-shaped cross section. The handle was large enough for the sword to be used two-handed and the cross-guards were rather longer than was usual for single-handed swords. This was an infantry weapon, for it was virtually impossible to wield a two-handed sword from horseback.

The second distinctively English weapon was the foot lance. The standard lance, or glaive, used by a man-at-arms was around 6m in length. When first ordered to fight on foot, the knights found these lances were too long and cumbersome. Many got their staff to saw off the rear end of the lance, then used the front half as a weapon on foot. Soon specific foot lances were being produced with a length of just under two metres.

What both the foot lance and two-handed sword had in common was that they were held with both hands. This meant that the left arm was no longer free to wield the shield. There is some evidence that men using these weapons had additional shoulder armour to give protection against blows coming down from an opponent on horseback. The most usual shoulder defences in 1346 were besagews, plates of steel attached to the front and back of the shoulder by leather straps. The more sophisticated epaulieres had first been developed only in the later 1330s, so at Crecy only the richest men could have afforded them. These were made up of a number of curved metal plates that hinged together. The uppermost plate was attached to the shoulder close to the neck and the others then flopped down over the shoulder itself. Alternatively, these men may have had small shields slung over the shoulder by means of a leather strap. Perhaps some had both.

What impressed foreign contemporaries about the English dismounted tactics was the density of the formation. Writing of a battle fought in 1359, Froissart states that 'The English dismounted and stood so closely together that they could not be separated'. Other chroniclers make similar comments. Clearly, the disciplined ranks of tightly packed armoured men was something entirely new to warfare.

Unfortunately, no contemporaries record how deep the English foot formations were on the battlefield at this date. It is possible, however, to make some deductions. The formation needed to be deep enough to convince charging horses that it was a solid and immovable object. It also needed to allow men from the rear ranks to step forward to replace men who were killed or wounded in the front rank as the fighting continued. At the same time, if there were too many ranks, the men at the rear would be effectively useless as they were simply unable to get their weapons to reach the enemy.

We know that in 1415 one English unit drew up four men deep, though whether this was typical or not we do not know. In all likelihood, the depth of a formation of men-at-arms on foot probably varied depending on how many men were present, how much frontage had to be defended and how much trust the commander put in his men to stand firm. Between four and eight ranks of men might be thought to have been usual.

If more men than this were to hand, it would make sense to put them into a separate formation placed some distance behind the first. From there they could be moved to plug any gaps that opened up in the forward formation, or moved to counter any new enemy thrusts.

In some situations the horses of the men-at-arms were kept close by. At more than one battle we read that the English mounted up to pursue an enemy that had been halted by the dismounted men at arms. Edward had done just this at Halidon Hill in 1333, to devastating effect on the Scots. The Scottish shiltron formations had been badly disordered by their repulse and were falling back to reform when the English mounted men-at-arms struck. On this occasion Edward had held back some 200 knights behind the battle line. These men were, therefore, fresh and untried by the initial fighting. When he came to draw up his army at Crecy, Edward will have remembered the success of this tactic.

Rather more numerous in the English army than the men-at-arms were the mounted men known as hobilars and mounted archers. Although the hobilars who rode to Crecy were almost exclusively English, this type of soldier had originated in Ireland. The name comes from the type of horse the men rode. The hobby was a tough, wiry pony standing about twelve hands high. Hobilars were a feature of warfare in Ireland for centuries, but are first mentioned outside the island in 1296 when Edward I hired 260 of them to join the army he was leading into Scotland. So useful were these men that soon English kings were asking Englishmen to come to war equipped as hobilars and by 1346 they were an established part of any English army.

Although the English hobilars rode English ponies rather than Irish ones, they rode to war equipped in similar fashion and were tasked with similar duties. The typical hobilar of the 1340s came equipped with an open-faced helmet which would have been considerably cheaper than those used by men-at-arms. There was sometimes a mail flap known as the aventail that hung down around the neck to give protection there.

For body armour the hobilar would have worn cheaper types of armour known as the haubergeon, the gambeson and the aketon. The records are imprecise, but it seems that a haubergeon was a form of mail tunic that reached to the elbows and mid-thigh with a split up to the crotch so that the wearer could sit on a horse. Mail was effective against all but the most determined blow by an edged weapon, though it was vulnerable to arrows and crossbow bolts.

The gambeson was made entirely of cloth. It came in the form of a long-sleeved coat that reached down to the knees and laced up the front to the neck. The garment was made as two layers of tough woollen cloth, between which were stuffed masses of raw wool, horse hair, old rags or pieces of leather. These were packed together with great force and, in theory at least, provided at least eighteen layers of fabric between the two outer layers. The whole was then quilted with lines of vertical stitching to hold the stuffing in place. A well-made gambeson would stand up on its own when new. With prolonged wear, it would mould itself to the wearer as the loose pieces of stuffing migrated about within the outer layers. The shoulders and elbows in particular needed to be broken in to achieve good flexibility.

These gambesons were surprisingly effective. A slashing blow would be absorbed without too much trouble, though a thrust from a lance or sword would probably penetrate the garment. An arrow would pierce a gambeson at close range, but if it struck at an angle or at such a distance that it had lost much of its momentum it would be halted. Some men liked to wear a gambeson over a haubergeon to combine the advantages of both. This combination was not only rather expensive for the average hobilar, but it left the man wearing a rather inflexible outfit that limited the speed and dexterity of his weapon-wielding movements in battle.

The aketon was a more expensive garment than either the haubergeon or gambeson. It originated among the Saracens and was adopted by European soldiers during the Crusades. The Saracen garment was known as the al qutun, which means literally 'cotton' and referred to the usual facing material in the Middle East.

Like the gambeson, it was based on two layers of woollen cloth between which was sandwiched the defensive armour. The aketon, however, had between the layers of cloth a large number of small iron plates, each of which was fixed to front and back cloth layers with a rivet. Each of the metal plates had to be carefully shaped with larger plates covering the chest and smaller ones covering areas, such as the stomach or shoulder, where flexibility was needed. Aketons came in a range of qualities, the better ones containing hundreds of small plates and being faced with coloured velvets or satins. A good aketon was almost as good for general combat as a cheaper suit of armour as worn by an esquire, and was correspondingly expensive. Few hobilars in the Crecy campaign would have worn an aketon, though they would become more popular as the years passed.

For weaponry, the hobilar carried a spear about three metres long, a single-handed sword and a heavy knife of the sort taken to war by most soldiers who were not men-at-arms. All these weapons were effective against men wearing similar types of armour, but would have made little impact on the better equipped knights.

The main role of the hobilars on campaign was off the battlefield proper. Mounted on a pony, the hobilar could travel quickly over rough terrain – such as was common in Ireland at the time. Such men were useful as scouts and outriders, ranging widely over the countryside some kilometres away from the main army. They could scout for enemy forces, report back on the lie of the land and identify which towns and castles had up-to-date, well-maintained fortifications, and which did not. Given their reasonably good arms and armour, hobilars could be expected to hold bridges and other positions of importance with a fair degree of success.

It seems that hobilars usually rode in organised groups of a dozen or more men. The larger forces were commanded by a knight or esquire who had definite orders of what he was supposed to achieve while detached from the main force. In some instances units of hobilars seem to have served as small armies in their own right, being separated from the main army for days at a time and being allowed much freedom to use their initiative as to what they should do. As we shall see, the hobilars were particularly effective at the strategy known as the chevauchée.

On the battlefield itself, hobilars vanish from the written record. So far as chroniclers and eyewitnesses are concerned they are simply not there. It is impossible that a commander would not use such large numbers of well-armed men, so the hobilars must have been fighting in some way that caused them to appear not to be hobilars. Given their arms, it is most likely that the hobilars fought on foot and blended into the ranks of the spearmen who were present in large numbers in any medieval army.

With their helmets and armour, the hobilars on foot could best be termed as heavy spearmen to distinguish them from their less-armoured colleagues. It was not just dismounted hobilars who fought as heavy spearmen: many of the men recruited by array did so as well. These men seem to have come more from the towns than the counties. The arrayed men usually had shields in addition to their various types of body armour and helmets, so perhaps the hobilars likewise had shields for foot combat.

The role of such men in battle was crucial in armies of this time. It was these men who patrolled city walls and guarded castles. It was they who held bridges and guarded fords. In major battles, it may have been the charge of mounted men-at-arms that was the prime offensive tactic, but it was the heavy spearmen who provided the defensive backbone to any force.

Only the best heavy infantry were expected to be able to stand up to a charge by mounted knights if caught in open country. Their less well-trained colleagues could, however, hold a position if they were protected by sheltering behind a thick hedge or were positioned above a steep slope that would make a mounted charge difficult. Many commanders used their infantry in this way to seal off parts of the battlefield and block them to enemy advance. Of course, if no enemy men-at-arms were to hand, heavy infantry could be used offensively against similar types of troops on the enemy side.

A key problem with heavy infantry of this type was that they very rarely did much training. The most that could be expected was that the men of a particular town would practise marching together and might have a grasp of basic tactics, such as forming up in a solid wall of shields. But the contingents from different towns and cities would come together only when the army was on the march – and by then it was simply too late to learn complex tactics. Much would depend on the unit commanders and their willingness and ability to co-operate with each other.

Heavy infantry tended to form up in dense masses, the front rank locking shields to form a solid wall. They mostly stood on the defensive, but could advance straight ahead to attack others of their own kind. If a block of such men was taken in flank or rear, however, they were lost. Unable to perform the complex countermarching needed to change front without losing formation, the organisation would collapse.

When used in combination with men-at-arms, however, the heavy infantry could be a highly effective element of the army. This was a tactic at which the French excelled, as we shall see.

Thus far the English army might appear to be a fairly standard mustering for the mid-fourteenth century. There was, however, one revolutionary new weapon that Edward took some pains over and which made a real impact at Crecy. Edward was taking guns to war.

In the financial accounts for 1345 we find King Edward paying Robert Aubyn eight pennies a day for his job as artillator at the Tower of London, and we know that Aubyn went to France in 1346 while his wife stayed in London and was paid by the king for manufacturing gunpowder. Several chroniclers, including Froissart and Villani, mention that the English used guns at Crecy. At this date, however, guns were a very new invention, so accounts of what types of weapon were used and how effective they were are not entirely clear.

Although firearms were new and much experimentation was going on, it is thought that there were three basic types of gun in 1346. The largest was the bombard which hurled a stone ball about 16cm in diameter over a distance of about 1.5km – though it was only even roughly accurate at about half that range. Their main use was in sieges when they could be used to smash stone walls to pieces. The mere presence of a bombard in the siege lines was usually enough to persuade a garrison to surrender.

Getting a bombard into position was, however, no easy task. To start with, a bombard was a very large piece of metalwork, weighing about 1.5

tonnes. Merely producing that amount of iron to a consistent standard called for metallurgical skills of a high order. The iron then had to be shaped into a number of identical tapered rods which were put around a wooden core to form the barrel. These were then bound together with precisely shaped iron hoops that were heated to be red-hot before being slipped over the rods. As the hoops cooled, they shrank and so bound the rods tightly together. Very few men could produce large pieces of iron to such precise measurements.

The final section of a bombard was the iron chamber that held the gunpowder charge. There would be two or three of these per bombard, each being cleaned and filled while another was being used. The chamber was put at the rear of the bombard, then secured in place by heavy wooden wedges. Finally, the ball was pushed down the mouth of the gun and packed into place with pieces of cloth and more wooden wedges. Again, manufacturing measurements had to be precise.

Then there was the not inconsiderable business of moving the gun. Each bombard was mounted on a heavy wooden sledge and dragged by a team of up to sixty oxen. This made a mess of the road surface, so the artillery usually came last in any army. Oxen pulling a load such as this are doing well to cover 15km in a day, and certainly cannot keep up that rate of progress for more than a two or three days.

Taking all things together, a bombard was too heavy and expensive to be risked on a campaign that was going to involve much in the way of marching. They were for use in sieges. Given that Edward knew his 1346 campaign would be one of movement, it is highly unlikely that he took a bombard with him. He did, however, ship three of them over in time to take part in the siege of Calais that followed the battle. Some believe that these three guns were with him throughout the campaign.

At the opposite extreme of firearm size were the poleguns. These were relatively cheap and easy to produce; almost any competent blacksmith could make one once he had been shown how. They were about the size and shape of a modern food tin, though made of iron and with much thicker walls. They were mounted on the end of a wooden pole about 1.3 metres long, hence their name.

A quantity of gunpowder was rammed down into the pot-shaped barrel, followed by a handful of scrap iron, pebbles or anything else hard and heavy that was to hand. When the gun was fired, the stones and iron would spray out the muzzle to a distance of around 40m. Such weapons were hopelessly inaccurate, but against a solid formation of men were effective enough. They were of only limited use, however. Given their short range, these guns could be fired only once at an advancing enemy before the two forces clashed. No doubt the English had many such guns with them on the Crecy campaign.

Between the poleguns and the bombards were a range of other firearms of various types and calibres. Known loosely as ribaudekin, these guns were mounted on carts that could be hauled by horses and so keep up with an army on the march. These guns fired metal or stone shot about five centimetres in diameter over a range of about 300m with some accuracy. They could be used against older or lighter fortifications, but were not much use against up-to-date fortifications. They could, however, be used in the field against enemy formations. It was probably guns of this type that were recorded as being in action at Crecy by the chroniclers.

What all these guns and firearms had in common was their complete unpredictability. Even in the hands of a trained and experienced gunner, the weapons would behave completely differently one day to how they did the next. The problem was the gunpowder.

At this date making gunpowder was more of an art that a science. Nobody understood the chemical reactions involved, so getting the mix right was down to trial and error, with each gunner fiercely guarding his own preferred method. Of the three ingredients, charcoal was by far the cheapest and easiest to source in the 1340s. Sulphur was more expensive, but again not too difficult to come by. It was saltpetre that really represented the problem.

Saltpetre, as its name meaning 'salt-rock' suggests, could be mined, but only in a very few places. Most countries resorted to manufacturing saltpetre. This was a messy and protracted business that involved collecting together large quantities of horse, cattle or sheep manure, mixing it with wood ash and piling it up inside a wooden barn which had a waterproof floor of rammed clay. The organic mass was then wetted thoroughly each week with human urine for a year. Then the wetting was stopped and the barn sealed shut to allow the rotting mass to dry out gradually. As the water evaporated slowly from the surface of the putrid mess, it brought to the surface raw saltpetre which precipitated out as white crystals. Each cubic metre of manure produced about 8kg of saltpetre.

The saltpetre produced by this method was a mix of various organic nitrates, the composition of which varied with the quality of the raw materials, the temperatures at which it rotted and the time allowed for drying. Each batch of saltpetre had its own qualities that affected the performance of the gunpowder that it was used to make. As we shall see, the crucial feature of this crude saltpetre at Crecy proved to be its hydrostatic properties. All saltpetre will absorb water from the air if left uncovered, but certain forms of raw saltpetre will absorb it more quickly than others. On damp days – and Crecy was fought on a famously humid day – the saltpetre will suck up moisture faster than ever.

Gunpowder in the fourteenth century was a simple mix of charcoal, sulphur and saltpetre for as yet no way had been found of combining the three into a stable powder. Each of these three has a quite different

An illustration of a heavy bombard taken from a manuscript drawn a few years after Crecy. The construction of the barrel with long iron rods bound with iron hoops can be clearly seen, as can the solid wooden carriage on which the gun rests. Such guns were used most often during sieges.

density, so if a barrel of mixed gunpowder was put onto a cart and trundled over the bumpy roads of the period for any amount of time the three components would separate out. Before a barrel of gunpowder could be used it had to be tumbled around the ground for quite some time to remix the ingredients. It was more usual, therefore, for the ingredients to be transported separately and for the gunpowder to be mixed only when it was needed.

The gunpowder then had to 'proved' before it could be used. This generally involved putting a measured quantity of powder into a polegun and ramming down a lead pellet of known weight. The gun was then fired, with the gunner watching carefully to gauge the force and sound of the explosion, as well as the distance the shot was carried. From this the gunner could then work out how much powder should be used to produce a standard explosive force. The powder would then be parcelled up into separate cloth bags accordingly.

As can be imagined, getting guns ready to fire was a laborious, lengthy and highly skilled business. Even then things did not always go right. As late as 1460 King James II of Scotland was killed when a cannon burst as he fired it.

Nevertheless, Edward clearly expected great things of his firearms in the campaign of 1346. Although we don't know what guns he took with him, we do know that he took enough ingredients to mix up about 3,500kg of gunpowder. This was not enough for a major siege (for which around 20,000kg would be needed), but was nonetheless a large amount of powder to cart about through enemy territory.

In the event, however, it was not the newfangled guns that would prove to be revolutionary aspect of Edward's army in 1346. It was not gunpowder that would change the face of warfare. It was a much older – even old-fashioned – weapon: the longbow.

IV

The Longbow

The longbow was not a new weapon in 1346. It had been around for generations and been an integral part of most armies raised in Wales or England for at least a century. Before discovering why it suddenly became a much more effective weapon in 1346, it is necessary to look at the weapon itself.

The longbows used by Edward's archers were made of yew staves almost two metres in length. Made from just one piece of wood, in technical terms they were self-bows, as opposed to composite bows that are made up of several pieces of different materials. Much skill went into the manufacture of a longbow, which was correspondingly expensive. Each bow cost about the same as two weeks' wages for a skilled labourer, and a sheaf of twenty-four arrows cost much the same.

Each stave had to be cut from a log of yew so that it was straight and tapered at each end. The stave needed to contain equal parts of heartwood and sapwood. The heartwood of a yew will withstand compression well, springing back into shape, while the sapwood is equally good under tension. By placing the sapwood on the outside of the bow where it will be stretched as the bow is drawn, and the heartwood on the inside where it will be squeezed, the bowyer was able to produce a powerful, tough and reliable weapon. After being shaped, the bows were fitted with tips of horn shaped to hold the bowstring securely. The bow was habitually kept unstrung to ensure that it kept its shape. It was only knocked, or bent to have the bowstring fitted, when action was imminent.

Until fairly recently it was not entirely clear how powerful the medieval war bow actually was. However, many dozen longbows were recovered from the wreck of the Mary Rose, a Tudor warship that sank in the Solent and was preserved in mud, and these have made it possible to produce accurate modern replicas. What these bows revealed about the technical merits of the medieval warbow was quite remarkable.

This archer could be either English or Welsh as by the 1340s bowmen from the two nations were dressed and equipped almost identically. He is dressed generally as he would have been at home on his farm. He wears a pair of black leather shoes over woollen hose that reach from his toes up to a leather belt to which they are laced. Over this he has a woollen jacket finished in the fashionable jagged hem. He had a separate hood to match his jacket, here shown thrown back. His head is covered by a padded cap, so he may have a cheap helmet of some kind for use in close-quarter combat. Around each wrist he has leather braces to protect his forearms when shooting. The bow is a standard longbow as described in the text. He carries a sheaf of arrows tucked through his belt. This was standard practice when an archer expected to shift position in action, when he was adopting a static defensive position the arrows would be pushed point down into the ground in front of him for quick shooting. This man carries a sword, presumably picked up as plunder from a battlefield somewhere. A long knife would have been more usual.

The strength of a bow is termed its draw weight, that is the weight that would be needed to draw a bow to its shooting position if it were hung on a wall and weights attached to the string. Modern hunting and target bows have a draw weight of around 35–45kg. The medieval warbows had a draw weight of some 70–80kg. This awesome power was necessary to do the job for which the bow was used.

Just as the bows of the Crecy campaign were more powerful than those of today, so the arrows were heavier. They weighed 100g or more, about twice the weight of modern hunting arrows. They were made of oak, ash, birch, beech or elder, though some craftsmen preferred chestnut. To withstand the enormous force inflicted on it when the bow was loosed, the arrows were relatively thick and had a noticeable thickening toward the centre and head.

The combination of heavier arrows and more powerful bow meant that each arrow had considerably more momentum in flight than modern arrows. In technical terms, a medieval war arrow imparted an impact force of some 100 joules; in layman's terms, about the same force as a blow from a sledgehammer wielded by a muscular blacksmith. It was this momentum that gave the medieval war arrow its tremendous punch and formidable killing power.

Merely being hit by one of these arrows would be enough to knock most men to their knees – or out of the saddle if they were mounted. That was merely the impact force. Of course, it was the arrowhead that did the real damage. In the medieval times there were a great many different types of arrowhead, each designed for a specific purpose.

The basic hunting arrowhead appeared pretty much as a modern person would imagine an arrowhead to look. It was triangular in shape with a pair of barbs pointing back from the needle-sharp point. The edges between point and barb were sharpened so that they would cut into the flesh of the animal being hunted. Once it had penetrated the hide, the arrow would be almost impossible for the animal to dislodge as the barbs would prevent it from being knocked out. As the arrow struck it might hit a vital organ and so kill the animal. Even if the arrow missed anything critical and merely hit muscle tissue, the fact that it could not be removed would ensure a steady loss of blood, which would weaken the animal and allow it to be followed and killed more easily.

There can be no doubt that the first war arrows were simply hunting arrows put to new use. Their effect on unarmoured humans would be much the same as on animals. However, humans going to war tended to wear armour, so new arrow designs were soon developed.

From at least the year 1000 the bodkin arrowhead had been developed to penetrate mail. When a normal arrowhead hit mail the width of the barbed head ensured that the force of the arrow strike was spread over several adjacent rings of metal. In most cases the arrow would not penetrate and, if it did, it might have only enough residual momentum to inflict a flesh wound.

The bodkin was a long, narrow arrowhead that could slip between the individual rings of mail to penetrate the body beneath. The arrow would thus reach the body with its momentum barely decreased and would be able to inflict deep, often fatal wounds.

Armourers soon realised that for the bodkin to work efficiently it needed to be able to slip through the gap in the centre of a mail ring. It soon became commonplace for knights to wear a second layer of mail over the shoulders and chest, those areas of the body where a plunging arrow was most likely to strike. The bodkin would get through the outer layer, but it was most unlikely the mail underneath would have its gaps in the same place as the upper layer, so the arrow would be stopped or at least have most of its force taken from it before it reached flesh. Owing to the sheer weight of such a garment, it was not practical to cover the entire body in a double layer of mail, so arms and legs remained vulnerable to the bodkin.

Meanwhile a new type of arrowhead had been developed specifically for use against horses. Medieval war horses were astonishingly valuable. The sort of pony ridden by a hobilar cost about £2 – the equivalent of almost three months' pay for the man who rode it. The destrier, ridden by a knight, was a much larger animal that had been trained for years to remain calm in combat and to respond instantly to the commands of its rider. Such an animal might cost £100 – more than ten years' pay for a hobilar.

A bodkin would penetrate deeply into a horse, often inflicting a fatal wound. A dead horse was no use to anybody, but one that was merely wounded could be rounded up after the battle, nursed back to health and sold at a good profit. There was a real financial incentive to the archers not to kill horses, so they developed the broadhead arrow.

This broadhead was effectively a modified hunting arrow. The width of the barbs was very much greater and the angle between the point and the barbs much less, producing a wide and fairly flat arrowhead. The wound such an arrow would inflict was wide, but shallow. Such a wound is most unlikely to hit a vital organ of an animal as large as a horse, but it would cause a sudden and dramatic blood loss. Since horses have a naturally high blood pressure, the loss of blood would be very pronounced. Within a very short time of being hit a horse would collapse and play no further part in the action.

The loss of the horse would make the knight who had been riding it unable to perform a mounted charge, and may have caused him to be wounded or at least stunned by the fall. The horse, meanwhile, would still be alive. So long as the battle was relatively short, it could be rescued and sold after the action, thus boosting the income of the archers. Even a maimed destrier was worth a tidy sum.

As we shall see when we come to study the French army in Chapter 8, new types of armour were being developed at this time. Primarily this plate armour was designed for use against swords, spears and maces, but it is important to look at how effective it was to be against arrows.

The developments were made possible by advances in metallurgy. Before about 1300 smiths had not been able to produce quality steel or iron in pieces larger than about 500g. This was good enough to produce mail or scale armour, but the production of a breastplate in a single sheet of metal was impossible. By 1310, however, smiths could produce quality steel in much larger sheets. Plate armour was possible, though it was to remain expensive for some years to come.

We shall look at this armour more closely later, but here it should be noted that the English archers were only just beginning to come to terms with the advent of the new style of armour. Bodkin arrows would penetrate plate, but if they struck the metal at much of an angle they simply glanced off. It remains unclear just how effective the English arrows were against the most modern plate armour worn by the richer Frenchmen at Crecy.

It is worth mentioning that in later years the French accused the English of using poisoned arrows, an accusation the English always denied. It has long been suspected that the archers' habit of pushing arrows into the ground to facilitate fast shooting may have caused tetanus or other germs to get on the arrowhead. In the last two decades it has also been found that the glue used to fix the arrowhead to the shaft included small amounts of copper sulphate, a chemical that will cause flesh to putrefy if introduced to a wound. Perhaps the French were right: although the English had made no deliberate attempt to poison their arrows, these may in any case have carried poison into wounds.

Such was the weapon that was to dominate the battlefield of Crecy. But as we have seen, the longbow and its arrows had been around for generations, so what was it that made it suddenly so formidable in 1346? The answer is to be found in tactics.

Before about 1300 archers had been raised among the infantry produced by commissions of array. Like the spearmen and heavy infantry alongside whom they served, these archers were expected to bring their own equipment at their own expense. On the battlefield, they were put with the other infantry in a mixed formation that combined long range striking power of the archers with the steady defensive power of the spear-armed infantry.

Such formations of mixed infantry had their uses on the battlefield. They could hold ground, even fending off charges by men-at-arms in favourable conditions. They could take the offensive against formations of similar men and were good for overcoming physical obstacles, such as fences or hedges, that would have halted a mounted charge.

For the archers, however, there were some drawbacks. Each archer was more or less on his own. Separated from other archers by the other infantry, effective co-operation or concerted action was impossible. Individual men would shoot only when they were reasonably confident of hitting something worthwhile. Given the high cost of good arrows, an archer was even less likely to take a speculative shot at a fleeting target. He would probably have only one sheaf of twenty-four arrows with him and would not want to waste any. There was also an understandable desire to keep at least half a dozen arrows in reserve in case the enemy launched a surprise attack.

It must also be borne in mind that the vast majority of men who went to war with longbows were not expert archers. Only foresters or gamekeepers needed the sorts of archery skills that meant they could reliably hit a moving, man-sized target at something over 150 metres. Most countrymen would be lucky to achieve that at 80 metres or so. With the strong, muscular torsos that these men built up working at hard physical labour in the fields from childhood they were easily able to pull their powerful longbows to send arrows flying over 200 metres, but they lacked the skill to do so with any accuracy.

The result was that arrow shooting was desultory and slow. There were some famous casualties to arrows, such as the wounding in the eye of English King Harold Godwinson at Hastings in 1066, but generally archers played a secondary role on the battlefield.

Exactly when the key change in tactics was made is not entirely clear. Chroniclers and eyewitnesses always preferred to write about the doings of famous men – or at least of the rich men who might give them patronage and jobs. The feats of humble archers and infantry can only be glimpsed when they achieve something special.

Most modern historians date the change in tactics to the Battle of Dupplin Moor on 9 August 1332. The ousted King of Scots, Edward Balliol, and a group of similarly exiled noblemen had recruited an army of English and German mercenaries to attempt to regain their throne and lands. These Disinherited landed in Fife, but had not got far when their scouts came in to report the approach of a much larger Scottish army led by Donald, Earl of Mar, and Robert, the illegitimate son of the recently deceased King Robert Bruce.

Balliol hurriedly fell back to a defensive position in a narrow valley. The valley floor was held by his 500 dismounted men-at-arms, while the mixed force of infantry and archers were put up on the slopes on either side where they would be less vulnerable to a mounted charge. The Scots trusted in weight of numbers and surged forward along the valley. The archers, seeing themselves under no immediate threat, poured arrows into the advancing Scots, reducing what had been a mighty charge to a disorganised rush. When the Scots struck the men-at-arms of the Disinherited, all order had gone and so the charge made little headway. Warming to their work, the archers continued to rain in arrows from the flanks, inflicting heavy casualties on the tightly bunched and disordered Scots. Finally, the Scots broke and ran.

A contemporary chronicler writing at Lanercost Priory in England recorded: 'The Scots were chiefly defeated by the English archers, who so blinded and wounded them by an incessant discharge of arrows that they could not support each other.'

The next step in the development of the new tactics is generally considered to be the Battle of Halidon Hill fought on 19 July 1333. Two veterans of Dupplin Moor were with the young Edward III at this battle, fought just outside Berwick against an advancing army of Scots. Sir Gilbert de Umfraville and Walter Mauny no doubt told Edward all about the successful deployment of dismounted men-at-arms flanked by archers, for he replicated the tactical deployment at Halidon Hill.

As at Dupplin Moor, the advancing Scots came on bravely enough, but their advance was disordered by the casualties inflicted by the archers and then stopped by the solid wall of men-at-arms. After some tense minutes of hand-to-hand struggle, the Scots fell back. As already noted, the retreat was turned to rout by a well-timed charge by English men-at-arms on horseback.

What had made the archery so effective at both these battles was the fact that the archers were now using a tactic that has today become known as the arrowstorm. Instead of the archers being dispersed among the arrayed infantry they were grouped together as solid groups of archers. This enabled them for the first time to come under the command of an experienced knight whose sole task was to direct the archery. Archers could be ordered to shoot at the same time at the same target.

What made the arrowstorm particularly effective was a realisation that the archers did not actually need to aim to hit a particular man, nor even a group of men. Such a feat was beyond most archers at ranges over 100 metres. Instead all the archers needed to do was to shoot in the given direction at a given range. Even the most average archer could put an arrow to within 20m or so of a chosen spot at 200m range.

A single archer making such a shot would have little impact, but by grouping the archers together in numbers and making them all shoot at once, the situation was transformed. A force of 200 archers would put 200 arrows simultaneously down into a designated area. The scattering of arrows by mediocre aiming would matter little, and indeed would help ensure that the arrows hit something.

The lack of a need for precision aiming speeded up the business of shooting. Instead of it taking up to twenty seconds to knock an arrow, choose a target, draw and shoot, archers could now knock, point in roughly the right direction and let fly in just ten seconds. If arrows were put point downward in the turf in front of the archer instead of being kept in the quiver, the shooting time per arrow was down to six seconds. It became usual for each archer to put about six arrows in front of him preparatory to shooting.

The combined results of these changes was awesome. The archery commander would watch the developing battle and select an enemy formation to be the target for his men. When the enemy came within range, the commander would point out the direction and call a range. The archers would then begin shooting, each man letting fly six arrows in twenty-four seconds or so.

At the receiving end the result was a veritable storm of arrows. Contemporary writers, awed by the sight, compared the arrows to falling hail or rain. A force of 500 archers could put 2400 arrows into an area of battlefield measuring 40m square with ease. Such a concentration of missiles in such a small space would guarantee that any man or horse in that patch of ground would be almost guaranteed to be hit by at least one arrow. No wonder contemporaries were so awed.

There would then follow a short pause while the archers got more arrows from their quivers and pushed them into the ground in front of them. The commander would use this time to assess the damage inflicted on the enemy, scan the battlefield for the next most urgent target and decide who to shoot at next. Again the commander would point and call out a range, again the arrowstorm would be let fly.

Of course, such tactics were enormously costly in terms of arrows, and arrows were not cheap. Archers who had to pay for their own arrows were unlikely to want to indulge in such extravagant shooting. By the time King Edward was preparing for his campaign of 1346 he knew that he would have to pay for and supply the arrows himself. Exactly how many arrows the English took to France that year is unknown, but the partial accounts that survive number 250,000 arrows, so presumably rather more than that were supplied in total.

Effective as the arrowstorm was, it did have its weaknesses. The most immediately obvious of these were linked to the performance of arrows. Although it packed a considerable punch, a 100g arrow was a relatively light projectile. It was likely to be deflected by even a relatively thin branch on a bush or tree. Archers could not shoot effectively either through or into woodland, and even scrubland was problematic. What was needed was open land with good sightlines.

However, such a landscape revealed the overwhelming weakness of archers as fighting men. They had no armour, no shields and precious little in the way of hand-to-hand weaponry. If men-at-arms or even heavy spearmen could get to close quarters with archers it would be a slaughter. Being only lightly equipped, archers could always run away from armoured men on foot, but no such escape was possible from mounted men. In any case, running away is no way to win a battle.

It is noticeable that at this date the archers from Wales were always recruited with and served with equal numbers of lightly armed spearmen. No doubt these men provided protection against attack by any enemy that managed to get to close quarters.

There has been an enormous amount of academic ink spilt on the subject of quite how the archers were deployed in battle. There is relatively little written evidence to go on, and most of that belongs to battles and events that took place many years after Crecy. By that time, the equipment and training of archers had become more standardised and was more closely linked to the new arrowstorm tactic. At the time of Crecy things were more in flux and tactical ideas were still being experimented with by commanders and by archers.

When writing about Crecy, Froissart mentions in an aside when talking about King Philip's actions that the 'archers were formed up like a herce'. The herce was a form of agricultural harrow, the precise design of which is unknown so it is difficult to know exactly what Froissart meant. Most harrows at this date were wooden frames in the form of a diamond grid with metal spikes pointing down from the places where the strips of wood crossed. Froissart may have meant that the archers were arranged like the spikes of a harrow, with the second rank shooting through the gaps in the first, the third through the gaps in the second and so on. Or it might mean that they were drawn up in a diamond shape. Just possibly Froissart was referring to the way that the spikes of a harrow all point in the same direction and so was contrasting the massed volleys of English archery to the desultory shooting in different directions of archers from other countries. There is some evidence that the herce harrow was a triangular shape, with the point facing in the direction of travel. Perhaps Froissart meant that the archers were drawn up in a triangular formation, point towards the French.

The chronicler known as the Bourgeois of Valenciennes says that at Crecy the archers were 'placed in two formations in the manner of a shield'. As with Froissart's 'herce' it is not entirely clear what is meant. Looked at from the front, most shields at this date were triangular in shape being rather longer from top to bottom than they were broad, with a straight top and curved sides. Seen from above, the shield would have had a distinctive curve designed to deflect any incoming missiles to one side or the other. If the Bourgeois meant that the archers were deployed in formations that had the shape of a shield, he might have meant they were triangular or that they were curved.

On the other hand, the phrase might mean that the archers were positioned like a shield. A shield is placed in front of the body, so the archers may have been pushed forward from the main body of the army. It is just possible that the Bourgeois meant nothing tactical at all regarding the deployment of the archers. He may have simply meant that the shooting of the archers shielded the rest of the army from attack.

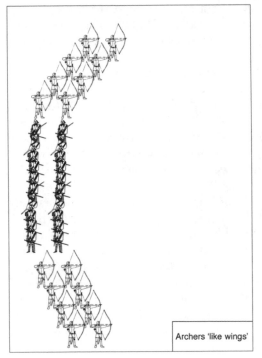

Archers 'like wings'

Archers 'like wings'. This shows the tactical deployment that is usually ascribed to the English armies during the 14th century. Men-at-arms are dismounted and drawn up in the centre in a dense formation. The archers are positioned on either flank and advanced slightly. The width of the formation would be such that no section of the line held by men-at-arms would be out of range of one or other formation of archers. If two or more such formations were put side by side there would be a triangular formation of archers between the blocks of dismounted men-at-arms.

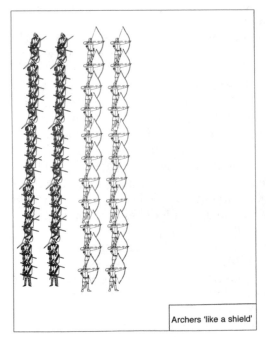

Archers 'like a shield'

Archers 'like a shield'. An alternative formation that would fit with some sources would be for the archers to be drawn up in front of the men-at-arms. The archers would shoot at the advancing enemy, then fall back through the ranks at the last moment to shelter behind the armoured men when it came to close combat.

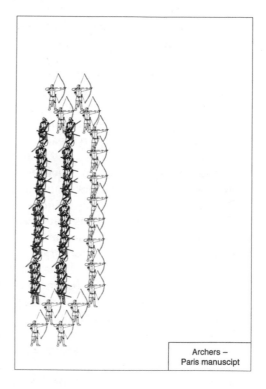

Archers –
Paris manuscipt

An illustration in a manuscript kept in museum in Paris shows an English army drawn up in this formation. The archers form solid blocks on either side of the men-at-arms while a single rank of archers covers the front of the army. It is not clear if the French artist had seen an English army in the field, heard first hand accounts of a battle or had merely imagined what he thought might have happened.

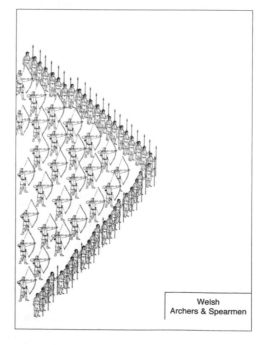

Welsh
Archers & Spearmen

Welsh Archers and Spearmen. Before about 1360 troops raised in Wales consisted of mixed units of archers and spearmen who served together. The few references to how they fought seem to indicate that the usual defensive tactical deployment was for the archers to draw up in a fairly loose formation that gave each man room to shoot easily. The spearmen formed a dense guard around the front of the archers to guard against enemy attack. The spearmen may have sat down while the archers shot, standing up only when needed.

There is an argument that the archers attached to retinues would have been kept with those retinues in battle, rather than sent off to form up with the arrayed archers. In this scenario, the retinue archers would stand in front of the men-at-arms to which they were attached. They would continue to shoot at the advancing enemy until the last moment, then slip back behind the armoured men for protection.

Some support for this idea comes from a well-known manuscript picture dating from about eighty years after Crecy and kept at the National Library in Paris. It shows an army of men-at-arms and archers drawn up for battle. The archers are arranged as a single line along the front of the army, with a group of archers four ranks deep on each flank.

On the other hand, retinues included hobilars, doctors, priests and cooks as well as men-at-arms and archers. Nobody suggests that these men were kept close to the men-at-arms in battle, so perhaps the archers too were free to choose their ground.

Whatever one might think about tactical deployment and effective use of troops, there is one factor that must always be borne in mind. No commander ever deploys his men in an idealised formation on the battlefield. Whatever the merits of putting archers on the wings or in amongst the men-at-arms, Edward at Crecy was the slave of the terrain. Armies must be arranged so as to take maximum advantage of the ground. As we shall see, the layout of the battlefield at Crecy was distinctive and unusual. It will have had a dramatic effect on how Edward drew up his archers, and on the impact those men had on the battle as it unfolded.

V

Normandy

As Edward gathered his army for the campaign of 1346 he was still unde-
cided where to go and what to do. It was the arrival of the Norman exile
Godfrey de Harcourt that made his mind up for him, for Harcourt had a
marvellous tale to tell.

According to Harcourt, Normandy was the ideal place for Edward to
land his army. The Norman nobility were, according to Harcourt, getting
fed up with the high-handed ways of King Philip and his haughty son
John, who had been made Duke of Normandy. Many were now regretting
the fact that they had turned down Edward's bid for the French crown
and were just waiting for the chance to support Edward. The landing of
an English force in Normandy would be that chance.

If Normandy did declare for Edward, it could make all the difference.
So far, Aquitaine had remained more-or-less loyal while Flanders and
Brittany had both recognised Edward as the true King of France, albeit for
their own selfish reasons. All three provinces, however, were only loosely
part of France and their rebellion against Philip was no great surprise.
Normandy was different. It was a central part of the French state and had
the king's own son as its duke.

Edward already knew that the county of Poitou was restive. Lying on
the southern border of Brittany, the county had suffered much at the hands
of the warring parties spilling over the border. Nor did the local barons
much enjoy being forced to supply the forces of King Philip with food that
they would rather sell for cash. In 1343 Philip had executed one leading
baron of Poitou, Olivier de Clisson, for suspected treason. If Normandy
rose, Poitou would almost certainly follow. And if Normandy and Poitou
abandoned Philip, who knew what might follow?

Harcourt was still regularly in touch with relatives and friends back
home in Normandy. He would have known the state of affairs in the
county, where troops were stationed and how people felt. To make the
prospect more tempting still, Harcourt and his men offered to show the
English where to land, which roads to use and all manner of other useful

things. Thus, he assured Edward, Normandy could tip the scales of the war and give the English king everything he wanted.

Of course, Edward will have known that his new guest was a man with a grievance. Harcourt had lost his lands and thirsted for revenge against his rival Robert Bertrand. Edward will have known that Harcourt had his own reasons for wanting the English to land in Normandy and might be willing to exaggerate matters – or even lie outright – in order to achieve that.

Even if Normandy was not as ripe for revolt as Harcourt suggested, an invasion there was still a tempting prospect. Unlike the northeast of France, where Edward had campaigned fruitlessly in 1339 and 1340, Normandy had not been fought over in living memory. The towns and castles were protected by out-of-date fortifications that might fall relatively easily to the modern English army. The towns and countryside of Normandy were known to be rich and prosperous. They would make ideal campaigning ground for that most medieval of strategies: the chevauchée.

A chevauchée is often caricatured as having been little more than a destructive murder raid, but that is unfair. A chevauchée was a much more subtle, if still brutal, technique. It must be remembered that at this date the vast majority of the economic wealth of a country was agricultural, as was some 90% of the population. Even when industrial businesses existed they were closely tied to agricultural products, as were the wool-weaving centres of Flanders.

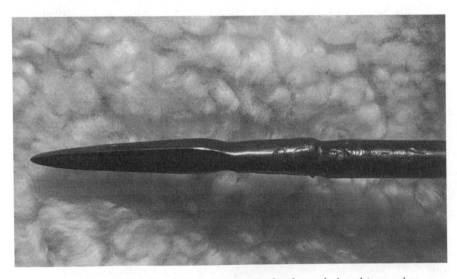

A short bodkin arrowhead. The short, but very stout head was designed to punch through plate armour, though it was prone to glance off the sloping surfaces that were being produced by 1346. With thanks to the Medieval Combat Society www.themcs.org

The sandy beaches south of the harbour at St Vaast le Hogue. Most of the smaller English merchant ships were beached here for unloading.

The ability of any state to wage war depends on a number of factors, but the two most important are having surplus manpower to do the fighting and having enough money to afford the weapons, supplies and pay that enable them to do so. It was these two key factors that a chevauchée was designed to destroy.

An army engaged on a chevauchée would fan out to cover as wide a front as possible, then advance through enemy territory in an organised and deliberate manner. As the troops advanced, they would kill all livestock, destroy all food stocks and burn all buildings. Anything of any economic value at all was to be utterly destroyed. If anyone were to be foolish enough to try to intervene, they would be killed. Bloodshed was not, however, a primary purpose of a chevauchée. If an army could wreak destruction over a wide distance then get home again without any blood being spilled at all, then the outing could be counted a success.

The aim was not simply to inflict as much economic damage as possible on the enemy, and so deprive him of tax revenues and income that could be spent on warfare; the deliberate smashing of farm equipment, demolition of bridges and razing of villages was designed to ensure that all available manpower was kept busy locally repairing the damage. If men were occupied building houses to shelter their families through the coming winter they would not be free to respond to a call to arms. If carried out thoroughly a chevauchée could render an area incapable of waging war for some years to come.

Naturally, the population of an area targeted did not take events lying down. The king whose lands were being devastated would attempt to muster an army and march to intercept the attacking force. Local people would meanwhile be taking their own precautions. Anything of value was gathered up and carried off to the nearest castle or fortified town. These strongholds were rarely attacked in a chevauchée. Reducing a fortress took both time and heavy siege equipment; an army engaged on such a mission would not have had much of either.

How much could be saved would depend on the warning the people had of an approaching army. At the very least the people themselves would rush to safety taking any money, jewels and other valuables that they could carry. With a day or two's warning, farmers could drive livestock into nearby forests or mountains to hide them, load farm tools and furniture on to a cart and get their families to safety. If several days were available, an entire village could be stripped of everything moveable. This tended to put a natural limit on the length of a chevauchée. After a couple of weeks the populace in areas ahead of the advancing army would be so thoroughly warned that there would be little left of any value to destroy.

Time was also against an army on a chevauchée simply on the grounds of safety. To operate the strategy effectively, the army had to be spread out across the landscape in a large number of small units operating relatively independently of each other. This made them highly vulnerable to attack by an enemy force that could muster even modest numbers. For the commander of an army on such a raid it was a delicate decision how widely to scatter his men.

Edward may have reasoned that Normandy offered a win-win opportunity. If Harcourt were right he would get an entire province to rebel against Philip, while if Harcourt were wrong the English could embark on a chevauchée on a grand scale and do immense harm to Philip's war effort. The decision was made: the target was to be Normandy.

Before Edward set out for Normandy, he had first to settle matters in the other theatres of war. Once marching through France there was no telling how easily he could keep in touch with his subordinates outside Normandy. First a few men were sent to help Sir Thomas Dagworth in Brittany. Dagworth's orders were simple: to keep Charles de Blois and as many French troops as possible tied down in Brittany. Orders sent to Lancaster in Aquitaine were equally straightforward, to hold Aiguillon and keep Duke John of Normandy in the south.

Sir Hugh Hastings was given a rather more complex mission. He was sent to Flanders with 250 archers, a handful of men-at-arms and wide discretionary powers. His basic task was to persuade the squabbling Flemings to put an army in the field and march as if about to invade France so as to tie down more French forces. If at all possible he was to attack Merville, then cross the River Lys into France proper and attack Béthune and Lilles.

Exactly when all this happened is obscure. Froissart tells us that Edward decided to sail to Normandy just days before the invasion fleet left England. It seems highly unlikely that such a major strategic decision would be left to the last minute. Harcourt had been in England since September 1345 and was certainly a well known figure at court by Christmas. It seems most probable that the decision to attack Normandy was made by Edward late in 1345, or very early in 1346, but that the decision was kept secret for as long as possible so as to take the French by surprise. Perhaps Edward made his announcement as the fleet put to sea, stating that he had only just made his mind up.

Whenever the decision was made, made it certainly was. The date of departure was delayed until late June due to various supplies and troops not arriving on time. While Edward kicked his heels in Portsmouth, he received very welcome news from Brittany. On 9 June Dagworth had won a stunning victory at St Pol de Leon.

Dagworth's official dispatch describing the battle has survived. In it he describes how he was engaged on a lengthy reconnaissance mission with 80 men-at-arms and 120 mounted archers, trailed by a few two-wheeled supply carts, when he ran headlong into the main army of Charles de Blois at St Pol de Leon. Powerful columns of French cavalry galloped off to cut the roads behind Dagworth, who had no choice but to fight. Dagworth hurriedly overturned his carts to form a rough defensive barrier and dismounted all his men.

Before the battle proper began there came a typically chivalrous event. William de la Heuse rode out from the French ranks and shouted loudly that he was taking a vow to bring Dagworth before Blois as a prisoner with his own hands. The French cheered; the English jeered.

While one force of French crossbowmen and men-at-arms approached the English on foot from one side, a column of forty knights mounted on horses protected by mail or scale armour cantered around to the rear of the English position. Both forces charged forward simultaneously. The English archers took a fearful toll on the French as they advanced, while Dagworth and his men-at-arms met the surviving French at the makeshift cart-barricades. Humiliatingly for him, de la Heuse was knocked unconscious while trying to scramble over a cart. When he came to, he was a prisoner of the very man he had sworn to capture not two hours earlier.

This initial French attack was thrown back, so Blois sent forward three more waves of assault, all of them on foot. Each time the English inflicted heavy casualties with arrows, then halted the attack in hand-to-hand combat. Each time the French fell back in confusion. At around 6.00 p.m., Blois decided he had had enough. He gathered his army together and marched back the way he had come. The fighting had lasted about eight hours.

Dagworth reported that several archers had been killed and every one of his men-at-arms had been injured. Of his 250 horses, 186 had been killed in the struggle. On the positive side, three French knights had been captured and Blois, sent packing. Dagworth and his men limped – literally – back to his base at Finisterre.

On 5 July the fleet put out from Portsmouth and neighbouring harbours, but was kept in the Solent by contrary winds. On 11 July the winds changed and the English fleet put to sea. At dawn the next day the long, low coastline of Normandy came up out of the horizon. The invasion had begun.

Guided by Harcourt, the English landed at the port of St Vaast le Hogue. The harbour itself was large enough to hold only the biggest warships in the English fleet, but to the south stretched several kilometres of sandy beaches. Here the smaller transports could be anchored so that they were left dry at low tide, and their cargoes unloaded over the sands. As soon as the English ships had been sighted, the population of St Vaast fled inland, taking whatever valuables they could cram into their pockets. The first troops ashore found no resistance, so they moved a short distance inland to set up a rudimentary defensive perimeter while scouts galloped further inland to seek news of the enemy. It would take several days to get the entire army ashore, but at least things had begun well.

In fact, the English were remarkably lucky at St Vaast. The port was one of those that had been earmarked by Philip for armed defence. A force of 400 Genoese crossbowmen, detached from the thousands brought north by Ottone Doria had been sent to man the walls. The fleet of warships commanded by Carlo Grimaldi was supposed to be cruising off the Normandy coast to attack any invasion fleet.

Unfortunately for the French, Grimaldi's fleet had not yet arrived. It had left Monaco on 6 May, already some weeks late, and collected King James of Majorca and his 500 men from Montpellier a few days later. Instead of heading for the Straits of Gibraltar, the fleet had then steered for the Balearic Islands. There King James had landed to harry the occupying Aragonese troops, perhaps in the hope of regaining the islands that gave him his title. The raiders were beaten off but then headed for the River Tagus. Only at the very end of June did the fleet finally set off for the English Channel.

If the mercenary fleet had not arrived, the Genoese crossbowmen on land performed no better – though this was not really their fault. Doria's men had arrived in St Vaast sometime in April. They seem to have spent their time repairing the tumbledown defences and scouting out the surrounding lands.

The Genoese were commanded by their own officers, but came under the overall authority of the local French Marshal who was responsible for the defence of Normandy. This was none other than Robert Bertrand, Harcourt's old enemy, now riding high in the favour of King Philip. Bertrand, however, had been unable to get the mercenaries' wages to be paid by Philip on time. On 9 July the Genoese had left St Vaast to march back to rejoin Doria at Rouen and complain about the lack of pay.

Faced by the sudden loss of his most reliable men, Bertrand had called a muster of local arrayed troops for 12 July, the day the English landed. If the Genoese had been paid, or the muster called for a day earlier, the English would have been faced by a defended shoreline. As it was, they simply strolled ashore into France.

Bertrand had not, however, been idle. He had met the first groups of refugees heading inland as he rode to the mustering. When he arrived, he found that about 300 men had assembled ready for duty. He formed these men up and led them gingerly forwards. Bertrand needed to get a clear idea of what faced him. Was this really a large army as the panicking refugees had told him, or merely a raiding force? He soon found out when his men clashed with the Earl of Warwick and saw the size of the English fleet offshore.

The *Acta Bellicosa* records this from the English viewpoint in suitably upbeat terms: 'The Earl of Warwick and his squire ... fought back boldly and killed some of the attackers. The rest, fearing they too would be killed, ... fled in haste leaving the way into Normandy clear for the king and the English army.' In his letter of 17 July to the Archbishop of Canterbury, Bartholomew Burghersh also mentions the fighting: 'My lord Warwick skirmished with the enemy and won the day honourably.'

Realising he faced a major invasion, Bertrand fell back. He sent messengers galloping off to all nearby towns and villages, as well as to the city of Caen and to King Philip himself in Paris. He alerted the local castles and town to the arrival of the English and ordered them either to defend themselves or flee. He himself rode south to the nearest town of any real size: Carentan.

Meanwhile, Edward had to attend to some important business. Donning his armour and ordering his attendants to unfurl the Royal Banner, he marched up the hill west of St Vaast to the little village of Quettehou where the church of St Vigor stood. Here, Edward formally announced his claim to be King of France and summoned all the nobles of Normandy to come to do homage to him for their lands. Right on cue, Godfrey Harcourt stepped forward to acknowledge the validity of Edward's claim, and to do homage to him for his lands.

This important piece of political theatre was accompanied by an equally important piece of chivalry. Edward knighted his own eldest son, Edward the Black Prince, and handed him his own banner. This, as custom dictated, was identical to that of the king except for the addition of a white horizontal bar along the top to indicate that it belonged to the eldest son of the man whose arms it bore.

Edward also knighted a number of other young men. Foremost among these the sixteen-year-old Earl of Salisbury, a great friend and companion of the Black Prince. Equally important was another teenager, Roger Mortimer. This young man was the son of the Roger Mortimer who had been executed for treason by Edward back in 1330. The Mortimers were a powerful family who could command a web of loyalties and contacts in the west of England. The young man was on his way to rehabilitate his family in the eyes of the king through dutiful service, but had not yet recovered the title of Earl of March.

In all Edward knighted about a dozen young men at Quettehou. It was a traditional ceremony for the start of a campaign. The king was recognising the rights of the young men to their status as knights in the adult world of chivalry; the men were affirming their pledge to serve the king. The coming campaign would give them ample opportunities.

The following day the landing of the army continued. Edward took the opportunity to make an important announcement to his army. The *Acta Bellicosa* preserves the fullest version, though in paraphrased form:

> The English king, feeling for the sufferings of the poor people of the country, issued an edict throughout the army that no town or manor was to be burnt, no church or holy place sacked and no old people, children or women in his kingdom of France were to be harmed or molested. Nor were they to threaten people, or do any kind of wrong, on pain of life or limb. He also ordered that if anyone caught someone in the act of doing these or other criminal acts and brought him to the king, he should have a reward of forty shillings.

This proclamation was a fairly standard one for the time. Edward was effectively reminding his troops that they were here to win over the people of Normandy, not to slaughter them. He was also making it clear that the campaign was not, at least yet, a chevauchée. Church property was specified for both religious and practical grounds. The king would do damage to his chivalrous reputation if he was thought to be targeting the possessions of God. Given the enormous prestige and power of the Pope at this date, Edward did well to avoid offending him. Interestingly, Edward does not ban the sort of pilfering of wine, food and household goods in which soldiers have indulged through all history. He was probably aware that he could not stop such acts, so did not bother trying.

In the event, the orders served only to curb the destruction and keep it to a fairly narrow range of countryside. Several houses in St Vaast were set on fire, and most of the neighbouring farms and villages were stripped of anything valuable.

By dawn on 14 July the big warships that had transported the king, his leading nobles and their staff had completed their unloading. Edward decided to put them to good use, so sent them off to attack the prosperous little port of Barfleur that lay a few kilometres to the north. Nearly all the troops were ashore by this point, so the Earl of Warwick was sent overland with a force to support the ships.

Whatever defences Barfleur had did not hold up the English for long and no source mentions any fighting. The English swarmed over the town, stealing any valuables they could find, then returned to St Vaast with several leading citizens. Presumably these men were to be questioned and kept as hostages. Meanwhile, the sailors were exploring the port at Barfleur. They found nine large warships and a variety of other craft. According to the *Acta Bellicosa*, seven of the warships were 'most curiously fitted out', whatever that means. All the ships were burned, after which the sailors went into the town to loot whatever the troops had left. Then the town was set on fire.

Burning a town is not as easy and straightforward as might be thought. People accustomed to reading about the speed with which flames spread during the Great Fire of London may suppose that all that is needed is to throw a flaming torch into a building for a major fire to erupt. However, the Great Fire and other destructive conflagrations were noteworthy because they were so rare. Even wooden buildings roofed with thatch are not so easy to burn as is often supposed.

The first task is to get the building itself to catch light. This usually involves piling up a quantity of kindling, smashed furniture or other smaller pieces of wood against a wooden wall. Most domestic walls were covered with daub, a mix of mud and other materials that does not readily burn. This would usually need to be smashed away with axes or hammers to reveal the wood beneath. The fire must then be lit and watched to make sure it neither goes out nor fails to spread to the main structure. While thatch will generally burn well, recent rain would make the roofs sodden so that they would smoulder and might well go out – certainly they could not be relied upon to spread the fire to the next building. In villages the individual houses, barns and storehouses tended to be more spread out, making it even less likely that flames from one would spread to another.

To make a really thorough job of burning a town or village, each building had to be set on fire individually. Then the attackers needed to stay close by to stop any of the locals emerging from hiding places to quench the flames. Soldiers were usually reluctant to do this until after they had searched premises for valuables. Effective burning of towns and villages could be a lengthy business.

The day after the Barfleur raid the ships, now accompanied by others that had unloaded, set out again. This time they headed for Cherbourg.

This was a strongly walled town, watched over by a castle with massively strong defences. To take such a place would clearly take many days of real siege warfare, for which the sailors were not equipped. They landed, raided some surrounding villages and then returned to St Vaast.

It was not until 18 July that the English army was ready to set off on its march through Normandy. The long delay – six days in all – had been caused largely by the landing of the supply train. Winston Churchill put his finger on an important point when writing of the British commander of a campaign during the Boer War: 'Sir Redvers Buller plodded from blunder to blunder without losing the trust of his troops, to whose feeding as well as his own he paid serious attention.' No army will get very far without food. Even in the fourteenth century it was not enough simply to hope to find enough to eat through pillaging.

Throughout the previous winter, Edward's officials had been preparing the food supply for the army. Purveyors had the power to purchase compulsorily surplus food stores at standardised national prices. The purveyors were not popular as it was they, not the owner of the stored food, who decided what was 'surplus' and who set the prices. Despite some complaints, and one near-riot in Somerset, the purveyors did their job well and without undue trouble.

The main bulk of the food supplies were sacks of oats, barley and dried beans. These were easy to transport and could be boiled up fairly quickly over a camp fire to provide a healthy, if not particularly attractive meal. There were also large numbers of barrels packed with bacon, dried meat, salted meat, dried fish or smoked fish. The royal household had several dozen cows shipped over live to provide milk, along with a number of chickens and geese to give eggs. Such live animals could be slaughtered if need be. It is more surprising to find no less than 500 barrels of wine being shipped over with the invasion army. Campaigning is notoriously thirsty work, but even so it seems a bit excessive to take quite so much wine to France.

All of this food and drink needed to be transported. Edward could not rely on finding a large number of carts left lying about by their owners in France, so these too had to be transported in the fleet. The most usual cart used on campaign was the cabriolet, a relatively light two-wheeled vehicle. These could negotiate narrower lanes and bridges than could heavy carts, but carried more than did packhorses or mules. Given that nobody could predict exactly what sort of terrain or roads would have to be negotiated, such light carts were the sensible choice.

The carts needed horses to pull them, so these too needed to be taken to France. Exactly how many horses went to France we do not know, but we do know that 20 ships were used to transport the horse fodder – even though horses were expected to find most of their food along the roadside. That fodder needed carts and horses to transport it, adding even greater numbers to the already lengthy list of transport. It is thought that perhaps as many as 500 wagons were taken to France. Clearly putting together the supply train was a massive organisational task in itself.

Again and again as the campaign progresses the supply train was to have an enormous influence on the decisions and actions of the English. While infantry can cover 25 km or so in a day without too much trouble, and cavalry considerably more, draught horses pulling carts cannot. An average of about 20 km is more likely. Greater distances can be covered for a day or two if necessary, but the horses will then need a day of rest. Not only that, but carts need relatively good roads along which to travel, and either bridges or secure fords when crossing rivers. In an emergency men and horses can swim rivers, but carts cannot.

Finally, all was ready. Edward divided his force up into the pre-arranged three divisions and gave the order to advance. The objective at this stage was clearly the city of Caen, for Edward ordered the fleet to coast eastward to Ouistreham and the mouth of the River Orne before moving upstream to Caen. This order was, in fact, a remarkable one. Apart from a handful of large warships, there was no navy as such. Ships were hired from merchants as and when required. Most were merchant ships that were transformed into warships simply by having soldiers put in them. A few might have prefabricated wooden platforms that could be erected and bow and stern to act as miniature castles for the soldiers, but the transports had no such conversions made.

Keeping a fleet together was an expensive business for both the king and the merchants. The king had to pay out cold cash for every day that the ships remained in his service. The merchants were paid only the running costs of the ships, mainly the wages of the crew, plus recompense for any damage they suffered. Most merchants could earn much more money using their ships to carry goods overseas. There was a real incentive for both king and merchants to have the fleet in being for the shortest time possible.

Previously, a transport fleet such as this was disbanded as soon as the army was landed. That Edward wanted to keep the fleet together and send it to the Orne is a clear indication that he was keeping his options open. If things went badly, Edward might have to cut and run back to England. If his strategic need was to achieve a success of some kind, he was no less desperate to avoid a disaster. A decision would have to be made at Caen.

Meanwhile, scouts and flanking forces of hobilars were sent off to guard against surprise attack or ambush, while the main body pushed south to Valognes. A short distance before the town, the advancing English were met by a deputation of citizens. When brought before Edward, the Frenchmen threw themselves prostrate and begged that their lives and those of the citizens of Valognes should be spared.

Edward was keen to show his magnanimity to those who surrendered promptly and acknowledged him as rightful King of France. He not only spared the civilian's lives, but issued orders that the town was to be guarded against looting of any kind. Discovering that Duke John of Normandy had a house in the town, Edward promptly moved in for the night.

The nearby town of Montebourg fared very differently. The inhabitants fled, leaving their town empty. The soldiers moved in, stripped it of everything of value and fired the houses. The different fates of the two towns made the choice facing others in the path of the English army brutally clear: acknowledge Edward as your king and survive unmolested; refuse and be sacked.

It was on this day, the 18 July, that Bertrand's messengers reached King Philip at his hunting lodge just outside Paris. He promptly sent out messengers to find out where his allies were. Count Amadeus VI of Savoy had promised to send 3,000 men to Paris, and King John of Bohemia was on his way with at least as many men, and was recruiting in Germany as he marched. Both men were some distance off, but Philip's envoys urged them to hurry. Philip also ordered the mustering of the forces of northern France to gather at Rouen, but made no effort to take the offensive. He waited to see what Edward would do.

At Carentan, Edward faced his first military problem. The city lay on the River Douve, which in 1346 was a wide, sluggish river flanked by extensive marshes. There was only one road across, a narrow highway that ran for three kilometres on top of a causeway and crossed the various branches of the river on a series of bridges. All these bridges had been demolished by Bertrand as he had passed by a few days before. He had also put a force of soldiers into Carentan Castle with orders to make a show of resistance to hold up the English, then slip away south.

By this date, Bertrand was in touch with the Count Raoul d'Eu, Constable of France. As the military commander second only to King Philip, d'Eu was a very important figure. He was the head of the wealthy and ancient Brienne family, which had married into not only the French royal family, but also into that of the Holy Roman Emperor. He was, however, fairly young and inexperienced, being just twenty-five in 1346. He was a close companion of King Philip, who trusted him completely. Even before the English had landed d'Eu had been sent to Normandy to get defences organised in case they were needed.

Between them, Bertrand and d'Eu came up with a plan. Bertrand was to fall back in front of the English, delaying them whenever possible but avoiding a real battle. In the time gained, d'Eu was to muster the forces of Normandy at Caen. The castle at Caen was one of the strongest in northern France and could confidently be expected to hold out for many weeks. D'Eu would await the approach of the English.

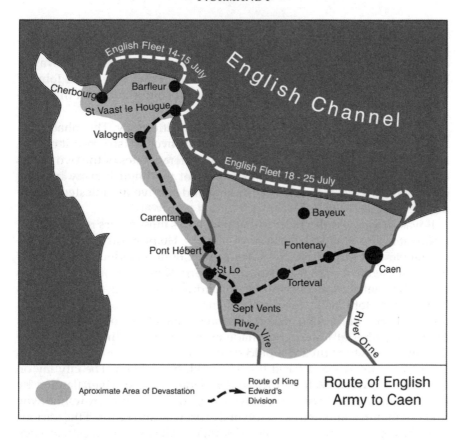

Route of English Army to Caen

Aproximate Area of Devastation

Route of King Edward's Division

Once he knew how many men he had and what King Philip was intending, d'Eu would decide whether to hold Caen, fall back or try to face the English in battle.

Carentan was intended to be the first holding action in Bertrand's retreat, but it did not work out like that.

Working by torchlight, the English carpenters repaired all the bridges on the night of 19 July. By dawn on 20 July the English army was deploying for the attack on the Carentan side of the Douve. Disturbingly for the small French garrison in the castle, a column of hobilars and mounted men-at-arms led by Harcourt was seen advancing from the southwest. According to le Bel, a number of English ships sailed up the Douve and made a brave show of launching an amphibious attack. Thinking their retreat was cut off, the garrison surrendered.

The English soldiers poured into Carentan to find vast stocks of wine and food. Some of the soldiers ran out of control, getting drunk and spoiling much of the food in their eagerness to feast. Edward was furious and, according to the *Acta Bellicosa*, had a new list of punishments drawn up and read out to his hungover men the following day. The army was then marched on towards Pont Hébert, where Bertrand had again demolished the bridge, this time over the River Vire. The summer of 1346 was proving to be exceptionally dry, but the Vire still ran fast and deep. Once again the carpenters went to work to build a bridge capable of carrying the army and its supply train.

Meanwhile Harcourt had been off on a little adventure of his own. He had led a small force of hobilars and men-at-arms to his old home at St Sauveur-le-Vicomte. All he found was an empty, roofless ruin. Bertrand had destroyed the castle some months earlier, and had rounded up any locals who might have remained loyal to Harcourt as soon as the English landed. Empty-handed, Harcourt returned to Edward.

As the English crossed the Vire on their new bridge, they saw the banners of not just Bertrand, but also of d'Eu. Reasoning that a combination of a Marshal of France and the Constable must mean that a major French army was present, Edward drew his army up for battle. For long, tense hours the English waited. Nothing happened. They cautiously continued the advance on St Lo.

In fact the Count d'Eu had ridden forward from Caen with a small escort to confer with Bertrand and have a look at the English army for himself. Despite the fortifications of the castle at St Lô and the walls that surrounded the town, d'Eu and Bertrand decided to abandon the place. There had been no warfare here for generations, and the walls and gates were in poor repair. The town clearly could not be held for long so the French commanders decided not even to try. They ordered the population of around 8,000 to evacuate, then d'Eu rode back to Caen taking Bertrand and his small force with him.

As soon as he realised the town was undefended, Edward acted fast. He did not a want a repetition of events at Carentan, so he sent a small force of trusted soldiers galloping ahead of the army to secure any stocks of food or drink and protect them from looting. And loot there was in plenty. The citizens of St Lô seem to have thought that their city would be defended, so had not shipped any of their goods away to safety before the evacuation order was given. In his letter of 27 July Michael Northburgh records that a thousand barrels of wine 'and much else in the way of goods' was captured.

While the English were stealing everything they could in St Lô, Harcourt was busy on another mission of his own. Three years earlier, three of his friends had been executed by King Philip at the instigation of Bertrand and their heads put up on spikes over the town gates of St Lô. They were still there. Harcourt had the heads taken down and solemnly laid to rest in a decent Christian funeral service at a nearby church.

It was at this point that Edward seems to have made an important decision. So far, the only places to have acknowledged him as king were those that were defenceless. Everywhere else the people had fled. Harcourt's boasts about how the Normans would rise to join Edward had been proved to be false. Now Normandy would know what the anger of a king could be like.

On the morning of 23 July the English army spread out for a chevauchée. From the coast inland, the army would move east on a front over 50km wide, stealing or destroying everything in its path. All buildings, except churches and monasteries, were ordered to be burnt.

While the English began seriously to destroy his lands and its wealth, King Philip took his first publicly important act of the campaign. He rode from Paris to the Abbey of St Denis that lay a few kilometres to the north-west. There he walked humbly into the abbey church accompanied by his standard bearer Sir Miles de Noyers and knelt in prayer for a while. The abbot then presented him with the most sacred and important military object in France: the Oriflamme.

This Oriflamme was the banner of St Denis himself and originated when that saint was executed in about 250 on the orders of the Roman Emperor Valerian. Denis is said to have picked up his severed head in a silk cloth and walked with it to the place where he wished to be buried before collapsing. The great abbey was founded on the spot and the blood-soaked cloth became the saint's banner.

The dark crimson flag presented so solemnly to King Philip was not the original cloth – that sacred relic was kept locked in a casket beneath the high altar – but it did have woven into it strands of cloth saturated with the saint's holy blood. The banner was about a metre tall and three metres long, ending in three tails each decorated with a green tassel. The flag was mounted on a wooden pole that was heavily gilded.

The taking of the Oriflamme was a highly symbolic act. It was handed over by the abbot of St Denis only when France itself was invaded by a foreign enemy – so Philip was announcing to the world that this campaign was not against a rebellious Duke of Aquitaine, but against an invading King of England. The move also demonstrated that King Philip would lead the army in person. Finally, the taking of the Oriflamme effectively announced that no terms or surrender would be contemplated. This was to be a war to the death. Away to the northwest in central Normandy the killing was about to begin in earnest.

VI

Caen

Just before noon on 25 July the English advance guard under Edward, the Black Prince, arrived at the village of Cheux. The few houses were quickly plundered, while the Prince's men secured the stocks of grain and other food in the great barns belonging to the local abbey. The village stood on a ridge, from which the Black Prince could look east down into the wide plain of the River Orne to the city of Caen, some twelve kilometres away. The soldiers dispersed to forage for food and cook their lunch.

Meanwhile, a monk dressed in the habit of the Augustinian canons was riding down from the ridge and heading for Caen. This was Geoffrey of Maldon, an eminent professor of theology who had been brought on campaign by Edward to provide him with advice on matters of theology and ecclesiastical law that might crop up. His mission this day was to carry Edward's offer of surrender terms to the defenders of Caen.

Given that the English were now embarked on a grand chevauchée, the terms were fairly generous. If Caen surrendered immediately the main English army would not enter the city; no looting would occur and the entire population could keep their personal possessions and lives intact. Of course, if the city did not surrender it would be looted and burned.

The monk was barely halfway through reading out the message to Bertrand and d'Eu when it was snatched from his hands by the Bishop of Bayeux. The Bishop, a relative of Bertrand who had been involved in the old feud with Harcourt, tore up the message and ordered Geoffrey to be thrown into prison. This was a serious breach of military etiquette and against all the customs of chivalry. The *Acta Bellicosa* records Edward's reaction when his messenger failed to return: 'This wicked action of the French meant that their own punishment was all the more severe.'

It was not until late in the evening that Edward finally realised that Geoffrey of Maldon was not coming back, and by then it was too late to take any action. So it was at dawn on 26 July that the English marched down the ridge from Cheux towards Caen. Scouts were sent out ahead to discover the lay of the land and the French position.

The church at Quettehou where the Black Prince was knighted on the day the English army landed. The church stands on steep hill that offers good views inland so that the English could keep watch for any advancing French troops.

Caen at this date was one of the largest cities in France and as big as any city in England except for London. The population was about 30,000 and its wealth was based on trading the agricultural produce of the rich Norman countryside. For centuries it had stood astride the River Petit Odon, surrounded by its ancient walls and protected by the massive castle to the north. To the west of the city stood the Abbaye aux Hommes, founded by the Duke William of Normandy who conquered England to become King William I. His tomb lay in the abbey, as that of his wife, Emma, lay in the Abbaye aux Dames that stood to the east of the city. Both abbeys were surrounded by walls of their own.

Over the long years of peace, Caen had spread outside the old city walls. A few areas of faubourg, or unwalled suburbs, lay to the west and north of the old city, but the major expansion had been on the Ile St Jean to the south. This island lay in the confluence of the rivers Odon and Orne, being surrounded on all sides by marshy rivers. About half the population of Caen lived on the island, and it was here that the homes and warehouses of the richer citizens were to be found.

The western defences of the castle at Caen, the largest fortified enclosure in northern France and, in 1346, one of the most powerful.

The Count d'Eu had about 4,000 men with him in Caen, mostly local men-at-arms and arrayed infantry but including some 400 or so Genoese crossbowmen. We do not know what his original plan was. He had too few men to fight a battle, but far more than were needed to defend only the castle. Whatever d'Eu intended, his mind was changed by two events that happened late on the 25th or early on the 26th.

The first was the arrival of a messenger from King Philip. This man brought no orders for d'Eu, but a message for Jean de Melun the Count of Tancarville and a trusted financial officer in the French government. Tancarville was promoted to the rank of Marshal of France with immediate effect. Whatever the reasons for the appointment, d'Eu seems to have taken it as a slight upon his honour and his competence.

The second event was the arrival of a deputation of citizens of Caen. There was still time for the civilians to flee the city before the English arrived, as the people of St Lô had done, but they had no wish to do so. They would have heard that St Lô had been thoroughly looted of anything of value and had no wish to lose everything they owned. They begged d'Eu to defend at least part of the city.

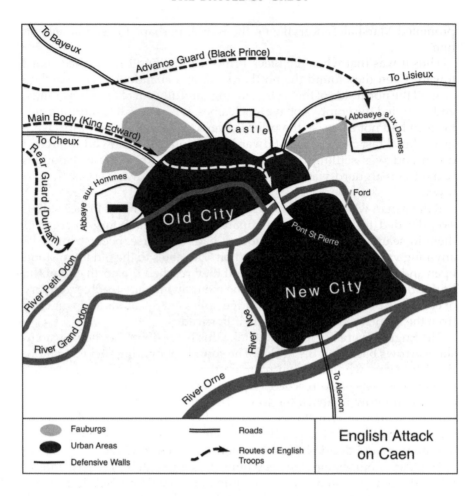

D'Eu decided that he would defend the Ile St Jean. The surrounding rivers and marshes made for reasonable defences, and there was also a stone wall along one side of the island and a solid wooden wall around the rest. There were only three ways on to the island, and each could be defended. There was one bridge into the old city in the north and a second leading out on to open fields to the south. The southern bridge was under no immediate threat until the English found another way over the Orne. The northern bridge was blocked by a makeshift wall manned by the men-at-arms while the houses overlooking it were packed with crossbowmen. The rivers at this point were tidal in 1346, and there was a narrow ford that could be crossed on foot at low tide. Boats packed with crossbowmen were put among the reeds on the island side to guard this crossing.

Bertrand and the Bishop of Bayeux were given the castle to defend, while d'Eu took the defences of the island. He decided to keep the newly promoted Marshal Tancarville on the island, perhaps to keep an eye on him.

Thus it was that when the Black Prince led the English advance guard toward Caen they found the northern suburbs abandoned. He marched around the north side of the castle, staying carefully out of crossbow range, and occupied the empty Abbaye aux Dames. It was now late morning and his men had not eaten, so the prince ordered a halt while campfires were lit and breakfast cooked. King Edward's division had meanwhile marched down and was settling down just north of the Abbaye aux Hommes while the rearguard was heading for the flat meadows west of the old town.

Rather than wait for breakfast, some men from the Black Prince's division decided to investigate the apparently empty faubourg in front of them in search of plunder. The houses had, of course, been stripped of anything valuable so the men pushed on. The gates to the old town stood open and deserted, and it was not until they reached the north end of the bridge that led to the Ile St Jean that the men ran into any trouble. A flurry of crossbow bolts flew across the bridge, followed by taunts and war cries from the French men-at-arms on their barricades.

The English were not inclined to take this lying down, so they began to shoot arrows back over the bridge. The sounds of fighting sucked in more English troops who had been roaming the abandoned houses in search of loot. The noise also reached Edward, who was eating a meal before deciding on how to attack the town. The king sent the Earl of Warwick with a few men-at-arms to see what was happening and to call a halt to the fighting. When he arrived at the bridge, Warwick quickly summed up the situation and decided to let the informal attack continue.

The Earl of Northampton was sent next, along with Sir Richard Talbot, Edward's personal steward. By the time they arrived at the bridge a real battle was underway. According to the *Acta Bellicosa*: 'When they saw the enemy, they did not hold themselves back but rushed on the enemy'. The houses at the southern end of the bridge had been set on fire to flush out the crossbowmen, so Northampton led a charge by armoured men-at-arms to try to take the barricades across the bridge.

Meanwhile, a force of Welshmen from the Black Prince's division had been trying to get across the ford. While archers lining the bank shot at anything that moved, the spearmen splashed through the mud to get to grips with the men in the boats among the reeds. Two of the French boats were set on fire and casualties among the crossbowmen mounted alarmingly. The tide was coming in by this point, forcing the Welshmen to swim back to the English bank. The crossbowmen and soldiers in the French boats decided enough was enough. Pushing their boats out to midstream, they paddled desperately downstream to get away from the deadly hail of archery.

For the French, this was the third time in the campaign that they had been let down by the Italian crossbowmen. First Grimaldi's fleet had failed to turn up and intercept the English ships. Then Doria's men had abandoned St Vaast just days before the English arrived. Now the Italians were rowing off downstream, leaving the French to face the English assault alone. No wonder some Frenchmen began to wonder if they had been betrayed by the Italians for English silver.

Seen from the point of view of the Italian mercenaries, however, things looked very different. Mercenaries at this date were professional, specialist soldiers who were hired for cash to carry out particular tasks in the business of warfare that the employer lacked either the skills or men to do himself. Of course they risked their lives, but they were not expected to throw them away. Nor were they expected to fulfil roles outside their own specialisation – crossbowmen were not expected to be men-at-arms, for instance.

The men guarding St Vaast had not been paid for some time. Mercenaries did not serve for promises or fair words, but for silver coin. They had not been paid, so they did not serve. If King Philip did not keep his side of the contract, the Italians saw no reason why they should keep theirs.

At Caen, the situation was rather different. The crossbowmen had held the ford throughout the period of low tide, as ordered. But they were not entirely at ease. The decision to hold the Ile St Jean was not a wise one given the less than impressive defences and the size of the advancing English army. The Italians were professionals who, unlike the youthful Count d'Eu, had seen it all before. Possibly the Italian commander spoke out against the decision, but once made dutifully put his men where they could do most good.

This was, however, the first time the Italians had faced up to English archery. Although in the confused conditions of the fighting at Caen the true arrowstorm was not unleashed, the Welsh would have been shooting their arrows in prodigious numbers with no care for the cost – something to which the Italians were not accustomed in warfare. Defending an island they thought should not have been defended and faced by awesome firepower, the Genoese probably concluded that the island could not be held. They were not being paid to die in a hopeless cause, so they decided to take advantage of high water to slip away and fight another day.

Whatever the rights and wrongs of the situations at St Vaast and Caen, they were unfortunate events that did little to foster trust between the French and Italians.

The water of the ford was by now at high level, but the Welshmen were nothing deterred. Some swam across, others rowed over in some light craft they found. They still faced the stout wooden walls around the houses on the island, but the sight of enemy troops on the island seems to have been enough to cause those defending the bridge to lose heart.

Warwick and Northampton got over the barricades and led their men into the new city on the island.

As the fighting men spread out through the narrow streets things became confused. According to Froissart, King Edward had himself come up to watch the fighting. He saw civilians on the roofs of houses throwing down stones and heavy wooden furniture that killed large numbers of English soldiers in the streets below. 'The king was so much enraged at his loss', continues Froissart, 'that he gave orders that all the inhabitants should be put to the sword and the town burnt. But Sir Godfrey de Harcourt prevailed with him to reverse this order and with the inhabitants to submit to quiet surrender'.

Nobody else mentions these events. Under the customs of war at the time, Edward would have been quite justified in massacring the inhabitants of Caen after the way they had treated his envoy, but it would have been highly unusual for him to have done so. At no other point in his career did Edward behave with such brutality. On the other hand, Froissart was writing for a largely English audience so it is odd that he would repeat such a story unless he had strong grounds for thinking it was true.

Whatever Edward did in the confusion that followed the immediate collapse of French resistance, we know some things that took place. Thousands of French civilians and soldiers alike streamed out across the southern bridge to make their escape over the open fields. Others were not so lucky.

The Count d'Eu was holed up in a house or warehouse somewhere near the northern bridge watching the English surging over and into the new city. Suddenly he spotted the distinctive one-eyed figure of Sir Thomas Holland striding through the crowd. The two men knew each other, having served together against the pagans in eastern Europe. D'Eu called out to Holland, who at once recognised his old friend. As a rich nobleman and Constable of France, d'Eu would be worth a large ransom so Holland did not hesitate to take him as a prisoner. Elsewhere in the confusion the newly promoted Tancarville was grabbed by a young knight named Sir Thomas Daniel, who thereby made his fortune.

In all, 95 of the French defenders were captured and some 2,500 killed before King Edward's household men managed to restore order. Churches and religious property had guards posted in them to prevent looting, and only those houses fired in the fighting at the bridge went up in flames. A huge amount of looting went on as the day turned to night, but most of the warehouses and their bulky contents seem to have been secured for the king.

The next day the serious business of organised looting began. Edward's orders ensured that the civilians were neither killed nor raped, but their property was entirely up for grabs. In his letter of 2 September, William Wynkeley reports: 'the town was stripped to its bare walls'. The quantity of riches plundered was enormous. The *Acta Bellicosa* says that the soldiers carried off 'a vast amount of treasure', while the amount of goods seized at the warehouses was so great that the English fleet could not find enough space for it all.

No doubt some of this is exaggeration, but there can be no doubt that the capture of Caen was a major success for Edward and the English army. It was not just the amount of loot that had been taken that was important. Edward had shown that his army could capture a major city, quite a result after the failed sieges of 1339 and 1340. And by capturing a Marshal of France and the Constable of France, Edward had inflicted a humiliating defeat on Philip.

The citizens of Bayeux hurried to surrender, asking that Edward spare them from plunder and death. Edward agreed, though unfortified towns and villages around Caen continued to suffer the full rigours of chevauchée.

Edward now had to decide what to do next. His fleet was in the Orne and eager to be off. His army was buoyed up by success and eager to march on to capture more cities and more plunder, and to defeat more French forces. Edward had achieved a great success, which is what he had been after. The capture of Caen and the huge amount of plunder that it produced may have been enough to placate Edward's critics in Parliament and allow him to continue the war. On the other hand, it might not. Edward would have been very much aware that he had as yet not crossed swords with King Philip nor faced the main French army that was even now mustering at Rouen.

Edward could now have returned to England in his fleet. He would have been able to bask in the glory of victory, but that victory may not have been enough. Alternatively he could have stayed in France and continued with his campaign of chevauchée. If he stayed in France, he could turn west to Brittany to continue the campaign there. Or he could risk the long march south to Aquitaine to link up with Lancaster. Finally he could head northwest to try to link up with Sir Hugh Hastings and the Flemings.

While Edward pondered his options, Bertrand remained defiant in Caen Castle. He had about 2,000 men, ample supplies of food and a secure water supply. He could hold out for months, so he sat back to watch the English.

At some point, probably on 28 July, an English soldier came across a cache of important official documents. These were sent to the king's household for inspection and one of them proved to be explosive. It was an agreement between King Philip, the then Count d'Eu (father of the current Count) and a number of leading Norman noblemen that concerned a planned invasion of England. The document set out in precise terms how many men and how much money each nobleman would provide:

59,000 men in total, with enough the cash to pay and supply them for six months. The expedition was to be commanded by Philip's son, Duke John of Normandy. Most dramatic of all was the stated aim of the invasion: to dethrone Edward and put John in his place. The entire nobility of England was likewise to be deprived of their estates and titles, while even the English Church was to be stripped of its landed wealth. Everything would then be divided up among the noblemen who had provided troops, with King Philip taking a major share of the spoils.

Edward was furious, as were his noblemen. Whatever Edward might have been planning, his mind was now made up. He sent the looted treasures of Caen back to England on the fleet, along with the sick and wounded – who included the Earl of Huntingdon.

On 31 July Edward got his army on the march once again. He was not heading for Brittany, nor for Aquitaine, nor for Flanders. He was marching on Rouen where King Philip was mustering the main French army. If Philip wanted a fight to the finish, he was going to get one.

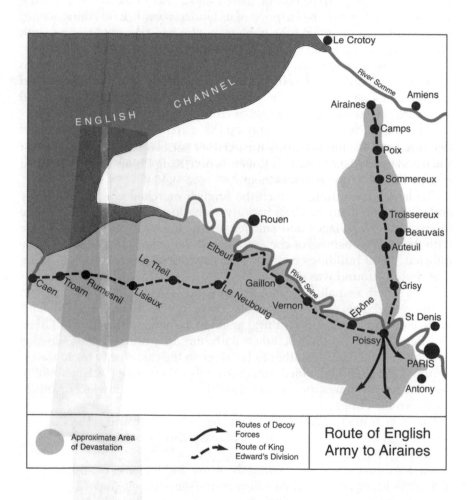

VII

The River Seine

On 31 August the English army turned their backs on the shattered city of Caen and headed east towards Rouen, where King Philip was gathering a mighty French army to defeat them.

The landscape through which the English marched was eerily empty and silent. The delay at Caen had given the local French plenty of time to evacuate the villages and smaller towns, taking everything of value with them. The business of chevauchée still demanded that desolation be inflicted, so all buildings except churches were set on fire and anything that could be found was destroyed.

Edward left a small force at Caen to watch Bertrand and his garrison in the castle. The *Acta Bellicosa* calls these 'a few men', while Richard Wynkeley and Bartholomew Burghersh fail to mention them at all. Given that Bertrand had some 3,000 men with him, it is unlikely that Edward gave his few men orders either to lay siege to the castle or to try to defeat Bertrand in battle if he sallied out. Presumably they were to hang about to keep an eye on things for a while, then ride off to find Edward or put to sea down the Orne.

The French made much of the fact that when Bertrand sallied out he defeated Edward's covering force with ease. But then the French were in need of some good news.

The 1 August was spent getting the army and its lengthy supply train across the River Dives and its adjacent marshes and swamps. There was just one narrow road across the soft ground, so the carts had to go in single file while the men splashed along beside them.

The following day the English arrived at Lisieux. The town itself was deserted, but the entire populace was sheltering in the walled precincts of the cathedral, guarded by a small body of armed men. The leading English soldiers watched the French warily, but did not attack. Edward arrived late in the afternoon and was probably deciding how to approach the Bishop to negotiate a surrender when he was interrupted by some unexpected arrivals.

Above: *A fourteenth-century cabriolet, or light cart. These vehicles were favoured for the transport of supplies on campaign as they could negotiate narrow roads and cope with rough surfaces, unlike the heavier carts.*

Right: *The eastern gate into the outer bailey of Caen castle.*

Led into his presence were two very important men. Cardinal Etienne Aubert was Bishop of Ostia, near Rome, while Cardinal Annibale Ceccano was Archbishop of Naples. The two men were on a personal peace mission from Pope Clement VI to try to find a way to resolve the dispute between Edward and Philip. First, however, the two cardinals complained that their horses had been stolen by Edward's scouts. Wearily, Edward gave orders for the horses to be found and returned, then promised to talk to the cardinals the next morning.

The meeting began with the two cardinals preaching a sermon to Edward and his nobles on the virtues of peace. Once this was out of the way, the serious talks began. The cardinals had already been to see Philip to ask him what terms he was willing to offer. These were to put the clock back to before the war began. Edward was to have Ponthieu and Aquitaine restored to him in full, though he had to give up his pretensions to the French crown. Philip also promised to find a rich and wealthy French heiress as a bride, apparently for the Black Prince.

Edward was unimpressed. At the very least he wanted some sort of guarantee that Philip would never again arbitrarily confiscate Aquitaine and Ponthieu. He gave the cardinals a lavish dinner of roasted beef, pork, venison and chicken. His cooks even managed to find a swan from somewhere and cook if for the cardinals. The next morning the churchmen were granted safe conduct, and were sent on their way with a small guard to escort them out of the English army.

While the negotiations had been dragging on, the English had thoroughly looted the abandoned houses of Lisieux. Perhaps out of respect for his ecclesiastical guests, Edward made no attempt to persuade the bishop to surrender, but simply continued the march. On 5 August the army passed through the little town of Harcourt. This was the home of the Count d'Harcourt, the head of the family to which Godfrey de Harcourt belonged. The entire area was abandoned, so clearly not even Harcourt's own family was willing to join the English.

The next day the army advanced slowly to Neubourg, while Edward sent a column of mounted men to probe towards Rouen. The scouts were led by Godfrey de Harcourt and included several knights as well as a sizeable force of hobilars. The hobilars fanned out with orders to burn everything, even church property. Two small monasteries went up in flames, but a leper colony was spared – perhaps because nobody volunteered to enter it and so risk catching that dread disease.

Some time after noon the column reached Rouen. The main city, surrounded by impressive walls, stood on the north bank of the Seine. On the south side was an unwalled faubourg, connected to the city proper by a bridge. Floating over the main gate of Rouen was the royal standard of France, showing that Philip was in residence. The English pushed through the faubourg only to find that the bridge had been broken and the far end barricaded.

The stage seemed ideal for a chivalrous episode, so Sir Thomas Holland, Sir Richard Marsh and Sir John Daunay rode out on to the broken bridge to brandish their weapons at the defenders on the far side of the river. 'St George for King Edward' bellowed the one-eyed knight. They were met by a barrage of crossbow bolts, one of which struck Sir John. The bolt plunged through his armour and inflicted a mortal wound. Chivalry was a dangerous business. The scouts rode back to Edward to report.

Those reports make no mention of the presence or otherwise of Grimaldi and his Genoese warships. Either the English did not see them, or they had not yet arrived. They certainly did arrive at about this time, however, and Grimaldi got a rough reception from King Philip. After some no doubt strained discussions about why Grimaldi was so late and how much his payments were going to be cut to recompense, Philip ordered the Italian to take his ships back down the Seine to Harfleur from where they could patrol the Channel for English ships. First, however, he had to land the bulk of his crossbowmen so that they could serve with Philip's army. King James of Majorca and his men also landed, hurrying to join Philip's army and make their excuses.

The following day the English army set off upstream to the town of Elbeuf. It is difficult to know exactly what Edward's intentions were at this point in the campaign. He later claimed that he was trying to find a bridge across the Seine so that he could attack Philip and the French army that he knew to be at Rouen. Certainly he had decided against returning home when he dismissed the fleet at Caen, just as he had abandoned any plans of marching to either Brittany or Aquitaine.

However, taking on the main French army was a daunting prospect. Edward would have known that Philip could raise an army much larger than his own, and that the French were widely accepted to have the best and most chivalrous army in Christendom. Like Edward, we know that his new tactics of the arrowstorm combined with dismounted men-at-arms in a defensive position had won him spectacular victories against the Scots. But the Scots were not regarded as a major army, good as they were at guerrilla tactics and swift raids. Sir Thomas Dagworth had done well against the French at Morlaix and St Pol de Leon, but they had been minor battles involving only small numbers of men.

Any battle between King Edward and King Philip, both with their main armies, would be a very different prospect. It would be a major battle fought with the utmost determination by both sides. The French royal army would be a tough opponent at any time, and supported as it would undoubtedly be by foreign contingents it would be even more daunting. It was forty-two years since a major French army had been defeated in battle, and no man alive would have been able to remember the last time a French king had lost a battle.

Edward probably realised that his only real chance of avoiding defeat was if the French army attacked his own over land suited to the arrow-storm tactic. This would be easier said than done. Such defensive positions were not easy to find, especially in foreign and relatively unknown territory. Even then the French had to be persuaded to attack. In the earlier campaigns of 1339 and 1340, Philip had shown himself to be a cautious commander who preferred to wait for his enemy to tire and run out of supplies rather than risk a major battle.

Perhaps Edward was counting on Philip's caution and expected the French not to attack. In this case he may have still been intent on conducting a large-scale chevauchée across northern France. With luck, Sir Hugh Hastings should by now have got a Flemish army in the field. If Edward could get over the Seine and if Philip did not attack, the English army would be clear to plunder their way north towards Flanders. It is a plausible scenario, but the fact is we do not know what Edward planned; we know only what he did.

At Elbeuf, Edward found the bridge was again broken down. On the north bank of the wide, tidal Seine a force of local knights and infantry stood to arms. Far away to the north a cloud of dust showed that Philip and his army had left Rouen and were marching up the north bank of the Seine. Edward ordered the town to be set on fire, then turned southeast and led his army towards the next bridge at Pont de l'Arche.

Seeing the English turn to leave, the French on the north bank began jeering. There was a legend among the French at the time that the English had tails, so a group of the French dropped their hose and waved their bare bottoms at the enemy. It was a taunt too far. Some of the Welsh spotted a few rowing boats lying unguarded on the north bank upstream and out of sight of the French. They swam over, took the boats back to the south shore where more Englishmen, including some men-at-arms, crowded in. They hurried back to the north shore and raced downstream to launch an attack on the surprised French garrison. Over a hundred Frenchmen were killed before the English had to row back over the river to escape the advancing horde of King Philip.

The English reached Pont de l'Arche early the next day. This town on the south bank was surrounded by modern defences and held by Viscount John de Boys. Seeing no prospect of a quick victory that would give him the bridge, Edward again ordered his army to push on, this time towards the bridge at Vernon.

As the English army streamed past, a small party of French knights came riding up the north bank and over the bridge demanding to be admitted to Pont de l'Arche. After a quick interview with de Boys, the knights rode out of the southern gates of the city under a flag of truce. They brought Edward an astounding offer: King Philip was challenging Edward to single combat.

It was the sort of chivalrous offer that Edward was likely to accept. In any case he was younger, stronger and more skilled that Philip. However, the English nobles and Edward suspected a trick. Edward's army was ahead of Philip's in the race along the Seine to find a bridge. The offer could simply be a means of slowing down the English to allow Philip to catch up. Even so Edward, the self-proclaimed perfect knight, did not want to refuse. He told the French messengers to ride back to Philip and tell him that Edward would meet him at Paris.

The next day the English crossed the Eure, a tributary of the Seine, and pushed on to Gaillon. There they found the town and castle held against them. The advance guard, under the Black Prince, attacked as soon as they came up to the place. The castle had a reputation for being impregnable, but its defences had not been well maintained. Sir Thomas Holland was injured leading the assault, but the defences were breached and the English surged in. The garrison promptly fled through the town, which had been emptied of civilians some days earlier, and hurried off toward Paris. Hobilars gave chase and many Frenchmen were cut down before the Black Prince called off the action. The town was stripped of whatever the population had left behind, then systematically torched.

Just after noon the English advance guard reached the village of St Pierre de Longueville and received a nasty shock. Trudging along the road on the far side of the river was the main French army. King Philip had caught up with them. In his letter of 3 September, Edward said 'This greatly annoyed us' – a remarkable understatement. By the time the English got to Vernon late that afternoon the French were already there in large numbers. Although the bridge was intact, there was no chance of crossing.

The next bridge was at Mantes, so the English set out before dawn in the hope of getting there first. But around noon the lead scouts met the two cardinals, coming back for another attempt at peace. This time the scouts did not steal the clerics' horses, but led the men straight to Edward. Out of respect for the Church, Edward halted his march while he once again listened to the cardinals. We don't know what peace terms were on offer this time. The *Acta Bellicosa* records only that 'the treaty was not to the liking of the English'. The churchmen were sent packing, though with great politeness, and the English march resumed.

The affair with the cardinals had cost Edward several hours' marching time. Even though the French had been forced to march around the outside of a bend, they were now ahead of the English. Edward decided to launch a raid over the river into the enemy's rear in the hope of causing confusion and getting Philip to halt.

The target for the raid was the castle and town of La Roche Guyon. Sir Robert Ferrers was chosen to lead the attack. As soon as it was dark, Ferrers loaded his men into boats and rowed over the river. As soon as they landed, the French sounded the alarm, but the English were into the town before serious resistance could be mounted. Taking the castle proved more difficult and a savage battle raged in which Sir Edward Attewoode from Staffordshire was killed.

The fight did not last long, for the garrison soon asked for terms of surrender. The reason for this was quickly apparent: the ladies and children of all the local noblemen and knights had taken refuge in La Roche and the garrison commander was worried about their safety should the English break their way in. Sir Robert was generous. He asked only that the French knights should pay him ransoms as if they had been captured, then allowed them to stay in La Roche to protect the ladies and children.

Quickly setting fire to the houses in the town to alarm the French army, Sir Robert paddled back over the river to tell King Edward all that had happened. His chivalrous behaviour was highly commended.

Next morning the march upriver continued. The English were now out of Normandy and in the Ile de France, the royal heartlands of France. The hobilars were ordered to fan out and do their work of devastation with renewed vigour. When Edward reached Mantes it was to see the main French army on the north bank of the Seine and the town walls on the south bristling with men. He bypassed the place and pushed on.

At dawn the next day the Earl of Northampton cantered off to the city of Meulan to try to take the bridge there by surprise. The city was on the north bank, and only a turreted barbican guarded the south end of the bridge. Northampton was confident that he could take the barbican, but when he moved up to begin the assault he saw that the bridge beyond it had already been demolished. He called off the attack.

There was now only one bridge left before Paris: Poissy. The English arrived there in mid-morning on 13 August. The town was undefended and empty. The royal palace lay abandoned, as did the Convent of St Dominic where King Philip's own sister, Isabelle, was prioress. Pushing through the silent streets, the English were unsurprised to find that the central span of the bridge had been demolished. What did surprise them was that the north bank was entirely empty of French troops. Before abandoning the town, the local commander had not put a guard to contest the crossing.

A messenger was sent off to gallop back along the English column to find William Hurley, the king's carpenter and his assistant Richard St Albans. These men were hustled forwards and hundreds of infantrymen ordered to drop their arms and get ready to work on whatever timbers could be found.

The carpenters had got four massive beams of wood across the broken section when the alarm was given. Coming over a hill a couple of kilometres to the north was a body of French troops. These were the arrayed troops of Amiens led by the Lord d'Aufremont and Lord de Revel. In all there were 1,000 mounted men and 2,000 infantry. Dragging along behind were a few catapults of some kind. The troops had been marching to join King Philip in Paris when they had been diverted to Poissy on royal orders.

The Earl of Northampton quickly ordered a body of archers to scamper over the narrow beams to the other side of the bridge. He was meanwhile getting his armour on and rounding up as many men-at-arms as he could find. Crossing a wooden beam some 30 cm wide and 20 m long suspended over a swirling river is a daunting prospect. To do so in full armour must have been even worse. If he fell into the river, Northampton would have been dragged down by the weight of his armour and sunk without trace. He did not hesitate, however, and neither did his men.

Seeing what was afoot, the French deployed hurriedly and charged across the meadows towards the bridge. The *Acta Bellicosa* describes the assault as 'like a ravening wolf on the sheepfold', echoing the Biblical description of the Assyrians attacking the Israelites. The initial rush carried the French into and through the English lines, allowing a handful of Frenchmen to reach the river bank. The English fought back, with reinforcements coming over the wooden beams as quickly as they could. Finally the French broke and ran.

Most of the defeated troops headed off back to their homes at Amiens and it was at least a day, possibly two, before anyone thought to send a messenger to Philip. That gave the English enough time to get a temporary bridge over the Seine that was strong enough to carry men and horses, but not the supply carts. That would take until 16 August.

Edward had no intention of being caught with his army divided by the Seine. To keep Philip guessing he dispatched strong forces from the vanguard to spread out to the south and east, burning all buildings as they went. King Philip's favourite residence, that at Chastel le Roy, went up in flames and one force under Harcourt burned a little village just three kilometres from Paris. If the intention was to alarm the citizens of Paris and keep Philip guessing, it succeeded magnificently. The Parisians begged Philip to help them.

Philip was by the afternoon of the 14 August camped with his army around St Denis blissfully unaware of events at Poissy. He thought that the English were still south of the river. The land had been stripped of supplies by the French, so Philip must have thought that his enemy was by now getting desperate. Short of food, unable to march towards his Flemish allies and cut off from the sea, Edward would be short of options. Perhaps this was why Philip sent the bishop of Besancon with a message to Edward.

Philip's message reminded Edward of his promise to meet Philip at Paris, and challenged him to lead the English army into battle at Bourg St Germain or Franconville – both being villages south of Paris – within the next five days. Edward must have realised that Philip did not know that the bridge at Poissy was almost repaired. According to the English sources, Edward did not give a firm reply, but instead told the bishop to tell Philip that he could find the English army any time he liked. He then dropped vague hints about not being bothered one way or the other about Philip's moves as he was off southwest, towards Aquitaine.

LE 12 JUILLET 1346
EDOUARD III ROI D'ANGLETERRE
DEBARQUÉ, LE MATIN, A St VAAST-LA-HOUGUE
ARMA CHEVALIERS
DANS L'EGLISE DE QUETTEHOU
EDOUARD PRINCE de GALLES
DIT LE PRINCE NOIR, SON FILS,
GUILLAUME de MONTAIGU,
ROGER de MORTIMER, GUILLAUME de ROOS,
ROGER de la WARE, RICHARD de la VERE
ET UN GRAND NOMBRE D'AUTRES JEUNES
GUERRIERS.

1. A plaque in the Church of St Vigor at Quettehou commemorates the knighting of the Black Prince and other young Englishmen. The ceremony was used by King Edward III to mark the start of his campaign.

2. The castle of St Saveur le Vicomte. This was the home of Sir Godfrey Harcourt, the renegade Norman nobleman who fought for the English during the Crecy campaign.

Above: **3.** The church at Cheux. The Black Prince climbed the church tower to get his first glimpse of Caen, some 12km to the east, while his men camped the night of 25 July in the fields around. The church was destroyed during fighting in 1944 and had to be almost entirely rebuilt.

Right: **4.** The mighty castle walls at Caen that defied the English army in 1346. Sir Robert Bertrand, who was defending Normandy for the French King Philip, took refuge here until after the English army had moved on.

5. The church of St Jean in Caen. The open square in the foreground marks the position of the now covered over River Odon. The bridge that crossed the river here saw the fiercest fighting of the English assault on the city of Caen.

6. The cathedral of Lisieux. The population of the city took refuge in the open square in the foreground, which in 1346 was surrounded by a defensible stone wall. While the citizens huddled under the protection of their bishop, the peace conference of 2 August took place outside.

Above: **7.** The modern observation tower that marks the site, and approximate size, of the windmill used by King Edward as a command post during the battle. This view was taken from the position occupied by the right flank archers of the Black Prince's division.

Left: **8.** The monument erected to commemorate the death of the King of Bohemia in the battle. The heavily weathered original cross was re-erected on the modern base in the early twentieth century.

Above: **9.** The main priory church at Airaines. The priory was much rebuilt in the later middle ages, then secularised and mostly demolished in the 18th century. This section of nave, however, remains from 1346 when the English army camped in the grounds.

Right: **10.** The west tower of the castle at St Sauveur le Vicomte. When Sir Godfrey Harcourt returned to his home here during the Crecy campaign it was to find that his luxurious home within the defensive walls had been torched by the agents of the vengeful King Philip.

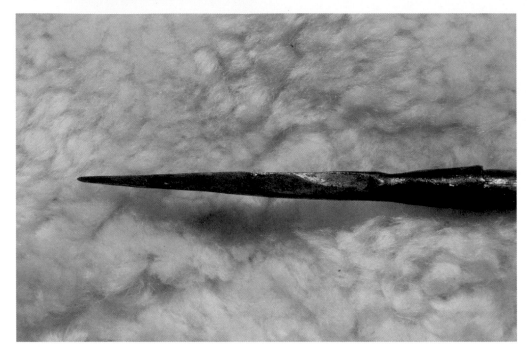

11. A long bodkin arrowhead. These weapons were most effective against chainmail. The point was designed to slip between the links of mail, prising them apart as it penetrated deeply into the man wearing the armour. The aim of such weapons was to kill. With thanks to the Medieval Combat Society www.themcs.org.

12. A broad-head arrowhead. These weapons were used against horses when the aim was to inflict serious wounds, but not to kill. With thanks to the Medieval Combat Society www.themcs.org.

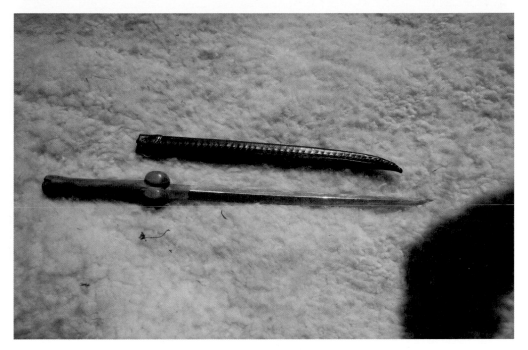

13. A "bollicker", a thin bladed knife designed to slip between the gaps in plate armour and so despatch the unfortunate knight. With thanks to the Medieval Combat Society www.themcs.org.

14. An archer's knife. These heavy-bladed, single-edged knives were carried by all archers. They could be used to repair fletching, joint plundered chickens and a host of other purposes. With thanks to the Medieval Combat Society www.themcs.org.

15. A fourteenth-century bombard mounted on its wooden firing sled and with the heavy lifting gear needed to position the gun after each shot. The gun weighs about 1.5 tonnes and has a bore of 38cm. The original on which it is based could fire a stone ball weighing 64kg over 1.5km. Bombards very similar to this were used during the siege of Calais. With thanks to the Company of St Barbara www. co-of-stbarbara.co.uk.

16. An archer prepares to shoot while standing beside the banner of Edward III. At Crecy these men were largely unarmoured, though many came equipped with helmets of various kinds and small shields. With thanks to the Medieval Combat Society www.themcs.org.

17. A pair of knights practise combat with swords. Both men are dressed in a style of armour that would have been modern by the standards of 1346. The knight on the right wears a bascinet with a pointed visor plus plate armour on his arms and legs. The figure on the left has an open-faced bascinet and less extensive leg armour. The tent behind them is typical of the type taken on campaign by richer knights. With thanks to the Medieval Combat Society www.themcs.org.

Left: **18.** An infantryman prepares to fire a polegun. These firearms had an effective range of about 35 metres and fired a collection of metal or stone pieces that sprayed out rather like the discharge of a sawn-off shotgun. With thanks to the Company of St Barbara www.co-of-stbarbara.co.uk.

Below: **19.** The key camping equipment of a medieval army on campaign: braziers and other cooking equipment.

Above: **20.** Edward III performs homage to Philip VI of France. Courtesy the British Library, Royal MS 20 C VII, f. 72v.

Right: **21.** A painting by Charles Doughty of Queen Phillipa begging for mercy from her husband Edward III on behalf of the six burghers of Calais. Edward had condemned them to death, but reprieved them as a result of his Queen's words.

22. Shield with arms of Edward III
from the tomb of the Black Prince in
Canterbury Cathedral.

Right: **23.** Edward III grants the title of
Prince of Aquitaine to the Black Prince.
Courtesy the British Library, Cotton
Nero MS DVI, f. 31.

24. The body – or funeral effigy – of Edward III lying in state.

25. Tomb of Edward III at Westminster Abbey: detail view of the effigy.
Courtesy of the Dean and Chapter of Westminster.

This soldier is equipped to a high standard for men produced by commissions of array who fought as heavy spearmen. His helmet, made of iron, is a close-fitting skull cap with a flared brim. It went by various names including 'chapeau de fer' and 'kettle-hat'. Under the helmet is a mail coif to provide protection to the sides and rear of the head as well as the neck. He wears a mail haubergeon over which he has put a sleeveless tunic of leather onto which are sewn metal scales. The large, triangular shield is made of wood and might be covered with a layer of tough leather. For the march it is slung over his should by a broad strap, but would be held on his left forearm in action. The shield would typically be painted with an heraldic device that identified the town from which he came. For offensive purposes he carries a three-metre spear and a short sword. The spear was almost mandatory, though sidearms might include axes, maces and knives as well as swords. This man is very well equipped for his type. Most men raised by array from towns had less impressive body armour.

The French sources, however, record the bishop coming back to Philip with a very definite reply. The challenge had been accepted and the battle would be fought on 17 August south of Bourg St Germain. Philip was jubilant. He had the larger army, knew the ground and was confident of success.

The 15 August was the Feast of the Assumption of the Blessed Virgin Mary, one of the holiest days in medieval Catholic Christianity. Both kings abandoned military actions for the day. According to the *Acta Bellicosa*, Edward 'announced that everyone was to make their devotions to the Mother of God. Nothing happened this day that is worth recording.'

The next day, however, Philip led his army through Paris, over the Seine and south towards Bourg St Germain. Edward, meanwhile, hurried his army over the repaired bridge at Poissy and headed north. The rearguard set fire to the town as they left (though Princess Isabelle's convent was spared), then demolished the bridge once they were safely over. That night the English army camped around Grisy, the French, at Bourg St Germain.

The 17 August dawned clear and bright, and as dry as every day since the English had landed. It was a grand day for a battle, so the French sharpened their weapons and got ready to teach the impudent English a lesson. But of the English there was no sign. It was not until almost noon that Philip finally accepted the words of his scouts. Not only were the English not coming to fight, they had crossed the Seine and were hurrying north.

Philip was furious, almost beside himself with rage. That evening he received a letter sent to him by Edward that morning. 'Philippe de Valois' the letter began, thus refusing to accept Philip's royal status and addressing him by his old title.

> … we have read your letters by which you say that you wish to fight us at St Germain or Franconville. On this we let it be known to you that with God's assurance and in the clear right which we have to the crown of France, which you wrongfully hold, to our disinheritance against God and right, we have come without pride to our kingdom of France, making our way to you to put an end to the war. But although you could have a battle with us, you broke down the bridges between you and us, so that we could not come near you or cross the River Seine. When we came to Poissy and repaired the bridge there which you had broken, we stayed three days, waiting for you and the army which you had gathered. You could have come there from any direction as you wished. Because we could not get you to give battle we decided to continue further into our kingdom to comfort our loyal friends and punish rebels, whom you wrongly claim as your subjects. And we wish to remain in our kingdom without leaving it to carry on the war to our advantage as best we can to the damage of our adversaries. Therefore if you wish to do battle with us in order to spare those whom you call your subjects, let it now be known that at whatever hour you approach you will find us ready to meet you in the field, with God's help, which thing we most earnestly desire for the common good of Christendom and since you will not accept or offer any reasonable terms for peace. We shall never be dictated to by you, nor will we accept a day and place for battle on the conditions you have named.

If Philip had been angry before, he was now apoplectic. He had been made to look a fool in front of his capital city, his allies and his own army. This was a real turning point in the campaign. Before reading the letter, Philip may have been inclined to wait out Edward and, as in 1339 and 1340, let a lack of supplies force the English to retreat. Now nothing less than the annihilation of the English would satisfy Philip. He wanted to see Edward a prisoner. The English must be destroyed.

VIII

The River Somme

Once the English army was north of the Seine, the pace of the campaign began to speed up. Again it is not entirely clear exactly what Edward was intending to do. On the day that Edward arrived at Poissy, Sir Hugh Hastings and the Flemings had finally marched out of Ypres to attack Mervilles. By the time Edward had got his army over the Seine, the Flemings had advanced as far as Béthune. The obvious move for Edward was to march north to link up with the Flemings, then turn to face the French army of King Philip.

However, Edward probably did not know where Hastings was, nor what he was doing. The territory between Béthune and Poissy was firmly in the control of the French. Armed men guarded all the bridges and key road junctions. The chances of a messenger getting through between Edward and Hastings were slim indeed, so slim that it is likely that neither commander considered even sending one. Getting a message through by way of the sea was even more problematic. Grimaldi's ships had been patrolling the Channel since the start of August. It seems that the last contact Edward had with English ships had been at Caen. Of course, Edward knew that Hastings was supposed to be marching south by way of Béthune, but given the instability of the Flemish alliance it was by no means certain that he was. Certainly to risk the safety of an entire army on what somebody was *meant* to be doing would have been very dangerous.

The chronicler Jean le Bel states that when Edward was marching north from Poissy, 'his chief intention was to lay siege to the strong town of Calais'. This was written some years after the event and may have been a case of talking with hindsight, though it cannot be discounted entirely.

There is just one fact that indicates what Edward might have been planning. Before leaving Caen, he had sent orders back to England asking for supplies of bows, arrows, food and men to be sent to join him at Le Crotoy by the end of August.

Le Crotoy was a small port on the north shore of the estuary of the River Somme. That put it in Ponthieu, the small county which Edward had owned before the war began and which he had visited several times during the years of peace. When he gave these orders they may have been nothing more than a contingency plan. By 16 August, however, the rendezvous at Le Crotoy might have become critical.

Although Edward had got north of the Seine, his situation was still serious. The army's food was running low, though starvation was still some way off. He was being dogged by a superior army, and as yet no place suitable for English tactics had been found. Just as Edward had probably considered using the rendezvous with the fleet at Caen to go home if things were going wrong, perhaps he now saw the meeting at Le Crotoy in a similar light. Alternatively, he may have been hoping for a sympathetic reception in Ponthieu; after all, he was friends with several of the local landowners and noblemen. Ponthieu might offer a haven in which to rest and resupply the army. Whatever Edward's aims were, they depended on staying ahead of the French army and on getting across the Somme. He had to march quickly.

On 18 August, the English reached the prosperous city of Beauvais. The Prince of Wales thought he could take the city, and sent a messenger back to the king asking permission. Edward refused, telling his son that since the French were following, it was no time to think of plunder. Despite this, some of the prince's men did slip into the faubourgs and abbeys outside the walls to engage in some private looting. Twenty of these men had the misfortune to be leaving the Abbey of St Lucien as the king himself was riding past.

Stressed by the way the campaign was going and already peeved by his son's behaviour, Edward was in no mood to be lenient. He ordered the men to be arrested and, as a tell-tale trail of smoke showed that they had fired the abbey, he had them hanged on the spot. The bodies were left dangling from roadside trees past which the rest of the English army passed, making it very clear what would happen to those who disobeyed orders.

The next day the English marched north to Sommereux, averaging almost twenty-three kilometres a day since leaving Poissy. Soon after dawn on 20 August Edward was disturbed to see a cloud of dust far to the east, and he sent out scouts to discover what was making it. Although Edward would not find out until late that evening, the dust cloud was being kicked up by the advance guard of the French army, commanded by King John of Bohemia.

King John had with him the Bohemian, Luxembourg and German contingents, plus an unknown number of French troops. In all likelihood this advance guard alone was as numerous as the entire English army. That would have been bad enough, but it soon became clear that King John was marching towards Amiens, where Philip had ordered the militias of Picardy to gather. If he got there first, the English would be caught south of the Somme just as they had previously been caught south of the Seine.

It is in the light of this rapidly worsening strategic position for the English that the strange events at Poix must be seen. At this date Poix was a prosperous town about the size of contemporary Lincoln or Leicester. It was surrounded by stout walls and protected by two castles, one considerably stronger and larger than the other.

According to the *Acta Bellicosa*, Edward had ordered the army to bypass Poix, just as it had bypassed Beauvais two days earlier. Some soldiers of the vanguard, however, felt that they could take the city and were obviously tempted by the prospect of rich plunder inside. The *Acta Bellicosa* makes this sound as if there were only a few men involved and that they were acting without orders. When some members of the king's entourage came up, 'they told the men attacking it not to make any further attacks'. The men fell back, but as soon as the riders had gone, returned to the fray.

The English tried digging mines under the walls, but this failed, so they set up scaling ladders, and under cover of archery clambered up to get a foothold on the town walls. The employment of engineers and ladders would seem to imply something more than a few hot-heads getting carried away.

The tale in the *Acta Bellicosa* continues with the English racing through the town to the larger castle, which they then attacked. Flaming torches were set to the gates and archers deluged the battlements with arrows. At this point, the castle commander surrendered on condition that all killing ceased immediately, though the English would be allowed to plunder. The next act is recorded as 'The Prince of Wales then gave the men-at-arms and archers and servants of his household...' And there the sole manuscript stops.

In his letter of 4 September, Michael Northburgh says that the vanguard and main body of the army marched around Poix and that it was the rearguard that took the town, later negotiating the surrender of the castle.

Jean le Bel tells a very different story. He states that the town and castle had been abandoned by the French military and that only local men with makeshift weaponry guarded the place. The civilians parleyed with the marshal of the army – presumably the Earl of Warwick, although elsewhere le Bel does name Harcourt as a marshal – and agreed that the town would be spared in return for a cash payment. Froissart broadly agrees, but names Sir Thomas Holland (apparently recovered from the wound he received at Gaillon) as the man who made the agreement. In these versions there is no fighting.

Both le Bel and Froissart mention that there were two aristocratic ladies in Poix who were in great danger of being raped and robbed by the English soldiers until Sir John Chandos and a fellow knight intervened and offered to protect them. These were the wife and daughter of Lord John Tyrel of Poix, who was riding with King Philip's army. The ladies were later given a small escort by King Edward and conducted

The monument to King John of Bohemia stands in a small, but carefully tended garden beside the road east of Crecy.

to Corbie, well out of the way of the campaign. The tale of two ladies about to be raped does not match the apparently peaceful picture otherwise painted by Froissart and le Bel.

The chronicle of the Bourgeois of Valenciennes also mentions the two ladies, giving their names, and states that there was a great slaughter of defenders, but without giving much detail.

Events get murkier the next morning. Michael Northburgh says that the local people of the area tried to ambush some English soldiers under the command of the Earl of Suffolk and Sir Hugh Despencer as they left Poix. The French were defeated, with over 200 being killed and 60 taken prisoner. Le Bel says that the trouble the following day began when the time came for the citizens of Poix to pay over the cash they had promised to the English. Seeing that the bulk of the English army was hurrying north at great speed, the French refused to pay and set upon the unnamed English knight who had stayed behind to collect the money. One of the English troops managed to get out of Poix and raise the alarm, whereupon 'the citizens were killed without mercy and the whole town burned, as it deserved to be.'

It is not unusual for different chroniclers to give slightly different versions of events, so the varied accounts of what happened at Poix may simply be the result of different points of view. Given, however, that the

English could see the dust cloud of marching Frenchmen to the east it is very odd that all this happened at all.

It may be that the Black Prince, smarting from being stopped from attacking Beauvais, decided to try again at Poix. The fact that mining engineers and ladders were involved would indicate that a senior commander had authorised their use. The *Acta Bellicosa* was written by a knight in the Black Prince's division so it is likely that he knew what those troops had been doing. It is equally likely that he may have implied that the soldiers acted on their own account to try to cover up the Black Prince's part in proceedings.

Northburgh may have thought that the rearguard took Poix if the place finally fell as the rearguard was passing. It would seem more likely that the surrender involved a cash payment than that the town was given over to plundering. Edward himself would have been on the spot by this time. He would have wanted to move on quickly, and plundering takes time. And if the unnamed knight in le Bel's account was the Earl of Suffolk, then his account can be squared with that of Northburgh. Even so, the events at Poix were all decidedly odd. No doubt there was rather more to the affair than the surviving records let on.

Whatever happened, the English left Poix on 21 August and marched north to Airaines. In itself this was a victory for the French, for it meant that Edward had given up hopes of reaching Amiens first and was turning northwest to avoid a confrontation with King John of Bohemia. While most of the army settled into the abandoned town to find quarters for the night, the vanguard was sent out to the east to form a protective screen facing Amiens, where Bohemia was known to be arriving at about the same time.

Bohemia also sent out scouts, and the two forces clashed. At first the English got the worse of the encounter, one Sir Thomas Talbot being captured and others 'beaten to the ground', according to Northburgh. The Earl of Northampton, as so often, was nearby and led a spirited charge that killed twelve Bohemian men-at-arms and captured eight more. Northampton pursued the enemy to within three kilometres of Amiens before breaking off and returning to camp.

The day after, Tuesday 22 August, the bulk of the English army rested at Airaines. Meanwhile, fast-moving columns of horsemen were sent out to scout out the Somme River and, hopefully, secure a bridgehead. The Earl of Warwick led a force towards Picquigny. The town was, however, well garrisoned and protected by high walls, so Warwick turned aside before reaching it.

He then marched northwest to Longpré. The unwalled town was abandoned, but the long causeway across the marshy Somme and the narrow bridge were heavily defended. Disturbingly, the banners of the French on the north bank included not only those of local knights but also of men from Bohemia's force. The main enemy vanguard had got there first. Longpré was set on fire as the English rode on.

The next bridge was at Long, but that too was defended and could be approached only by a long causeway cutting over wet marshes. Warwick passed by yet again.

It was getting late in the day by the time Warwick reached Pont-Remy. The causeway here was shorter and the French banners showed only local men to be present. Warwick, who according to le Bel was by now joined by a force under Harcourt, decided to try an attack. In the event, it was not only local arrayed men who defended the bridge at Pont-Remy, there was also a force of Genoese crossbowmen. Hampered by being forced to stay on the causeway, the English proved easy targets for the Italians. Warwick called off the attack and rode back to Airaines.

King Edward himself had meanwhile led a separate force to Abbeville. This city was surrounded by modern walls and the bridge was heavily fortified. After a brief skirmish with the men led by the mayor, Lord Collard-en-Ver, Edward withdrew. Le Bel puts this raid on 23 August. On whichever day it took place, the results were the same: Edward could not cross at Abbeville and fell back.

It was by now imperative that the English get across the Somme. The kitchen accounts show that only the most basic food was being served to the king, so it must be assumed that the rest of the army was similarly on fairly poor rations. King Philip with the main French army was arriving in Amiens and would soon be marching towards Airaines. There was no good defensive position suited to English tactics in the area, so even the hope of fending of French attacks with dismounted men-at-arms and archers could not be relied upon. Edward had his back to the sea and his face towards a vastly superior opponent. It was time to get away.

Fortunately, there were two ways out for Edward. The first was the English fleet that might be able to evacuate the army or bring in reinforcements. It was due to be at Le Crotoy within the next few days. Although Le Crotoy was north of the Somme, there was another small port south of the river: St Valery. If that port could be taken, it could be used by the fleet. Captured ships could be sent over to Le Crotoy to summon the fleet if it were there, or sent to England to hurry it along if not. Perhaps the English army could hold at St Valery until the fleet arrived.

Early on 23 August Edward sent Harcourt to investigate St Valery. It was a long ride from Airaines and so it was not until well in to the afternoon that Harcourt arrived at the port. He found it surrounded by good walls behind which the English could indeed shelter for some days from King Philip. Unfortunately, the banner of Count de St Pol fluttered from the battlements. St Pol was an experienced commander and he had with him a sizeable force of men-at-arms sent by King Philip some weeks earlier. St Pol marched out boldly to face Harcourt's men in the open. There was a short skirmish, but the English soon realised that they could not take St Valery without a major effort Harcourt turned back eastward.

Edward, meanwhile, had left Airaines and was marching the main body of his army in the footsteps of Harcourt. When he reached the small town of Oisemont, Edward found a force of local French troops drawn up to block the road. A quick attack of men-at-arms backed by archers was enough to send the French fleeing across the fields. Oisemont was burned and the English marched on to reach Acheux by nightfall. It was there that Harcourt rode in to report failure at St Valery.

Edward now had only once choice: the tidal ford that crossed the broad, marshy Somme somewhere near Saigneville. There were, however, problems in both finding and using it. According to le Bel, Edward did not know the ford existed, and Froissart repeats the story. This is highly unlikely. The English were now on the borders of Ponthieu and the ford lay within that county. Edward had himself visited the county several times, and there were men in the army who had worked in Ponthieu as administrative officials for years at a time. That none of these men knew that a tidal ford existed stretches credulity.

What is far more likely is that none of these men had ever actually used it. In the days of peace it would have been far more convenient to use the bridges at Abbeville, Pont-Remy or Longpré than to splash through a ford that was passable only part of the time. It is most likely that the English knew the ford was there, but were rather hazy about where it came out on the southern bank of the Somme. They were probably little better informed about the state of the local tides and how they affected the ford.

No doubt efficient scouting would have found the ford within a day or so, but Edward did not have the time. Some time after noon King Philip had arrived in Airaines, only four hours or so after the English rearguard had left. He sent his scouts out to follow the English, then led the rest of his army to Abbeville. There he camped overnight to await firm news of the retreating enemy before continuing the pursuit.

According to le Bel, Froissart and others, Edward went to see the prisoners captured at Oisemont as soon as Harcourt had reported in. Edward offered to pay 100 golden crowns and to set free up to four men if anyone would tell him where the ford was. The knights and men-at-arms stayed silent, but then a man named Gobin Agace stepped forward to claim the reward. Agace was a simple peasant to whom the 100 gold coins would have represented a fortune.

The ford of Blanchetaque was destroyed in the early nineteenth century when the Somme was dredged out and the surrounding marshes drained to create productive farmland. In 1346, it was as much a causeway as a ford. The central feature of Blanchetaque was a solid causeway of chalk – whether natural or manmade is unclear – that ran across the valley of the Somme just north of the village of Saigneville. The chalk path was about fifteen metres wide at its narrowest point. At high tide the seawater rushed in and made the ford impassable, but at low tide the white chalk path was exposed across most of its length. Only in a few places was the path underwater, and then only to a depth of about 15 centimetres or so.

Just as useful to the English was the fact that the marshes either side of the chalk ridge were not the muddy morass that they were elsewhere. If they did not mind getting muddy, both men and horses could get over the marshes at low tide. The total width of the marshes at this point was approaching three kilometres. At low tide there were only the various shallow, muddy channels of the Somme where the men would get more than their feet wet. In places, these channels may have been waist deep, but no more. The summer of 1346 was a dry one and there had been no real rain since the English army had landed six weeks earlier, and possibly for some time before that. The Somme would have been running low by this time.

Lacking a bridge, Blanchetaque seemed an ideal place to cross. But when was the next low tide? Agace knew that too: just after dawn.

While it was still dark on the morning of 24 August, trumpets sounded throughout the English army. The men were roused from their sleep around Acheux and ordered north. The army trailed through Saigneville in the grey light of dawn and trooped down to the edge of the wide, marshy valley of the Somme. The tide was ebbing strongly, with masses of swirling water heading out to sea to reveal the white path of Blanchetaque. But all was not well. The French had got there first.

Sitting at the north end of the Blanchetaque ford was a force of 1,000 men-at-arms, a few hundred Genoese crossbowmen and 3,000 infantry under the banner of a Burgundian soldier of fortune, Sir Godemar du Fay. The banner of a gold stag on a blue field would have been instantly recognised by the English heralds, for du Fay was a well-known and competent soldier who had served the French before.

Edward now had no choice. He had to get across the river, and that meant defeating du Fay and his men. His heralds would have told Edward that apart from du Fay, all the banners visible beyond the river were of poorer or unimportant knights from Picardy. Edward will have known that he was facing a good commander, but one who had largely inexperienced men under him. Edward laid his plans accordingly.

There are several sources for the Battle of Blanchetaque. Edward himself in his letter of 3 September and Michael Northburgh writing a day later both mention the fight, but give no details. Le Bel gives a brief outline of events, but it is Froissart – as usual – who adds the details and names in his account.

A strong force of mounted men-at-arms, archers and spearmen was put under the command of Sir Hugh Despencer and sent on to the chalk causeway. Despencer served in the rearguard, so Edward must have had some special reason for asking him to lead the army here. Perhaps he had some useful experience.

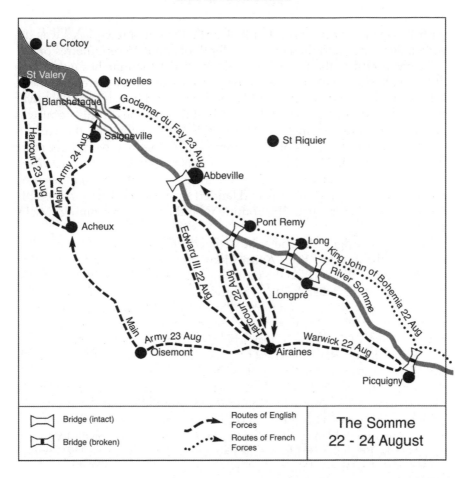

Le Crotoy
St Valery
Noyelles
Blanchetaque
Godemar du Fay 23 Aug
Saigneville
Harcourt 23 Aug
Main Army 24 Aug
Abbeville
St Riquier
Acheux
Edward III 22 Aug
Pont Remy
Long
King John of Bohemia 22 Aug
River Somme
Harcourt 22 Aug
Longpré
Main Army 23 Aug
Oisemont
Warwick 22 Aug
Airaines
Picquigny

⊠ Bridge (intact)	→ Routes of English Forces	**The Somme**
⊠ Bridge (broken)	⋯→ Routes of French Forces	**22 - 24 August**

While the armoured cavalry rode forward along the firm ford, the archers and spearmen splashed their way through the adjacent marsh. As they came within range of the Genoese, the English began to be hit by crossbow bolts. The archers shot back, but they were hampered by being scattered across the marsh and not having secure footing. The exchange of missiles was going the way of the French.

Despencer now led his men forward through the infantry to deliver a charge of heavily armoured cavalry, such as had won the day for Derby at Auberoche. He unfurled his banner and led his men in delivering a loud chant. Then he put his spurs to his horse.

Du Fay beat him to it, leading his men-at-arms in a furious charge down into the shallow waters of the ford. The French charge seems to have been well delivered and effective. It was at this moment, with Du Fay and his knights personally engaged in the shallow water and with all his infantry watching the battle to the front, that Edward pulled his masterstroke. Erupting from the flank of the French force came the Earl of Northampton leading a charge by a hundred mounted men-at-arms, backed up by some mounted archers or hobilars.

Exactly where and when these men had crossed the Somme is not made clear. Richard Wynkeley says only that they 'went in front of the main army'. Perhaps they had splashed across the marshes while everyone's attention had been focussed on the fighting along the ford. Perhaps they had crossed the night before and been hiding in nearby woods to await their chance.

However Northampton had managed to get undetected on to the French flank, his attack was decisive. 'He drove them off by force', Richard Wynkeley continues, 'killing that day two thousand or more and the rest fled.' All that King Edward says is 'the enemy were defeated'. Michael Northburgh is more informative, saying that the French 'fled right up to the gates of Abbeville, and a large number of knights were taken'. Du Fay himself was injured and fell back northward. He did not go far, but halted near Noyelles to keep an eye on English movements.

The French chroniclers record the fight at Blanchetaque in a similar, but rather different way. They may have been looking for somebody to blame for the way the English escaped Philip's trap – nobody was going to point out to the king that his plan had been flawed. In any case, the French writers of the time are all agreed that du Fay did not put up much of a fight. The arrayed infantry are said to have fled as soon as the fighting started, leaving du Fay and his men-at-arms to face the English alone. At this point du Fay fled so the local French knights had no choice but to fall back. But then du Fay was a foreigner from Burgundy, so it was safe to blame him.

Having secured the ford, Edward now had to get his army and its supply train across before the tide came back in. Depending on how long the fighting had taken, the English had between four and six hours to get the job done – assuming that the French did not intervene once more. It was a nervous time for Edward. With his army divided by three kilometres of marsh between north and south banks and his supply train strung out along a single track causeway, he was desperately vulnerable. If the French attacked now, the English would be helpless.

King Philip was, in fact, hurrying to do just that. He had left Abbeville shortly after dawn, riding west south of the Somme. The latest news that Philip had at this point was that brought in by scouts returning to Abbeville after nightfall on 23 August. These had reported the English army marching north from Oisemont toward Acheux, beyond which lay St Valery and the Blanchetaque, both possible targets for Edward.

No doubt Philip sent out scouts to ride hard to the west to find the English. He would have anxiously scanned the western horizon himself for the columns of smoke that marked the burning towns and villages left by the English chevauchée, but there were none. It is likely that Philip knew even less about the ford at Blanchetaque than did Edward. If he had been told that it was a causeway like that at Longpré or Pont-Remy he will have been confident that du Fay and his men could hold it, as those others had been held two days earlier. If Philip knew that men could walk over the marshes, he did nothing to act on that knowledge.

So far as Philip was concerned, Edward was trapped. He had the river to the north, the sea to the west, devastated land to the south and the advancing French army to the east. There was no rush.

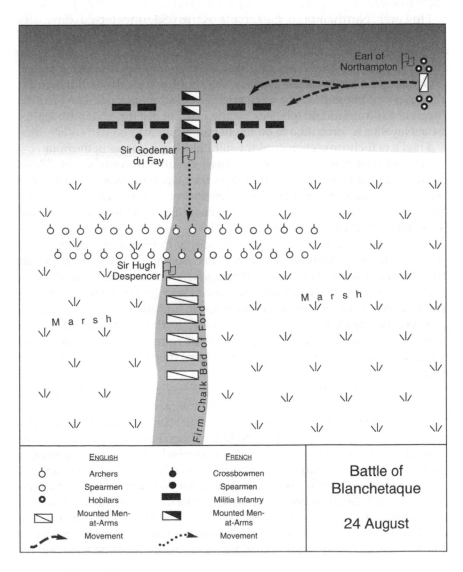

ENGLISH		FRENCH	
Archers		Crossbowmen	
Spearmen		Spearmen	
Hobilars		Militia Infantry	
Mounted Men-at-Arms		Mounted Men-at-Arms	
Movement		Movement	

Battle of
Blanchetaque

24 August

It would have been mid-morning by the time the French scouts found that the English had left Acheux heading north to Blanchetaque. Philip likewise turned toward the ford. As the French army advanced, they ran into the expected English scouts. There does not seem to have been any skirmishing, the English simply fell back as the French advanced. Philip reached the ford about 2.00 p.m. The sight that greeted him threw him into another fury.

The retreating English scouts were splashing their way over the chalk road as the tide came flowing in. Already the waters were almost reaching the horses' bellies. Apart from a few broken and abandoned carts, the entire English army was on the far side of the wide, swampy valley.

In his letter of 3 September, Edward wrote: 'We waited there and took up battle positions, and stayed like this the whole day.' Froissart adds his usual colourful detail. A French knight rode his horse into the deepening waters to shout a challenge to the English. Sir Thomas Colville of Bukdensike, Yorkshire, answered. He rode out to meet the Frenchman in mid-stream to the cheers of the watching armies. After some jousting at each other with lances, the rising waters forced the two men to part. They saluted each other, then rode back to their respective armies as the chivalrous heroes of the hour.

Once he was certain that his prey had escaped him yet again, Philip did not waste much time. It would be dark before the tide fell again and crossing a marsh in the dark under threat from enemy arrows was not something he fancied. 'He did not wish to cross over to us', recorded Northburgh, 'and returned to Abbeville'.

Having been forced to return humiliatingly to the town, Philip was in vengeful mood. He declared that du Fay must have made way for the English deliberately, and that the Burgundian had obviously sold out for English cash. Du Fay was a traitor, declared Philip, and demanded that the knight be executed by the first Frenchman to find him.

As those survivors of du Fay's force who fled to Abbeville came in and were questioned, it became clear that the Burgundian had, in fact, done his best. Even so, Philip would not listen and it was some months before du Fay dared show his face.

Meanwhile, the English were north of the Somme and Edward was moving fast. He sent Sir Hugh Despencer with a strong mounted column to gallop around the estuary marshes to reach Le Crotoy. The small garrison was quickly overwhelmed and killed. Food stocks found in the town were large, and Despencer loaded them on to stolen carts to haul back to Edward and the main army. But of the English fleet there was no sign.

It may have been at this point that Edward finally realised that he would have to fight Philip and so face up to the most powerful army in Christendom. Fortunately for Edward, he was now on his home ground of Ponthieu. He knew the landscape and he knew what it had to offer. He ordered his men to march to a small village a few kilometres to the north. Its name was Crecy.

IX

The French Host

While King Edward led his English army to Crecy, King Philip was at Abbeville doing everything he could to ensure that the English would be wiped off the face of France. The instrument he chose was the vast army that was gathering, and which proved to be so large that Abbeville could not hold it.

Philip had delayed summoning an army to face Edward until he was reasonably certain of Edward's intentions. The result of this was that some of the troops were still arriving, indeed some arrived after the battle had been fought. In part this delay was caused by Philip wanting to make sure that he mustered his army in the right place at the right time, but a primary consideration was money.

The French crown directly owned extensive estates that produced profits, both in money and kind, for the use of the king. The king could also levy a number of traditional taxes, such as the gabelle on salt, which produced regular cash income. The problem with the taxes was that they had been established some generations earlier and no longer reflected the economic conditions of modern France. The kingdom of France was booming in prosperity with trade and commerce, but the king of France was still trying to raise taxes on vanishing agricultural practices. Just as galling was the lack of a central tax collection system. The money owed in taxes was collected by local nobles and authorities, who then passed it on to the crown. Inevitably there were delays in passing the cash on, and varying percentages were deducted for 'expenses' by the collectors.

The king could ask for additional taxes or payments, but usually only for a particular purpose. Since France was a very decentralised state at this time, this meant that the royal officials had to approach dozens of local assemblies independently to ask for money. In 1346 Philip had begun this process in January, hoping to have it completed by April. Many towns and provinces did produce money by the deadline, but others did not. Perhaps something over half the expected amount had come in by the time Edward

This crossbowman is typical of the mercenaries from northern Italy and Provence who served on the French side during the Crecy campaign, but who could be found in the ranks of almost any medieval army whose commander could afford them. His crossbow is of the foot-spanned variety with a wooden stock and bow, but metal stirrup and trigger mechanism. The two metal hooks that hang from the front of his belt were used when spanning the weapon. He would bend down so that his foot was in the stirrup to hold the bow firmly on the ground. He would then slip the hooks through the bowstring and straighten up to use his leg muscles to pull the string back and engage it into the hook on top of the stock. The crossbow is shown here spanned and ready to shoot. He carries a selection of bolts in a leather pouch slung from his belt. On his head he wears a palet helmet with an open face and with mail hanging down to cover the neck and shoulders. He wears a short-sleeved mail shirt, over which is a tough leather jerkin reinforced with small metal plates and studs. Over his knees he wears the flanged metal coverings that seem to have been peculiar to northern Italian crossbowmen. His legs are otherwise unarmoured.

landed at St Vaast. Philip borrowed the outstanding amount, hoping to pay it back when the taxes were paid.

In theory, the main source of manpower for the French army in 1346 was the *ban de l'ost*, a feudal system broadly similar to the English commissions of array. Each area was expected to send to fight for the king a certain number of men armed in a particular way. The area paid for the men's equipment, and for their pay and supplies for the first forty days of service, after which the king paid. Just as taxation suffered from local administration, so with the ban. It was down to discussion between royal officials and local authorities to decide how many men should be sent and of which type. Nor was it always certain that everyone would turn up.

Beyond the *ban de l'ost* there was the *arrière ban de l'ost* which covered all men aged eighteen to sixty. These men were not expected to come equipped for war (though many did carry improvised weapons), but were used as manual labour during sieges and to transport supplies. The *arrière ban* was generally invoked only for service in the area where the men were raised.

As in England, the summoning of the feudal host was on the decline, though the process was not as advanced in France. While the English king issued indentured contracts to men supplying units of men, the French kings were issuing *lettres de convenances*. Few of these documents have survived from the period of the Crecy campaign so it is difficult to know exactly how widely used they were. There is one clear difference between terms and conditions in the two kingdoms, however. The French king claimed that all noble prisoners who could be expected to pay a ransom had to be handed over to him, but in return he would pay ransoms to free those of his men who were captured. The raising of troops by *lettres de convenances* had the advantage that the king and his commanders would reliably know how many men would be available and how they would be armed. The same could be said of the mercenaries who, as we shall see, were hired in large numbers by French kings.

Whether raised by the *ban* or by *lettres de convenances*, the soldiers serving in the French armies at this time conformed to various types. Rural areas produced large numbers of lightly armed infantry that went by names such as *ribaud* or *brigante*. The fine distinctions such terms imply have been lost, if they ever really meant much at the time. These men came to war carrying light arms, such as short swords, axes or spears about 2.5m long. A few had crossbows. For defensive purposes the *ribauds* wore a similar type of padded cloth armour to that favoured by English hobilars. They almost always wore a helmet of some kind and most would have had a mail coif to give protection to the neck and throat.

For some reason the *ribauds* that are shown in manuscript illustrations are always a very colourful lot. Their clothing comes in various shades of blue, red, pink, brown, buff, green and yellow in the most astonishing combinations. One man may have a red jacket with green sleeves over blue leggings, another have differently coloured legs and arms with a jacket the body of which is itself boldly striped. There does not seem to have been any attempt at uniform colours or outfits even within the ranks of units raised in the same area. Why the French rural infantry should choose to be so attired is unknown, but it would certainly have made for an impressive sight.

The chroniclers often refer to the *ribauds* as being present on campaign, sometimes in large numbers, but hardly ever do they mention what these men actually did. Presumably, they supplied the numbers needed for less important campaign duties such as watching crossroads, guarding bridges and manning town walls. No doubt these men were good enough to carry out such tasks in areas where no major enemy force was expected. They were able to provide the sort of security and confidence needed by civilians, and would reassure the army commanders that no enemy force would suddenly appear in an unguarded area.

But these *ribauds* also fought in major battles, so they must have performed some useful function that escaped the attention of the chroniclers. The most plausible scenario is that they formed back up and support to the next class of soldier that formed a regular element in French field armies of the time: the heavily armed infantry.

The armoured infantry raised in the country or from the estates of noblemen are often termed sergeants. However, the majority of these men seem to have come from towns and cities where they formed the militia. In origin the town militia were units raised to man the town walls in time of siege or to patrol and guard the surrounding land in more general times of war. By the 1340s, however, it was usual for at least some of a town's armed force to be sent to join the royal army.

Each town or rural area was responsible for arming its own men, so details of equipment varied greatly, even within the ranks of a single militia. Generally, these men wore a hauberk of mail that reached to the knees and elbows. Each man would usually have a coif to protect his head and shoulders, as well as an open helmet to give additional head protection. By the 1340s some of these men were beginning to acquire more sophisticated armour that their fathers would have thought belonged to knights. They wore metal plates over their shoulders and may have had leg and arm armour made up of strips of iron sewn on to leather clothing.

Each man also carried a large shield. These are generally shown as being about a metre long and some 60cm broad and forming the curved triangular shape which was standard at the time. Some shields carried a badge or heraldic device that identified the town from which they came, but others simply carried the blue field and yellow fleur-de-lys that showed they served the King of France.

A very few men in manuscripts are shown carrying even larger shields (about 1.7 metres tall and 1 metre wide) that wrap around the body. When

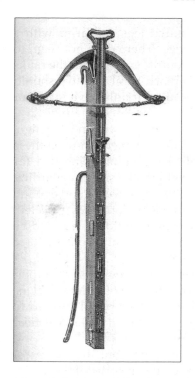 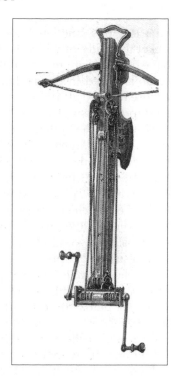

Above left: *A simple handspanned crossbow. The crossbowman would plant the nose of the weapon on the ground and insert his foot into the metal stirrup before hauling back on the string with a metal hook. The weapon was discharged by lifting the metal trigger underneath the stock.*

Above right: *The much heavier and more powerful windlass crossbow. It is not entirely clear when this more powerful, but more cumbersome weapon entered general use. At the time of Crecy it may have been reserved for siege warfare and would probably not have been seen on the battlefield.*

such a shield was rested on the ground, a man kneeling behind it would have been protected against any incoming missiles. Perhaps these men formed the front rank of a militia unit. All militia men and sergeants were armed with spears, often over 3m in length. They would also have side arms, such as a short sword or hand axe.

The militia, and to a lesser extent the sergeants, were adequately trained as well as being better armed than their *ribaud* colleagues. Most towns held regular training days, probably once a fortnight, at which the militia turned out to have their equipment inspected and to practice battlefield manouevres.

These consisted of variations on the theme of a solid phalanx of men, drawn up shoulder to shoulder to a depth of six or so ranks. The men were probably trained to march forwards and backwards, to turn about to form from column into line and back again and to change direction when advancing in column. Such movements are relatively straightforward so long as there are sufficient experienced men to keep the others in order. Trying to alter direction when advancing in line calls for rather more discipline and so perhaps only some units could be relied upon to perform such a movement reliably.

On the battlefield these armoured infantrymen had a variety of uses. They could push aside formations of *ribauds* without too much trouble, whether on the attack or defence. When facing men of their own kind, armoured infantry would depend on numbers and position for success. Their main tactical role on the battlefield was to serve as solid defensive formations around which the commander could move his more mobile troops.

In the French armies of the 1340s, it was the cavalry which formed the main offensive arm available to any commander. Modern historians refer to the heavily armoured cavalry of the time by the generic term of men-at-arms. This term masks a wide variety of men, arms and equipment. It was one of the major problems facing a French field commander at this date to sort out his men-at-arms into formations that would be able to fight as useful units on the field.

As we have already seen, the kingdom of France was a politically and socially decentralised state at this time. Historically, the social elite were those families who could claim the title of *seigneur*, and who were always addressed as '*mon seigneur*' from which comes the polite modern French form of *monsieur*. These had originally been men who owned estates producing enough income both to buy the military equipment of a knight and to free the owner from the need to work so that he could spend all his time training to fight as a knight.

Over the years, however, the status of such men had changed. The social prestige of being a *seigneur* was very great, so fathers tended to pass the title on to all their sons together with a share of the family lands. This inevitably led to a larger number of men claiming to be *seigneurs*, each with less land than the previous generations.

By the 1340s, it is thought that somewhere around 50,000 men in France claimed to be *seigneurs*. Some of these men were in reality little more than the richest farmer in the village, though their ancestry gave them the coveted title to which they held proudly and jealously. In fact only about 5,000 men throughout France held enough landed wealth to train and serve as knights. There were perhaps another 15,000 or so who could afford a reasonable suit of armour and warhorse, but who could not afford to train full time. In England such men would have been classed as esquires.

Of the remaining 30,000 or so men of gentle birth we have very little idea how they would have shaped up for military service. It is very likely that some would have owned enough old armour and a horse to show up for a *ban* claiming to be able to serve as a knight, though their effectiveness on the battlefield would have been questionable.

Others might have had little more than great-grandfather's sword hanging over the fireplace to impress the neighbours. Such men would undoubtedly have felt that their honour demanded that they turn out for the *ban*. It is likely that many of the men who feature as sergeants in the records are in fact impoverished seigneurs.

There was, therefore, a wide variation within the types of armour worn by the men-at-arms within the French army. The poorer men would have come to battle wearing mail armour that covered them from head to toe. On their heads would have been a helmet known as the great helm. This consisted of a number of iron plates riveted together to form a cylindrical helmet that wrapped right around the head from below the chin to the forehead, then sloped in to form a conical crown. This was good from the point of view of protection, but it was heavy to wear and was inflexible. It was either on or off.

By the 1320s the richer men were sporting sheets of plate armour on their limbs. These were held in place by leather straps and were worn over the mail. The advantage of plate was that it gave a smooth surface that encouraged weapon points to glance off. In most cases, however, it was the mail backing that provided the real strength to the armour. By the 1340s the vast majority of knights would have had some sort of plate armour on their arms and legs.

Many knights were also wearing additional body armour. This might have been the padded garments favoured by infantry, usually worn over the mail, or it might have taken the form of strips of iron sewn on to a cloth or leather sleeveless jacket which was usually put on under the mail. These garments came in a wide variety of designs and forms as they were still rather experimental, as was the wearing of shaped plates of iron over the shoulders and around the throat.

By the time of the Crecy campaign, any knight with any money would have given up the great helm in favour of the bascinet style of helmet. This was a lighter piece of hardware that was hammered into shape from a single piece of steel. The helmet was padded within with thick, folded layers of cloth finished off with a smooth lining to make the wearer more comfortable. The bascinet relied on the smooth, curved shape to deflect incoming weapons as much as on the strength of the steel. The main piece of steel covered the head, but left the face open. A second piece of steel was shaped to fit over the face, with holes left for seeing through and for breathing. This visor was hinged at the sides or top so that it could be lifted up easily to allow the wearer to look around him or catch his breath. This gave the wearer the benefit of keeping his head protected while having his face clear, something not possible with the older great helm.

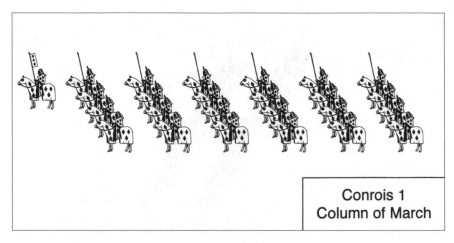

Conrois 1
Column of March

This shows a conrois of men at arms on the march. Most roads of the period could accommodate four mounted men riding abreast. Only one man has a banner on his lance to serve as the rallying point for the conrois in action. He rides at the head of the column. In this instance all men in the conrois carry the same coat of arms on their shield, indicating that they are esquires serving a single knight. In reality most conrois included several men entitled to bear their own arms on their shields.

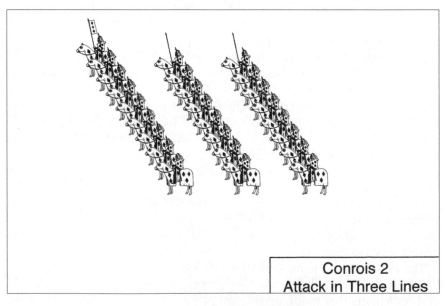

Conrois 2
Attack in Three Lines

Here the conrois is drawn up ready to charge an enemy formation. An attack in three lines was the usual deployment for a conrois. Enough space was allowed between the lines so that if a horse fell the riders behind stood some chance of veering to one side to avoid tripping and falling in turn. The banner was positioned in the front rank, usually to one side.

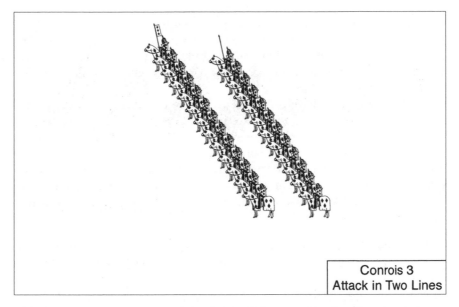

Conrois 3
Attack in Two Lines

If the frontage to be covered was wider than could be covered by three lines a conrois might deploy in two lines. This lessened the impact of the charge but prevented the conrois from being outflanked by the enemy.

It took a great amount of skill to produce such a helmet, so the bascinet was correspondingly expensive. Since it protected the head, however, it was generally the first bit of modern armour a knight would buy to upgrade his older suit.

Since they were trained to fight mostly from horseback, the French knights retained the long lance. This was usually held underarm and secured in place by a vamplate which not only guarded the hand but also allowed the wielder to brace the weapon against his chest. The lance was used in the charge to spear enemies, or at least to knock them flying if the lance tip hit a shield.

French knights generally had a single-handed sword to use once the lance had been broken or discarded after the initial impact. Some men carried a secondary weapon, either a short sword, axe or mace, in case the sword was lost or broken.

The one unifying feature of these men was their social pride and self belief. As *seigneurs* they were very definitely superior to the peasants and merchants that made up the rest of the population. Their views and opinions counted, even if for no other reason than that they believed they did, as thought the peasants. It was this pride that could make them so difficult to command. A touchy rural knight in poor-quality armour would refuse to accept that he might be less effective in battle than a richer man in modern equipment, and would refuse to step back to a rear rank. Each *seigneur* was as good as another, at least in his own opinion. It was just this pride and determination that made the French knights such a devastating weapon on the battlefield. In the hands of a competent commander they were simply unstoppable.

The basic tactical unit of the French armoured cavalry was the conrois. These came in a wide variety of sizes from a dozen or so up to over a hundred. They were men who knew each other and wanted to serve together. Usually they came from a small area of countryside or owed allegiance to a particular lord. Although each knight carried his own coat of arms on his shield, the members of a conrois would proclaim their membership by some means. Attaching a small pennon embroidered with a badge or design was one method used, as was painting the lances in matching colours.

Each conrois would practice and train together to a greater or lesser degree. There were only two basic offensive tactical formations: the line and the column. When forming up in line a conrois might be between two or five ranks deep, depending on how many knights it contained. It was highly unusual for a charge to be delivered with a conrois more than five ranks deep. Having more ranks would do little to add impact to the charge and would mean that the rear ranks would have no real chance of getting at the enemy.

If there were more knights available than were needed to deliver a five-rank deep charge at the selected target the commander would hold back some of his conrois to deliver a second charge if the first were unsuccessful. Successive waves of mounted charges were the accepted offensive method that was thought to offer the best route to victory.

Before about 1300 the French had developed a standard set of battlefield tactics that proved to be highly effective. Naturally the details would depend on the terrain over which the battle was to be fought and the formations adopted by the enemy, but the general aim remained clear. The army would draw up so that the line was held by armoured infantry militia formed in dense phalanxes. If there were any sections of the line that offered naturally strong defences, such as riverbanks, walls or hedges, these would be allocated to the *ribauds*. Otherwise these light infantry would form up behind their armoured comrades.

The knights would form up behind the infantry, most often in lines three ranks deep. The various conrois would be grouped together to produce a number of formations of roughly equal size. These would be posted at intervals across the front.

The French believed in offensive action whenever possible, so the army commander would be constantly watching the enemy army for a weak point. This might take the form of a section held by fewer men, or might be indicated by the behaviour of the men in an enemy formation. Nervous men

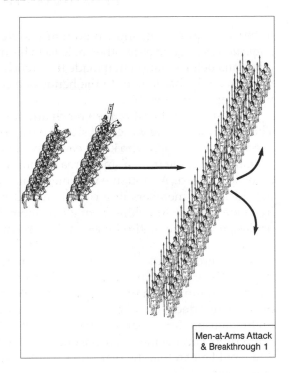

A conrois of men-at-arms drawn up in two ranks is about to charge a formation of infantry. The infantry shown here are Welsh spearmen, but they could just as well be any arrayed infantry or one of the less well-trained town militia. The infantry are in a dense phalanx shown here two ranks deep, though in reality such formations could be up to six ranks deep.

Men-at-Arms Attack & Breakthrough 1

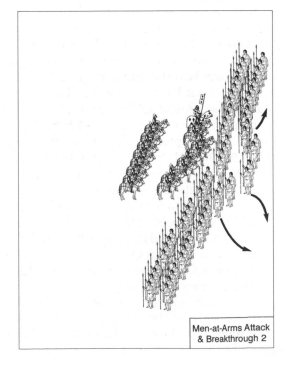

Even before the men-at-arms make contact the infantry phalanx begins to break up as men in the direct path of the charge begin to back away and run before the awesome sight of knights in armour advancing at the charge.

Men-at-Arms Attack & Breakthrough 2

121

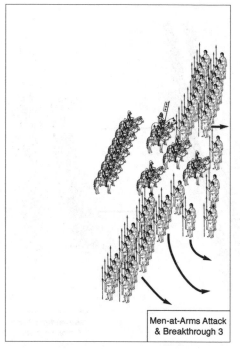

Men-at-Arms Attack
& Breakthrough 3

The central section of the infantry formation has crumbled under the impact of the mounted charge. Those infantry closest to the scene also begin to break ranks and flee, while those furthest from the action are as yet remaining in their ranks. The front rank of the men-at-arms are pushing into the gap to begin the pursuit of the infantry.

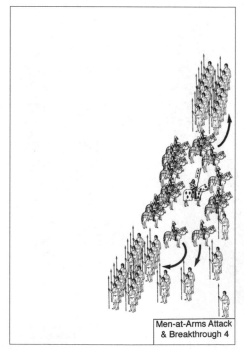

Men-at-Arms Attack
& Breakthrough 4

The entire centre of the infantry formation has vanished as the men flee. The leading men-at-arms swerve sideways to attack from the rear those infantry on the flanks who are still in position. The rear rank of men-at-arms surges through the gap to continue the pursuit of the fleeing enemy.

When faced by more reliable infantry, such as dismounted men-at-arms or the better-trained town militia, a force of men-at-arms would need to employ more sophisticated tactics than a simple charge. The attack in two phases was one option. Note that the infantry are shown here drawn up two ranks deep, but in reality might be up to six ranks deep. Each wave of men-at-arms is shown here to be one rank, but in reality would be composed of two or three ranks. The attack begins with the first wave of men-at-arms advancing while the second remains stationary.

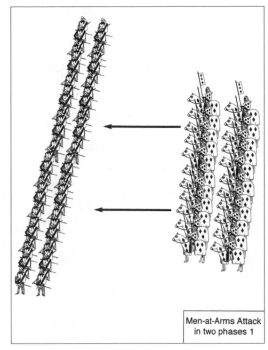

Men-at-Arms Attack
in two phases 1

The front rank of attacking men-at-arms makes contact with the infantry. They are unable to break through so close quarter combat between the horsemen and those on foot begins. The rear rank of mounted men-at-arms remains stationary.

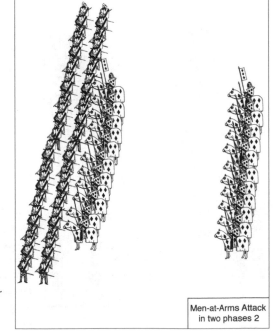

Men-at-Arms Attack
in two phases 2

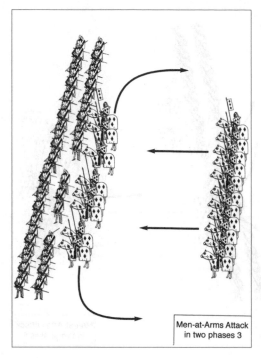

Men-at-Arms Attack
in two phases 3

As the first wave of mounted men-at-arms begins to tire a prearranged trumpet or drum signal orders them to withdraw. The horsemen turn outward to the flank before retreating. By this time the infantry formation will have taken casualties and have been seriously weakened. As the first wave turn aside, the second wave of attacking men-at-arms begin to advance.

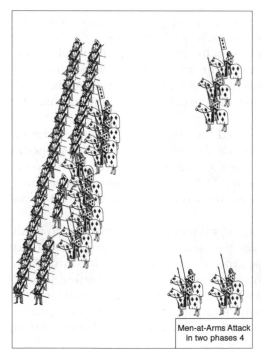

Men-at-Arms Attack
in two phases 4

If the attacking commander has timed things correctly the second wave of mounted men-at-arms will strike the infantry just as the first wave gets clear and before the defenders can reorganise their depleted ranks to meet the new threat. The second wave of attacking men-at-arms strikes home into the infantry formation, aiming for the sections most weakened during the fighting of the first wave. Again no immediate breakthrough is achieved. The retiring first wave have now halted and have turned to watch the combat develop. Their horses are blown and the men tired. They are unable to attack a solid formation again, but prepare to cover the retreat of the second wave or to join the pursuit – whichever event takes place.

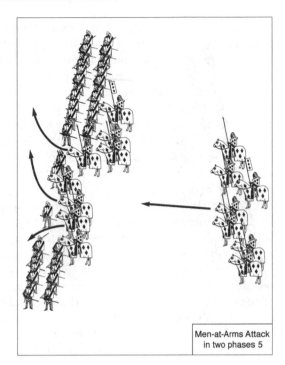

Men-at-Arms Attack
in two phases 5

After a period of close combat, the second wave of attacking men-at-arms breaks through the weakened section of the infantry formation. The tired first wave now spur forwards to join the pursuit as the enemy infantry turn to flee.

will not fight as well as confident men. An experienced soldier would be able to spot signs of such unease from across a battlefield.

A formation of infantry might be sent forward to probe for weaknesses. By launching an attack on foot, the commander could test the quality of the enemy troops and see how his opposite number reacted. At the least, some of the enemy would be killed and the defensive abilities of that section of the line reduced.

Once the commander had identified the target for his mounted charge and judged that the moment was right, the knights would begin to move. Led by the marshals appointed for the task, the mounted men would get themselves opposite the selected target. As the horses moved forward at the walk, the lines of infantry would move aside to let them pass.

Formed up in dense masses, the knights would break into a trot to build momentum while preserving formation and direction. The lances would be lowered and tucked under the arms as the men moved forward. With about 100 metres to go, the knights would let rip with their battle cries and speed up to a canter. Moving as a solid, surging block of armoured ferocity, the mounted charge built up massive momentum and awe-inspiring determination. To those standing in the path of such an avalanche of warriors it was a terrifying sight.

Many men simply turned and fled as the knights approached. Others tried to stand and fight. Generally, the crashing impact of the knights simply rolled over opposition. If the enemy did not flee, the knights would throw away their lances after the first impact and draw their swords, axes or maces. After a few minutes of hand-to-hand fighting, one side or the other would give way.

The French commander would be watching events carefully from his own lines. If it was the French knights who pulled back, having failed to drive through the enemy army, he would order forward his second force of knights. Again, the infantry would move aside as the next wall of steel and horseflesh moved forward.

The retreating knights would ride back through the gaps in the infantry line. The wounded would be sent to the doctors to the rear, while the uninjured sought out their conrois comrades and began once again to form up in solid ranks and rows. It was highly unlikely that the same knights would be asked to charge a second time. The horses would be tired, as would the men. Any attack they might deliver would be less effective than the first. Instead, they formed up behind the shelter of the infantry to await the next stage in the battle.

The key and most difficult decision of a commander was to choose when and where to unleash his massed charge of knights. If they were sent forward too early or against steady troops, the charge might fail. If they charged too late, the enemy army might have already begun to retreat in good order and so rob the French of the type of overwhelming victory that they sought to achieve.

If all went well, the second wave of charging knights would achieve the desired result. They would cut a gap in the enemy defensive line and push through, fanning out as they did so. This was the moment for any fresh unit of knights to hand, or for the re-formed first wave. Forward they went to ride through the gap opened up in the enemy line. Turning to left and right, the horsemen would launch new charges against the flanks and rear of the enemy units on either side of the gap.

Meanwhile, the French infantry would be marching forward to launch a general attack along the whole breadth of the battlefield. With infantry coming from the front, and horsemen attacking from the rear, the enemy army would collapse. Unit after unit would turn to run. Once the order of the enemy had been broken up, the pursuit could begin. Men would be cut down as they fled, or rounded up as prisoners. Any fresh horsemen that remained would be urged on to chase the fugitives as far and as long possible, giving them no chance to reform or try to hold a defensive position.

If, on the other hand, the mounted charges failed to punch a hole in the enemy line, the French commander would seek to extricate his army intact and in good order. If he occupied a good defensive position, this might involve staying put. More likely, it would mean retreating back to the safety of a fortified town or city. As the infantry fell back, the reformed conrois of knights would be used to threaten any enemy that got too close. A charge might be delivered if absolutely necessary, but usually the mere presence of formed-up knights was enough to deter an enemy pushing the pursuit too closely.

That, at least, was the theory. In practice, much depended on how well the men fought, how the enemy reacted and often simply on luck. The general plan had worked well on many occasions, rarely better than at Benevento in 1266. Charles, Count of Anjou, was leading a French army in Italy when he was attacked by the forces of King Manfred of Sicily. Leaving his infantry to form a motionless block on a hillside, Charles sent his first cavalry charge down to strike one unit of Manfred's heavy cavalry as they deployed to charge. The first French attack was beaten off, so a second was sent in that burst through the Sicilian heavy cavalry, sending the survivors in flight. A third force of French knights raced in to follow their comrades, then wheeled to attack a second force of Manfred's cavalry. These men fled without striking a blow, causing the rest of the Sicilian army to break up and run. Manfred was killed in the confusion.

As the French were perfecting their offensive tactics, their enemies were trying to find ways to counter them. One method was to try to find a defensive position that did not give the French knights a clear, smooth approach over which to deliver a charge. At the Battle of Courtrai in 1302 a force of Dutch infantry led by John de Renesse did exactly this. They formed up behind a stream backed by a hedge and with their flanks secured on marshy bogs. The French commander, Robert d'Artois, ordered his knights to charge, but they made little headway and were driven off with heavy loss.

The French were adaptable enough to confront the situation. Although they still retained faith in the charge by knights as the ultimate battle-winning tactic, they realised that something more was needed. The French army needed to acquire an effective missile arm. In 1304 at the Battle of Mons-en-Pevele they tried hauling heavy catapults on to the battlefield, but found they were too weighty to move around once battle was joined. The answer came in the form of the crossbow.

This weapon had been used in large numbers across Europe since about the year 950. It had traditionally been used in siege warfare, owing to its great power and accuracy, and to the way in which it operated. The weapon was ideal for shooting from a fixed position, protected by stone walls and with a supply of ammunition readily to hand. It was not so obviously suited to open fields, but the French made it so.

There were two types of crossbow, categorised by the way they were loaded or 'spanned'. Both types consisted of a basic pattern. There was a stock, usually made of walnut, about a metre long. At the far end of the stock was the bow, at first made of yew but by the 1340s sometimes made out of laminated strips of different woods. The fact that the bow crossed the stock at right angles gave the weapon its name.

The foot crossbow was loaded by putting one or both feet into a metal stirrup at the bow end of the stock. While the feet held the crossbow steady, the string could be hauled back by both hands until it engaged with a hook towards the rear of the stock. A bolt was then slipped on to a smooth runner that ran the length of the stock and knocked on to the string. When a trigger was pulled, the hook was pulled down and the string released, shooting the bolt. By the 1300s most foot crossbows were spanned with the help of a pair of metal hooks attached to a stout leather belt. The crossbowman bent down to attach the hooks to the string. As he straightened up, he was able to use the muscles of his legs as well as those of his arms to pull the string.

The winch crossbow was a larger and more powerful weapon. It had a detachable set of ropes and cogs that was attached when the weapon needed spanning. The string was pulled back by metal hooks operated by handles that allowed much greater force to be exerted than by the simpler foot method.

The two methods of spanning a crossbow produced different types of weapon. The foot crossbow was a lighter weapon which shot a less-powerful bolt, but could be used more quickly – perhaps three or four times a minute. The winch crossbow was bigger, heavier and more power-ful but even the most experienced man would struggle to shoot it more often than once a minute.

The fact that crossbows of both types were shot by means of a trigger made them highly accurate. The crossbowman would span his weapon, then lift it so that the stock rested on his shoulder and the bow pointed toward the enemy. He could aim at his leisure before pulling the trigger. A longbowman, by contrast, was unable to hold his bow at full draw for more than a second or two.

The bow of a crossbow was shorter and stouter than that of a long bow, making it considerably more powerful. While an English long bow had a draw weight of around 80kg, a foot crossbow of the 1340s had a draw weight of some 140kg. A good winch crossbow might have a draw weight in excess of 500kg.

The bolts shot by these weapons were thicker and heavier than longbow arrows. A typical bolt was about 30cm long and weighed around 140g. The head was usually smooth, without tangs, and square in cross-section. The Latin term for a square, *quadrus*, gave these war bolts their alterna-tive name of quarrel. Such quarrels could punch through chain mail with ease and could penetrate plate armour, unless striking at a very oblique angle.

The fact that the crossbow shot small, heavy bolts affected its perform-ance. The bolts had great momentum behind them, which gave them such effective armour-piercing qualities, but their weight meant that they had a low speed and so lost flying power quite quickly. An average effective range of about 200m seems to have been normal in 1346 for a foot cross-bow – much the same as for a long bow. The winch crossbow had a range of some 400m.

The upshot of the various performances of the different types was that winch crossbows were used almost exclusively in sieges. Rapid rate of fire was not really an issue in the long, drawn-out business of a siege, but accuracy and range were. Men shooting winch crossbows from the battlements would have a pile of bolts beside them. The weapon would be spanned, then the man would wait for a likely target to be seen before shooting.

The men doing the besieging used their weapons in a rather different way. Faced with shooting from the open, these men used a form of mobile shelter called a pavise. This was made of wood thick enough to stop a bolt shot from a winch crossbow and stood about two metres tall and one metre wide. The crossbowman stood behind the pavise to span his weapon, then stepped out to one side to shoot it. Most pavises had a spyhole in them so that the user could peer through at his target without exposing himself. Some had a notch cut out of one top corner so that the crossbow could be shot while the man kept most of his body behind cover. These pavises were large, cumbersome and heavy, so most crossbow units had teams of men whose job it was to put them in place.

Some men adopted a smaller type of pavise which was used more as a large shield. Before going into action, this light pavise was strapped to the crossbowman's back so that it just about covered him from head to toe. The man would turn his back to the enemy when spanning so that the light pavise protected him. He would then turn around to shoot. This form of pavise was more mobile than the traditional form, but was still heavy and cumbersome. No man wearing such a contraption could do more than shuffle along.

It was the lighter foot crossbow that the French adopted as their missile weapon of choice for open battle. Their use was grafted on to the traditional tactical plan with ease. Now the battle would open with a long-range missile assault by the crossbowmen. Such an onslaught would inflict casualties on the enemy army, but there was more to it than that.

The heavy bolts shot from crossbows of great power were able to punch through fences, hedges and undergrowth to kill or injure the man sheltering behind it. The crossbows had been brought in by the French to deal with the tactical problem of infantry sheltering from cavalry behind field obstacles of just this type. If properly conducted, an assault by crossbows could actually force infantry to abandon these defences and pull back to more open ground where they would be vulnerable to mounted charges.

The problem for the French in using crossbowmen in open battle was that they did not have enough of them. The vast majority of crossbowmen in the French army were infantry raised by the *ban* system. As we have seen, one of the key drawbacks of the system was that no French commander could predict in advance how many men would turn up nor how they would be armed. If the new crossbow-reliant tactics were to work, the commander needed to know how many crossbowmen he would have.

The only effective way to have access to reliable numbers of trained crossbowmen was to hire them as mercenaries. French kings had been hiring specialist crossbow mercenaries from Provence and northern Italy since around 1250, and Philip followed the lead. Historians writing about the crossbowmen who fought in the Crecy campaign generally refer to them as Genoese. This is largely because Froissart and other contemporaries call them so. In fact, it was the commander, Ottone Doria, who was from Genoa. The men themselves had been recruited widely across northern Italy.

As we have already seen, the fleet led by Carlo Grimaldi of Monaco arrived too late to meet the English invasion fleet at sea, so Philip ordered him to put ashore some of his crossbowmen to fight on land. The total number of 'Genoese' mercenaries available to Philip was around 8,000. Not all of these were crossbowmen. Some were workmen tasked with heaving the pavises around, others were armoured infantrymen equipped with shields and spears whose task was to fend off any attacking enemies who got too close. There were perhaps 5,000 crossbowmen. Some of these were sent off on detached duties, such as those that had fought with du Fay at the Blanchetaque ford, but most were kept with the main army.

These men were arguably the most professional and experienced coherent body of troops in the French army. Although they were hired afresh for each campaigning season, the men served together under the same commanders year after year, only the employer and the place of employment changing. They practised weapons and tactics constantly so as to be ready for their task when called upon. Having fought in several theatres of war, these men had seen all types of battle, skirmish and siege.

Each man paid for his own equipment, but there was not as much variety of armour and weaponry as in less professional forces. Each man had a mail haubergeon, often covered by a padded tunic or coat of plates to make it even more effective against missile weapons. The head was protected by a steel helmet over a mail coif, the lower flanges of which spread over the shoulders. The lower arms and legs were often protected by plate armour or by strips of iron sewn on to leather. Most crossbowmen had a large leather pouch slung from their belt in which were kept a dozen or so bolts for immediate use. In addition to the crossbow, most such mercenaries carried a short sword or heavy knife.

The personal equipment of a crossbowman was, therefore, heavy enough. It was usual for the pavises and additional stock of bolts to be loaded onto carts which trundled alongside the men as they marched. Before going into action the men would want their pavises to be put into position and to have large supplies of ammunition readily to hand.

The Genoese were not the only foreigners serving with King Philip. Grimaldi's fleet had brought north King James of Majorca and his small mixed force of men-at-arms and infantry – probably less than a thousand men all told.

More significant were the forces that had marched north from Savoy in the Alpine foothills. Count Amadeus VI was a child at the time, so the Savoyards were led by Count Louis of Vaud. Count Louis was almost sixty, but an active soldier and one of the most experienced and respected diplomats in Christendom. He had been present at the coronation of Edward's father, King Edward II, back in 1308 and had been appointed a Senator of Rome.

The Crecy campaign was not the first time that Count Louis had led Savoyard troops north to fight for King Philip. He and his men had been present during the campaign of 1340 when Edward had fruitlessly marched about north-eastern France, failing dismally to capture a single city. Count Louis had been part of the French army that trailed the English as they retreated back to Flanders, making the humiliation worse by watching them go.

Count Amadeus had promised to send a thousand men-at-arms to arrive in Paris by July, along with an unspecified number of infantry support – perhaps 3,000 men in all. In the event, the Savoyards did not reach Paris until early in August, and there were not as many men as had been promised.

More reliable and certainly more important were the allies brought by King John of Bohemia. The fifty-year-old King John was, at this date, rather better known in Europe than either Edward or Philip. He was the son of the Holy Roman Emperor Henry VII and grandson of King Philip III of France. He had spent most of his childhood in France before, in 1310, his father married him to Eliska, heiress to the Kingdom of Bohemia.

King John, as he now was, hurried east to take control of his new kingdom. Working with his wife, John first of all reformed the kingdom's finances and administration then set about reducing to obedience various minor states in eastern Europe which had thought to escape Bohemian dominance. By the 1330s King John was becoming bored. He had become estranged from his wife and his son Charles was now effectively running Bohemia, the nobles preferring a grandson of their old king to a son-in-law. He spent some years fighting on crusade against the pagan Lithuanians, then embarked on a spectacularly successful tour of tournaments across Europe.

In 1340 King John came to France to serve with King Philip and took part in the campaign against Edward. He was accidentally injured, losing the sight of one eye immediately and having the other eye damaged.

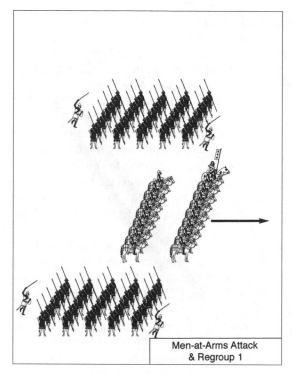

Men-at-Arms Attack
& Regroup 1

It was usual practice for a mounted charge by men-at-arms to make provision for an orderly withdrawal in case their attack failed. One option was to employ a formation of more reliable infantry to act as a mobile defensive screen. The men shown here are from a town militia, but dismounted or mounted men-at-arms would serve equally well. Less reliable militia or arrayed men might be employed, though only if there was no real prospect of an organised enemy counterattack. Here we see the mounted men at arms moving forward through a gap in the infantry formation to begin their attack.

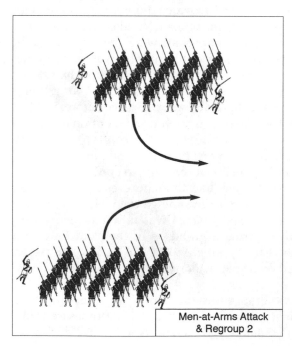

Men-at-Arms Attack
& Regroup 2

While the mounted men-at-arms are delivering their attack the knights commanding the infantry manoeuvre them forwards to form a solid defensive line.

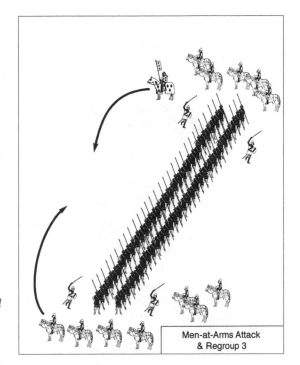

Men-at-Arms Attack
& Regroup 3

The infantry are now drawn up in a phalanx. They are shown here two ranks deep, but in reality may have been drawn up in as many as six ranks. The defeated survivors of the mounted charge are making their way back around the flanks of the infantry, following their banner as a guide.

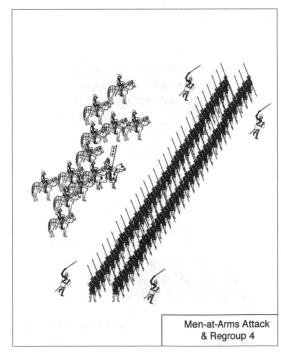

Men-at-Arms Attack
& Regroup 4

The mounted men at arms have halted behind the infantry and are now in the process of mustering on the banner. Men with minor wounds will remain in the ranks for the time being, while the more seriously wounded will be sent back to receive medical treatment. The immediate task of the infantry will be to ward off any enemy counterattack. They may then go on the offensive themselves, or fall back slowly to cover the retreat of the men-at-arms.

Despite the injury, he continued to travel through Christendom in luxurious style lending his military advice to whoever asked for it.

In 1346 Philip asked King John to return to campaign against Edward and the English once again. The summons found King John at Trier where he and his son Charles were attending a Diet (an assembly of nobles) of the Holy Roman Empire. The Diet had been called to elect a successor to the ailing Emperor Ludwig of Bavaria, and young Charles was one contender. John would not leave the Diet until it ended on 11 July with the appointment of Charles as King of the Romans, the traditional title bestowed on the acknowledged heir to the Imperial throne.

Then John and Charles both headed west towards France. As the new King of the Romans, Charles was able to recruit from among the lands over which he would soon be emperor. In any case, Germans were already accustomed to serving as volunteers in the army of the King of France, both to gain experience and to seek royal favour. We know of six German counts who agreed to march with the two kings. Given that John and Charles had left Bohemia with about a thousand men to attend the Diet, they must have brought an impressive force with them when they arrived at Paris about the time that Edward was marching to Poissy. No records survive, but with two kings and six counts it is likely that the Bohemian force numbered around 4,000 men or so.

Even before Charles had been elected King of the Romans, three counts from the Holy Roman Empire had already volunteered to join King Philip. The first of these was Count John of Hainault. The old Count William of Hainault, Edward's brother-in-law, had died in January and with him died Hainault's alliance with England. The new Count John was a remote cousin who had no close links to Edward. He was quickly approached by the Count of Blois who offered him a massive cash sum to change sides. Count John took the money.

When Hugh Hastings landed in Flanders it was to find that the army of Hainault – probably about 3,000 strong – was now no longer prepared to march to assist him. In fact Count John had ridden to join King Philip. He quickly established himself as a key adviser who was rarely far from the king's side. When Hainault changed sides he set an example. Two other local nobles who had thus far remained neutral now decided to support Philip. Count William of Namur and Count Simon of Salm were neither so rich nor so well connected as Count John, but between them they may have brought some 2,000 men to Abbeville.

Fitting these various foreign contingents into the structure of the French army was not going to be easy, but it did not cause as many initial problems as might be expected. The reason for this was that the command structure of the French army was a rather flexible and informal affair that was based as much on the social rankings within French society as on military discipline.

As king, Philip was the commander in chief whenever he was present with the main army. To act as his chief military advisor and to take command if he were to be absent, he had the Constable of France. The serving Constable was the Count d'Eu, who had been captured by the English at Caen and sent over the Channel as a prisoner. Philip had not appointed a successor, perhaps because he thought that he did not need one since he was leading the army himself.

Philip also had two Marshals of France, Charles de Montmorency and Robert de Saint Venant. Montmorency came from one of the grandest families in the kingdom and was an old friend of Philip. St Venant came from more humble stock, and seems to have been promoted for his ability. The main task of the Marshals was to look after the men-at-arms and their needs. The Marshals had to welcome each conrois as it arrived, allocate it to a place in the army and ensure that the men and horses received the necessary rations and support. They were also in charge of the scouts, sending out mounted men to mark out a route for the army to follow and to try to find the enemy.

Once battle was imminent, the Marshals were given the task of getting the men-at-arms sorted out into suitably sized units, ensuring that each man knew his task and smoothing over any ill feeling among the notoriously prickly *siegneurs*. Finally, they would lead the men-at-arms in to battle.

As the care of the men-at-arms was the duty of the Marshals, the care of the infantry was the domain of the Master of Crossbowmen, currently Galois de la Baume. It was this man's task to ensure adequate supplies for the various infantry units that came in, and to allocate them places to camp whenever the army halted.

Thus the administrative and supply systems were in the hands of men, most of them noblemen, appointed by the king. The command structure in the field was quite different. Each of the *grands seigneurs* had the right to be commanded in battle by nobody but the king. In theory, this meant that the king would need to divide the army into as many divisions as there were senior noblemen present. In Abbeville that August, Philip had with him eight such men, plus the Kings of Bohemia, Majorca and the Romans as well as the Savoyards. Dividing the army into twelve divisions might have been impracticable, though there is some indication that Philip did just that.

Philip did, however, organise three main divisions of his army. The first was under the command of King John of Bohemia, probably the most experienced and successful of the senior commanders. The second was kept under the king's personal control. The third was given to Count Charles d'Alencon. This d'Alencon was Philip's younger brother and had campaigned with Philip several times.

The main problem with this system was that there was a lack of any real organisation between the senior commanders appointed by the king and the leaders of the individual units. The militia of a town would be told that they were to serve in the division of the Count d'Alencon, King of Bohemia or King of France, as were the rural infantry units and conrois of knights. Each senior commander would have a team of assistants to take his orders to the units within his command, but there was no real mechanism to enforce orders on the different units. Each conrois or militia looked to its own commander for leadership. In the hands of a competent commander the system would work well enough, and the flexibility of having direct links from senior divisional commander to small units could be turned to advantage.

Unfortunately for the French, there were two factors in the Crecy campaign that made the system vulnerable to pressure. The first was that Philip had delayed mustering the army until almost the last minute. This meant that there was no real chance to divide the many different units between the three great divisions with care to produce three balanced and integrated fighting organisations. There was also the problem that those units that had arrived most recently would be unfamiliar with both their commander and his messengers. A knight might ride up to give orders to a unit only to be met by blank stares and questions about his authority.

The second, and in many ways more serious, handicap was the character of King Philip himself. The king was not very good at delegating. This may have been due to the way that he had inherited the throne, making him feel uneasy about his position and suspicious of the loyalty of others. Certainly, he disliked giving command of troops to men who might have a motive to use them against him. He was unwilling to give credit to men who commanded troops outside his immediate influence, and was famously unwilling to stir himself away from his command post to see what was going on elsewhere.

In the context of a medieval army this was a serious drawback. King Philip was not only the military commander but also head of both the civilian government and of the social elite. Any ambitious young man or powerful nobleman who wanted to gain military or social advancement would want to gain the favour of the king. Given Philip's style of command it was no good simply getting on with doing a good job and hoping that your commander would mention you to the king. It was necessary to be seen to be doing well by the king himself.

One of the great unanswered questions of the Crecy campaign is the size of the army that Philip had managed to muster in Abbeville by 25 August, the day he allowed his army to rest and reorganise. No precise French military records survive for 1346 so it is impossible to know with any certainty, but it is possible to come to some conclusions.

It is worth reading what the contemporaries have to say. Richard Wynkeley who was at the battle on the English side said that the French army 'was very large, estimated at 12,000 knights and 60,000 others'.

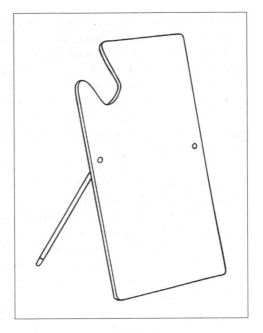

The pavise shown here is of the heavy, self-supporting type. It was made of wood about seven centimetres thick, so as to provided protection from incoming crossbow bolts and arrows. It was some two metres tall to protect the man while he spanned his crossbow. The notch cut out of the top corner allowed the man to peer at the enemy while keeping most of his body covered. The face of the pavise was usually painted with an heraldic device linked to the commander who had hired the mercenaries. For the Crecy campaign they would most likely have been painted with the golden lilies of France.

Edward III also counted 12,000 armoured cavalry, but thought only some 8,000 of them were 'gentlemen, knights and squires', and he gave no estimate as to the numbers of others. Writing a few years later Jean le Bel stated that there were 20,000 mounted men and 100,000 infantry. Froissart stated that there were 20,000 men-at-arms and 60,000 infantry, then added the Genoese as an additional force of 15,000 men. Villani, writing in Italy, believed that 6,000 Italians had marched to Crecy.

Although the official records for 1346 have been lost, those for 1340 survive. These show that King Philip was paying wages to 22,500 men-at-arms, 12,700 infantry and 2,000 crossbowmen to take part in the campaign in north-eastern France. Of course, the campaign of 1340 was very different from that of 1346. The majority of the men-at-arms were stationed in castles and fortified towns and very few were with Philip's field army. It is likely that the same is true of the infantry. Since the royal purse was paying 12,700 of them, it seems that this figure represents those with Philip. The militias on duty guarding their home towns and cities were paid by the local authorities, not the king. The total numbers of infantry would, therefore, have been much higher than 12,700.

In 1346 the position was reversed. Only a minority of the available force was held in garrisons and the majority was in the field. If Philip could muster a total of 22,500 men-at-arms in 1340 it is likely that he could do the same in 1346, and he would have had the additional men brought by his allies. He might have had a total of around 25,000 or so men-at-arms at his disposal for the campaign. Some of these would have been further north dealing with Sir Hugh Hastings and the Flemings, while others would still have been needed on garrison duty. Even so, the English might well be right that Philip had around 12,000 men-at-arms – about half his total – with him in the field army.

We can also be reasonably certain about the Genoese crossbowmen. Writing in distant Florence, Villani would have had no reason to misrepresent the figures and he would have had access to reliable data. He is probably correct when he says that there were 6,000 Italian mercenaries with Philip. Not all of these would have been crossbowmen for the total included pavise carriers and armoured infantry as well. Perhaps 4,000 crossbowmen is a realistic total.

As for the French infantry, we really have very little idea. We know that Philip mustered out the militias and infantry from a wide area of northern France for the battle, but we also know that they did not all arrive in time since their summonses had been sent out late. There may have been 20,000 of them at Abbeville preparing to march with Philip, there may have been 40,000. We don't know.

However many there were, the army that Philip was mustering was significantly larger than the English army it would shortly face. It was composed of various types of soldier, each of which had its role to play in the tactical attack plan developed and perfected by the French over the years. King Philip had himself used these tactics against Flemish rebels at the Battle of Cassel in 1328.

On this occasion he used his crossbowmen to render ineffective the Flemings' field defences. The Flemings then charged forward to get to grips with the French infantry. While the infantry were struggling for dominance, Philip sent a mounted force of men-at-arms riding wide around the flank of the Flemings. These knights delivered a traditional charge of crushing power into the rear of the Flemish army, which then collapsed. In the pursuit that followed, about half the Flemings were killed or captured.

There can be little doubt that Philip intended to repeat the basic plan of the Battle of Cassel against the English in 1346. He would thin them out with his crossbowmen, charge them with his cavalry and slaughter them with his infantry.

Such was the military juggernaut that Philip was gathering in order to crush Edward and his impudent army. All Philip needed to do now was to find them.

X

The Field of Crecy

While Philip had been reorganising his vast army at Abbeville on Friday 25 August, Edward had also been busy. After receiving the news that the English fleet had not arrived at Le Crotoy, he led his army into the dense woodlands of the Forest of Crecy. All that day the bulk of the army marched in the shade of the ancient trees – it was yet another dry, sunny day. By late afternoon the army was nearing the far edge of the wood. There Edward ordered his men to camp. There was, he said, no hurry.

According to le Bel and Froissart, Edward made a speech to his assembled army. 'Let us post ourselves here,' said Edward. 'I have good reason to wait for the enemy on this spot. I am now on the lawful inheritance of my lady mother [actually his grandmother], which was given her as her marriage dowry. I am resolved to defend it against Philip of Valois.'

As with his letter sent to Philip after crossing the Seine, this was a good piece of chivalrous theatre. Edward was now in Ponthieu, so he was making a serious political point by fighting there. He had inherited Ponthieu through the female line and nobody had objected, but he had been blocked from inheriting France by the same means. He was also defying Philip's right to confiscate the county. However, Edward had no more intention of defending Ponthieu in 1346 than he had had in 1337 when he had abandoned the place to Philip. Without easily defended castles or cities, the county could not be held against heavy odds.

In fact, Edward had other reasons to fight in Ponthieu. Sir Hugh Hastings and the Flemings had been defeated on 22 August by a well-organised sally launched by Godfrey d'Annequin, the defender of Béthune. Despite the pleas of Hastings, the Flemings began to retreat. The news would have been flashed south to Philip by d'Annequin. Perhaps Edward learned of his allies' defeat from Frenchmen captured at Le Crotoy or Blanchetaque and realised that he no longer had anywhere left to run. In any case, the English army was short of food and had been marching hard for many days. If Edward did not stand and fight now, his army might prove to be incapable of doing so when the time came.

A leather hauberk. These garments were lighter and cheaper than mail armour of similar design, but were considerably less effective against most weapons. Some, such as this example, had reinforcing strips and metal studs to add to their effectiveness.

It is likely that for several days, Edward had been looking for a place where he could use the new English tactics of archery in co-operation with dismounted men at arms. The gentle hills and open fields of Ponthieu would offer just such a place. Indeed, Edward or one of his men might have already known of the landscape around Crecy from their days in Ponthieu before the war.

Whether or not the English had prior knowledge of the military possibilities of Crecy, they soon found them. Scouts were sent out to search the surrounding countryside. By early afternoon Northampton, Warwick, Harcourt and Sir Reginald Cobham were at Crecy. They splashed across the ford in the River Maye, through the deserted village and on to the hill beyond.

To understand why the ridge above Crecy was chosen by Edward for the battle it is necessary to look at the wider strategic position. The English had got across the Somme just ahead of the pursuing French. Assuming that Edward was going to try to reach the relative safety of Flanders, he would need to change direction by moving north-east, away from the coast. The best road would be that which ran to Hesdin on the River Canche, then pushed on through Merville to Ypres. From his camp around Abbeville, Philip would seek to cut off Edward's route. He was closer to Hesdin than was Edward at Blanchetaque and so was most likely to make that his first target. If they got to Hesdin first, the French would then have the English trapped between the Canche, themselves and the sea just as they had thought to have them trapped south of the Somme.

What Edward needed to find was a defensive position suitable for English tactics that blocked Philip's route either to Hesdin or between Hesdin and the sea. The road from Abbeville to Hesdin crossed the Maye just east of Crecy and was dominated by the ridge north of the village. Philip could not get to Hesdin without first getting past an English army drawn up on that ridge.

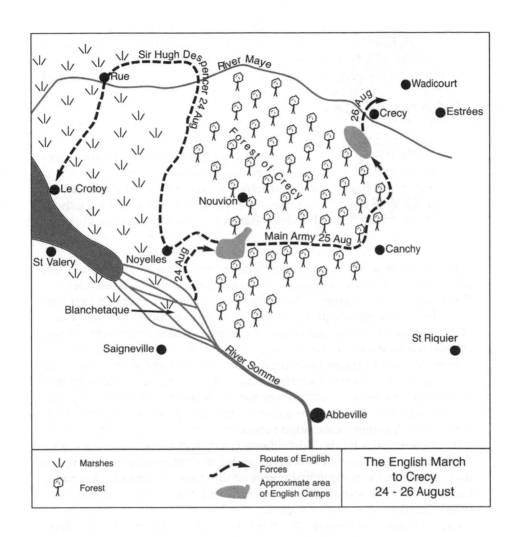

The English March
to Crecy
24 - 26 August

What clinched the matter was that the ridge north of Crecy was peculiarly suited to English tactics. It is likely that after making his speech, Edward rode forward with his Constable and marshals to view the position they had found. It was no doubt at this point that Edward, Northampton and Warwick decided how the army would be drawn up.

The ridge that they found was almost 2,000 metres long and ran in a generally north-easterly direction. In the south, the ridge ends abruptly at a steep slope that drops about 40 metres down to Crecy and the Maye. In the north, the ridge ended at the village of Wadicourt, the defensive properties of which were increased by orchards and gardens.

In front of the ridge, from the English viewpoint looking east, was a small valley the floor of which was about 200 metres wide at the southern end and something more than half that in front of Wadicourt. While the ridge stood 40 metres above the valley bottom at Crecy, it was barely 10 metres high at Wadicourt. The name of this valley at the time of the battle is unknown, so the name 'Crecy Valley' will be used. As we shall see, the events of the battle later caused it to gain the name Vallé des Clercs.

The drop from the ridge to the valley floor was not consistent, nor was the ridge straight. Immediately north of Crecy, the ridge was steep and made more so by almost sheer drops of up to two metres in height, caused by terracing of the slope. Beyond this the slope became much gentler, the summit of the ridge falling back to the west by some distance. This gentle slope from valley floor to the ridge is some 300 metres wide. Beyond that the slope steepens again and is once more fronted by almost sheer terracing. After a further 200 metres or so the terracing vanishes and the slope is no longer so steep. This slope continues towards Wadicourt with the rise diminishing as it goes. Just before Wadicourt itself there was a final steep section of terracing. Beyond this steep, but not especially high, knoll, another section of gentle sloping ground cut back in front of Wadicourt. The floor of this cut-back slope was masked from the ridge to the south by the knoll.

On top of the Crecy Ridge were a few features of note. A road ran along near the summit linking Crecy with Wadicourt. Towards the southern end of this road, standing on a little patch of high ground, was a windmill. From the rise immediately above Crecy, another road ran back away from the ridge itself to reach a manor house named Crecy Grange. This was surrounded by walled grounds and to its south lay a small but dense patch of woodland.

From a defensive point of view, the ridge was a good position. The almost sheer terracing was effectively impassable to closely packed formations of cavalry. A man on foot could scramble up a steep two-metre slope with ease. Even a horseman could probably manage it. But a horse carrying a man in armour would have difficulties. If that horse were hampered by being pushed up against several hundred others the feat would become impossible. Effectively, these sections of ridge were denied to the favoured French tactic of the mounted charge.

Nor was that all. To the east of Crecy Valley the land rose again to the Rathuile Ridge. This ridge is not quite so tall as the Crecy Ridge, being about five metres shorter along most of its length. Running almost the entire length of this ridge, facing down into the valley, is a long length of terracing. This terrace varies in height between two and five metres and, like that to the west, would have been impassable to dense masses of horsemen. At its southern end the Rathuile Ridge drops down to the River Maye more gently than does the Crecy Ridge. To the north it simply peters out on to the high ground that extends north and east of Wadicourt. To the east of this ridge the land fell again down into the Vallée Maté.

Across all this ground the dominant form of ground cover in late August 1346 would have been newly harvested grain fields. This area of France was one of those that specialised in the bulk production of wheat and barley. There were, no doubt, fruit trees and pig pens around the villages, but the countryside between had been cleared and ploughed for grain production. Such crops are generally ripe for harvesting by the last week of August. Even if the farmers would ordinarily have not yet been cutting the grain, the news of an approaching armed force would have induced them to get the harvest in as quickly as possible and cart it off to the nearest walled town for safe keeping.

It was probably an almost unbroken scene of stubble and piled-up straw that greeted Edward as he surveyed the view. This gave his archers a clear and uninterrupted shooting area. It also presented no obstacle to the French mounted charge.

The River Maye that runs across the southern end of the parallel system of ridges and valleys is today a small stream. In 1346 the banks of the river will have been rather wider than today and there were probably stretches of marshy ground. Close to Crecy village itself there were fairly extensive water cress beds. None of this would have been impassable to either men or horses, but the water features would have caused delay and confusion to moving formations. Even given the long dry summer of 1346, the cress beds and marshes of the Maye would have been less than ideal ground over which to manoeuvre bodies of men.

Overlooking the Maye from the south was a high, wooded hill: Mont St Remy. From their camping ground on the edges of the Forest of Crecy, the English would approach the battlefield from the southwest. They would ford the Maye and the water cress beds around the village, then climb on to the ridge at its steep southern end before deploying.

The French approach up the road from Abbeville would be by a more easterly route. This road is now known as the Chemin de l'Armée, the Army Road, in honour of the use put to it by the French on the day of the battle. This road skirts the eastern edge of the Crecy Forest, then strikes north to

The Chemin de l'Armée crosses the River Maye by way of a culvert. In 1346 the river was wider, bordered by marshy meadows and could only be crossed by a ford.

cross the Maye some two kilometres east of Crecy Village. It then enters the Vallée Maté before climbing the Rathuile Ridge. Just before the road strikes the steep terrace that runs up the western side of the Rathuile Ridge, it veers sharply to the north. At the end of the terracing, it turns back to the northwest to dip down into the Crecy Valley before climbing again to Wadicourt.

On the day of the battle, sightlines from this road would prove to be crucial. A man riding up the Chemin de l'Armée from the south in 1346 would leave the flank of the Crecy Forest at the hamlet of Marcheville. He would then be crossing open farmland with the Maye and the Vallée Maté to the north and the Mont St Remy blocking his view to the west and northwest.

As our rider got to the ford across the Maye, a small gap would have opened up between the Rathuile Ridge and Mont St Remy. Through this gap could be seen Crecy Village and the very southern tip of Crecy Ridge. Moving on into the Vallée Maté the view to the west would again be blocked, this time by the Rathuile Ridge. As our rider moved forward along the road and up to the crest of this ridge, the whole battlefield would suddenly come into view. Gazing out across the newly harvested grain fields, the rider on the Chemin de l'Armée would be able to see the landscape from Crecy to Wadicourt laid out before him. Not until he got a bit closer, however, would he become aware of the terracing along the western face of the Rathuile Ridge and find his direct route down into the Crecy Valley blocked.

Such was the landscape across which the Battle of Crecy would be fought. Both King Edward and King Philip had their preferred tactics and battle plans. Both would need to adapt their plans to the terrain and to the actions of the enemy. It was Edward who got there first.

XI

Crecy – Morning

The morning of 26 August dawned bright and clear. At Abbeville King Philip of France awoke early, along with the vast army he had gathered to crush the English invaders. His first duty was to hear mass at the Abbey of St Peter, for a Christian king had to set a good religious example on such a day. According to Geoffrey Baker, Philip held a quick council of war with his senior commanders to decide how best to proceed.

Late on the evening of 24 August the English had chased the survivors of du Fay's force who had fled west as far as the gates of Abbeville. Those manning the walls of the town had watched the English horseman as they came to a halt outside crossbow range and rode about scouting the town. The Englishmen had then left, riding northwest into the setting sun and keeping close to the banks of the Somme.

At dawn the next day, columns of smoke had been seen rising from Le Crotoy, indicating that the English were in that direction. While the army rested Philip had sent out scouts to find the English and discover what they were doing. Those who rode along the Somme clashed with English scouts near Noyelles. The French scouts sent north toward Hesdin found a few isolated English riders moving about north of the Forest of Crecy – presumably these were Warwick, Northampton and their men scouting the ground around Crecy.

Now Philip and his commanders discussed what these reports meant. King John of Bohemia may have been almost blind, but he could see more clearly than most. He stated that the English would stand and fight. Nobody else agreed. Philip himself believed that Edward would continue to run north. Baker tells us that several French noblemen 'reproached the King of Bohemia for being foolish'.

Still, it seems that Philip wanted to harry and chase the English rather than trap them. Presumably, he hoped that hunger and fatigue would reduce the English army to impotence and save him the bother of a major battle. He gave the order that the French army was to continue the pursuit. Le Bel says: 'King Philip urged his men on to follow the English'.

A modern re-enactor dressed as a herald from the 1340s stands in front of a camp. The heralds were tasked with carrying messages between the rival commanders as well as being expected to recognise coats of arms displayed by knights in the opposing army. With thanks to the Medieval Combat Society. www.themcs.org

It must be said that the events of the campaign so far favoured Philip's interpretation rather than that of John of Bohemia. In both 1339 and 1340 Edward had marched about north-eastern France making much noise, but eventually retreating to Flanders when he ran out of food and supplies. Now, in 1346, Edward had marched across Normandy, Ile de France and Picardy looting and boasting, but fighting only when he had a clear advantage. He had been given the chance to fight outside Paris, but instead had run. He had been running ever since, and there was nothing to indicate that he would do anything other than continue running.

Later French tradition has it that the French army set off down the north bank of the Somme towards the rising columns of smoke coming from Le Crotoy. It must be admitted that the contemporary sources do not state the direction of march. North of the Somme does, however, fit the known facts.

If Philip was determined to chase the retreating English until their discipline broke down and supplies ran out, then this was the correct way to go. If he had marched directly north to Hesdin, the English might have turned around and slipped behind him past Abbeville and marched east. Edward had already pulled off a similar stunt at Poissy and might be expected to try it again. If he did, the English would again be a day or two ahead of Philip and so would have enough time to capture a town or two and so replenish their supplies.

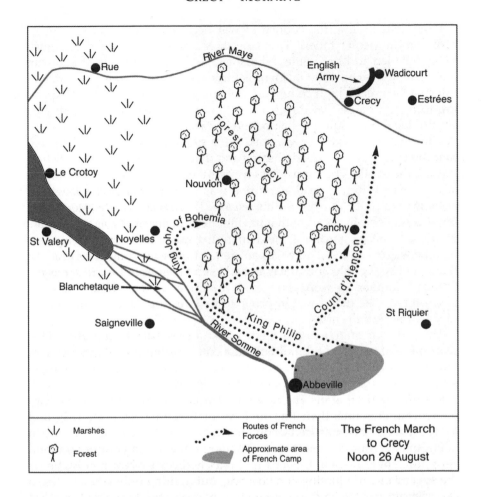

		The French March
∖∕ Marshes	•••► Routes of French Forces	to Crecy
🌳 Forest	Approximate area of French Camp	Noon 26 August

But if Philip marched to the north end of Blanchetaque, picked up the English trail and followed it, he would ensure that he was following the English step by step, keeping his sword in their backs. The countryside had been stripped bare of food, now stored in castles and towns. There would be no time for the English even to think of attacking a fortified position with the French hurrying them along. It was a sound strategy and fits in well with le Bel's comment.

There is another reason to accept that Philip set off down the Somme. Froissart tells us that the French march began soon after dawn. If Philip had marched directly up the Hesdin road, he would have reached Crecy around noon with his army in good order. But the French army did not begin to arrive at Crecy until mid-afternoon and it was in a disorganised state. Clearly something had happened to it between leaving Abbeville and reaching Crecy.

Baker tells us that the council of war between Philip and his nobles broke up in jocular mood. The King of Majorca 'asked for the English king to be left to him' while 'others asked for the Prince or the Earl of Northampton'. This little incident is important as it reveals the frame of mind of the French high command. Bohemia apart, they were not expecting to fight a battle that day. They believed that they would merely be continuing the pursuit that had begun at Paris.

The prospect of victory was taken for granted. The French believed that the English were already beaten and that it was just a matter of sharing out the spoils. The capture of an enemy nobleman was a key aim for any combatant in medieval warfare. It was usual practice for a knight or nobleman to pay a ransom for his release. There was no set scale of fees, but it was generally thought that paying the equivalent of a year's income would be a bit niggardly, while demanding much more than five year's income was excessive. There was an element of bargaining involved, but that could begin only once the man had been taken prisoner. So far as the French commanders were concerned, the English were already as good as captured. The mood would prove to be infectious and would spread rapidly through the army.

The order of march as the French host streamed out of Abbeville is reasonably clear. King John of Bohemia commanded the advance guard, which left first. Philip himself commanded the central division, leaving as soon as Bohemia's men had got on their way. This may have been around 8.00 a.m. or a little after. The rear guard was commanded by the Count d'Alencon. This final division could not realistically have begun getting away from Abbeville much before 10.00 a.m.

Philip had good reason to give the rear guard to his younger brother. As a prince of royal blood, d'Alencon had the social clout to give orders to the ever proud and prickly French lords. And although d'Alencon was an experienced and talented commander, he was inclined to be rather rash. In the rear of the army he would be safely away from any difficult decisions calling for guile or caution.

What is utterly obscure is how Philip had divided his troops between the three divisions. King John would, of course, have had his Bohemians with him and most likely the various German contingents that he had recruited after the Diet at Trier. King Charles of the Romans was most likely somewhere in this advance guard as well, but later events will show that he was not riding at the side of his father. Perhaps he had command of some sub-division. We know that Count John of Hainault was marching with the king because le Bel says so and since the count was le Bel's main source for the French side of things we must assume he knows what he is saying. Of the composition of d'Alencon's rear guard the contemporary accounts say nothing.

The usual practice at the time was for the three divisions to be of approximately equal size, but for the king to keep specialists under his own command. If this were the case on the morning of 26 August, each division would have numbered about 4,000 men-at-arms with a larger number of infantry – perhaps between 6,000 and 10,000 – marching in their respective local units. Given that King Philip had to find individual commands for each of his high nobles, it would make sense if each division was broken down into smaller units, each containing a mix of men-at-arms and infantry, though there is no way of knowing if this was the case.

As specialist soldiers and expensive mercenaries, the 6,000 Genoese would have been with the king's central division. There was another reason for Philip to keep Doria and his Italians close. The Genoese had abandoned St Vaast just before the English landed, and had abandoned Caen in mid-battle. There might have been good reasons for this, as no doubt Doria had explained at length, but Philip was in no mood to trust the mercenaries out of his sight. At Blanchetaque only two days earlier another foreign mercenary captain, du Fay, had let Philip down. Philip wanted the Genoese where he could see them. Whatever the precise order of march, the French army trailed out of Abbeville marching west soon after dawn.

At the same time Philip or his marshals Charles de Montmorency and Robert de Saint Venant had sent out scouts. Some rode ahead of the army towards Noyelles, but others rode up the road towards Hesdin. No doubt others fanned out in other directions to screen the French line of march and keep an eye on the rear and flanks. It was the scouts riding north to Hesdin who found the English. In his letter written on 3 September, Edward puts the arrival of the French scouts at Crecy as 'in the morning', and nobody else is even this precise. Since it is about fifteen kilometres from Abbeville to Crecy, it is likely the scouts arrived around 10.00 a.m. There seems to have been some skirmishing with English scouts for an unnamed English knight was killed. Clearly, the French scouts saw enough to convince them that they had found the entire English army, not just a party of foragers. Putting spurs to their horses, the scouts headed off southwest to find King Philip.

Given the marching speed of a medieval army and the time it had taken to get out of Abbeville, the scouts would have found Philip somewhere over halfway to Blanchetaque. We do not know who these scouts were, but they were not knights or nobles. Philip was wary of accepting their report at face value. He was expecting the English to be hurrying north as fast as they could, not to be drawn up and calmly waiting for battle.

To verify the report, Philip sent four of his most experienced knights cantering north. These were: Miles de Noyers, the king's personal standard bearer; Henri le Moine, who had seen service in the crusades against the Lithuanians; Olivier d'Aubigny, a greatly trusted member of Philip's household; and Count John of Hainault. Presumably, the four knights took with them a mounted guard to protect them. They rode off at speed.

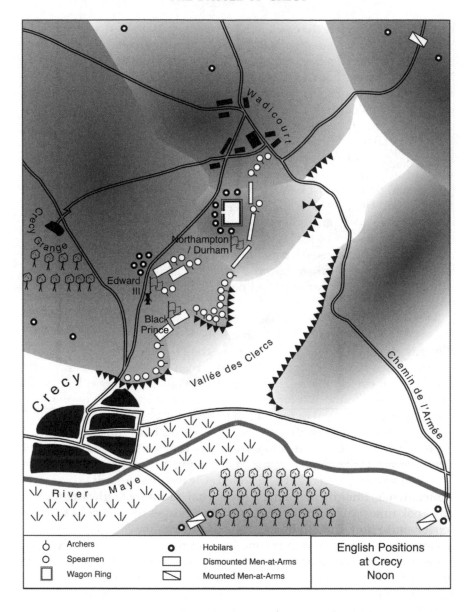

Crecy Grange

Wadicourt

Northampton / Durham

Edward III

Black Prince

Crecy

Vallée des Clercs

Chemin de l'Armée

River Maye

♂	Archers	⊙	Hobilars
○	Spearmen	▭	Dismounted Men-at-Arms
▢	Wagon Ring	▱	Mounted Men-at-Arms

English Positions at Crecy Noon

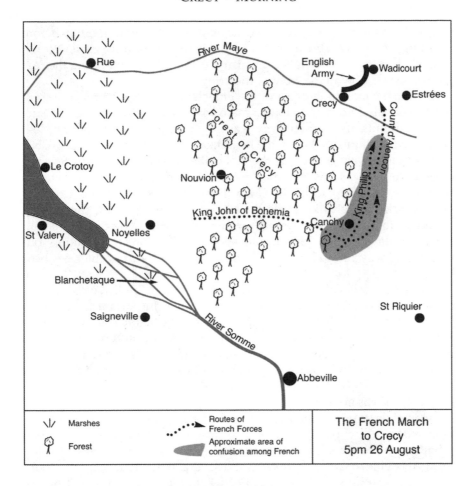

		The French March
|/ Marshes	Routes of French Forces	to Crecy
Forest	Approximate area of confusion among French	5pm 26 August

Meanwhile, Philip ordered the army to change direction towards Crecy. This took time. Philip's orders could be transmitted only as fast as a messenger could ride. The arrival of such a drastic change of direction would have led to a degree of questioning and confusion. This will have been made worse by the already slightly informal and unstructured nature of the French command system and the fact that some units were only recently arrived.

Philip's division will have turned first as the messengers reached the various conrois and infantry units. As the riders pushed on down the line they passed on the orders to progressively more distant units. King John of Bohemia may have been as far as Blanchetaque by the time he got the orders to turn aside. He can't have been too surprised as he had already predicted the English would fight. In the rear, the Count d'Alencon would have received his messenger from Philip about the same time as did King John of Bohemia. There is some evidence that he had already heard that the English were at Crecy, perhaps one of the scouts had found him before reaching Philip. Whatever the case, d'Alencon was now closer to the English than the rest of the French army. Although commanding the rear guard, he was now in the front of the army.

At once the marching order of the French army began to get confused. Instead of being arranged along a main road in a previously agreed succession of units, the French army was now trying to march more or less abreast cross country. There were lanes heading in the right direction, but none of them was as wide as the Abbeville-Noyelles road and few ran directly to Crecy. King John had particular problems. At Blanchetaque he had the vast spread of the Crecy Forest between him and Crecy. It would make sense to keep his division in marching order, then swing round to follow the same road through the woods that Edward had used two days earlier. This would keep the division in formation, but was a long way round and would bring King John out of the trees near Canchy.

It must be recalled that the French believed that the English were already beaten. For the nobles and knights at least, it was important to get to the scene of action in time to get a share of the spoils. In any case, the diffuse nature of the command structure encouraged conrois and militia units to act independently under the command of their own leaders. Faced by the need to push through narrow lanes or over open country, the French unit commanders would have been undaunted. They turned north and headed for Crecy. It was about noon.

Meanwhile, Edward and the English had been getting ready for the battle that they fully expected to fight. The day had begun more leisurely than it had for the French. Edward knew that even if Philip marched directly from Abbeville to Crecy there were still several hours before battle would be joined. The king and Black Prince heard mass, accompanied by the leading nobles. The rest of the army also attended divine service and most men confessed their sins to one of the various priests and monks with the army.

Edward then led the army out from their camp to splash over the ford into the village of Crecy and up on to the ridge beyond. Scouts were sent out in all directions to keep an eye open for the French. Philip was expected to arrive along the road from Abbeville, so no doubt particular care was taken in that direction, but other French units might be about and Edward did not want to be surprised. While the scouts cantered off, Edward and his noblemen got the army positioned as they wanted, then ordered the men to stand down to eat and drink, and to rest. It was now about nine o'clock in the morning.

Edward had plenty of time to study the landscape and to decide how best to position his men. Unfortunately for the military historian, the contemporary accounts give only sparse detail. They were, of course, writing for men who understood precisely how a medieval army should be drawn up for battle. They did not need to give technical details which everybody then knew, but which is now no longer so obvious. This has led to some confusion over who was where and what they were supposed to do.

However, by studying what the contemporaries do tell us, in conjunction with what is now known of the capabilities of medieval weaponry and in particular with the layout of the battlefield, it is possible to put together a likely scenario. It must be admitted that it is by no means certain that what follows was actually the disposition of the English forces. However, it is not contradicted by any contemporary account and does fit in well with everything that we know for certain.

The general organisation of the English army at least is beyond dispute. Throughout the campaign the army had been divided into three divisions. Froissart and others make it clear that this same organisation was retained for the climactic battle. The advance guard was commanded by Edward the Black Prince under the watchful eye of the Earl of Warwick, Sir Thomas Holland, Sir Reginald Cobham, Sir Godfrey Harcourt and other veterans. Froissart rather cheekily adds to this list of veterans the name of his friend Sir John Chandos, although in 1346 Chandos would have been a young and insignificant knight ignored by most. In the latest version of his Chronicle, Froissart records that the Black Prince had 800 men-at-arms, 2,000 archers and 1,000 infantry. Le Bel gives him 1,200 men-at-arms, 3,000 archers and 3,000 infantry. The rear guard was nominally under the command of the Bishop of Durham, but at Crecy was firmly in the grip of the Earl of Northampton, supported by the Earl of Arundel, the Earl of Suffolk and a number of other experienced men. Again Froissart and le Bel are the only contemporaries who give figures for the numbers in the division. Froissart says there were 800 men-at-arms and 1,200 archers, le Bel makes it 1,200 men-at-arms and 3,000 archers. The central division was commanded by King Edward himself. Froissart gives Edward 700 men-at-arms and 2,000 archers le Bel again gives larger numbers with 1,600 men-at-arms and 4,000 archers.

These figures mean that Froissart reckons the English army at Crecy to have had a total strength of 8,500 men, while le Bel puts it at 17,000. We know that around 15,000 combatants landed at St Vaast. There had been fighting along the way, and no doubt some men were taken sick. Even so, Froissart's figures seem on the low side, and le Bel's are clearly too high. What both writers agree on is the relative strengths of the three divisions and who was in command. Presumably the true strengths of the three divisions is to be found somewhere between the two. It should be noted that neither le Bel nor Froissart mention hobilars at Crecy. The English fought on foot, so these men must be presumed to be included among the infantry and archers.

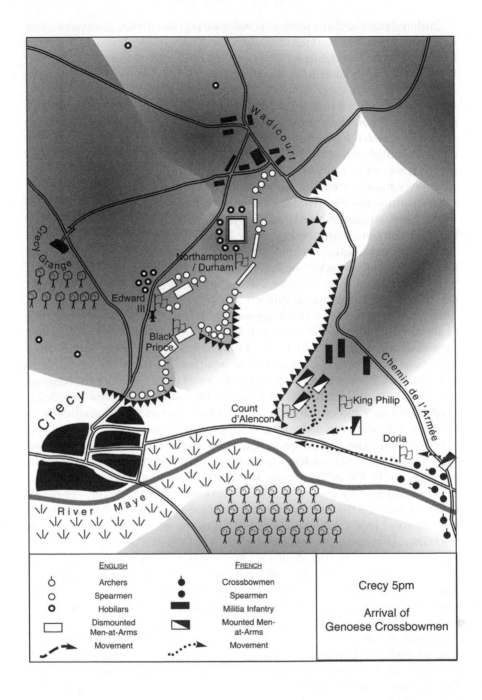

ENGLISH

○ Archers
○ Spearmen
◎ Hobilars
▭ Dismounted Men-at-Arms
➤ Movement

FRENCH

● Crossbowmen
● Spearmen
▬ Militia Infantry
◪ Mounted Men-at-Arms
•••➤ Movement

Crecy 5pm

Arrival of
Genoese Crossbowmen

Crecy Grange

Northampton / Durham

Edward III

Black Prince

Crecy

River Maye

Wadicourt

Count d'Alencon

King Philip

Chemin de l'Armée

Doria

Quite where the three divisions were put on the ground requires more detective work. Froissart gives no specific details of the deployment of the three divisions, though as he describes the battle it becomes clear that the Black Prince's division took the main brunt of the initial French attacks and that the King's division was being held in reserve. He later implies that Northampton's men were attacked by the French, but not so fiercely as those of the Black Prince. Le Bel says that Edward's division was in the centre, between the other two divisions. The St Omer Chronicle is not very clear, but implies that the English divisions were not in a single line, but that at least one of them was in the rear.

None of these accounts is definitive or complete, but taken together they seem to imply that the advance guard under the Black Prince and rear guard under Northampton formed up side by side. King Edward kept his division behind these two, positioned centrally. Since the Black Prince was the most heavily engaged at the start of the battle, this would put him closest to the French line of advance, on the right wing of the English army.

There are other clues to the layout of the English army. Several accounts agree that Edward stationed himself beside a windmill on top of the ridge. This makes sense. He would have wanted to have the best view possible of the battlefield, which would put him on its highest point. A man up the windmill could see even better. Edward may have climbed up himself from time to time, but certainly would have had a trusted man on duty to scan the distance for enemy movements. Until fairly recently there was a windmill named 'Moulin Edouard III' on the ridge. This stood beside the road from Crecy to Wadicourt, about a third of the way up from the south. Edward's position can, therefore, be fixed with some accuracy.

Baker says: 'The archers were put apart from the men-at-arms so that they were to the side of the army almost like wings. In this place they did not hinder the men-at-arms, nor could they be attacked head-on by the enemy, but they could reach the enemy with their shooting.' Froissart famously tells us that the 'archers were formed up like a herce', whatever that means. He also says that the men-at-arms were 'at the bottom of the division'. The Bourgeois of Valenciennes says that at Crecy the archers were 'placed in two formations in the manner of a shield'. As we have already seen, Froissart's herce and the Bourgeois' shield could both mean a triangular formation. Froissart's 'bottom of the division' for the men-at-arms is almost as obscure as his herce, though it has been speculated that he was using a then current term for the rear.

These comments are ambiguous and vague. Reading them as they stand does not tell us very much, but turning to the actual layout of the Crecy Ridge things become a bit clearer. If the French cavalry could not charge head-on at the archers, as Baker maintains, then there must have been something to stop them. The only physical features on the battlefield that could do this are the stretches of terracing.

There are three sections of terracing on the western face of the Crecy Ridge. At the northern end is the knoll in front of Wadicourt. At the southern end are two more. One lies directly north of Crecy Village and the other is some 300 metres north. Both these sections of the ridge project forward from the main line of the ridge itself in bulges that could – at least at a pinch – be said to be triangular. Between them is a gentle slope leading up from the valley floor to the top of the ridge.

The English formation that best fits the written sources and the nature of the ground is the archers massed on these two projecting bulges of high ground and the men-at-arms standing at the top of the gentle slope between them. This would fit Baker's description exactly. The archers were protected from French cavalry attacks, they were to the sides of the men-at-arms and they were within bow range of an enemy advancing up the gentle slope. The triangular shape of the high ground occupied by the archers matches the Froissart's herce and the Bourgeois' shield. Moreover, it makes sense of Froissart putting the men-at-arms at the bottom, or rear, of the army. With the archers thrown forward on the high ground, the men-at-arms would indeed have been toward the rear.

However, this stretch of ground occupies only the southern end of the Crecy Ridge. If the entire English army were drawn up there it would have been leaving its left flank wide open to a French attack. The slope up to the ridge south of the Wadicourt knoll was not so smooth or gentle as that further south, but it could easily be negotiated by a formed mass of knights that would then wheel left to take the English army in the rear. And, as we have already deduced, Northampton's rear guard was to the left of the Black Prince. This would put Northampton's force along the northern stretch of the ridge. What Froissart, Baker and the Bourgeois seem to be describing is the layout of the Black Prince's division. Since it was this division that saw the most action it is natural that they would want to describe it in great detail. Taken together, the layout of the land and the written sources do seem to be describing a fairly clear layout for the English army. It was divided into three divisions. The reserve under the king was held back around a windmill on top of the ridge. The advance guard under the Black Prince held the right wing of the front line with his men-at-arms blocking a slope up which the French could advance and his archers posted on either side to shoot down on any French force that tried to do so. Northampton's rear guard was strung out along the rest of the ridge. Nobody describes the positioning of the units with Northampton's division.

There remain two other features of the English disposition that need to be dealt with. We know that the English had guns with them on the Crecy campaign and that they were used in the battle. Most chroniclers also mention a park for and made from the wagons of the baggage train. Neither Froissart, Baker nor le Bel tell us much about the position of the wagon park. Le Bel says that Edward 'had an enclosure with only one entrance prepared from all the carts of the army, and placed all the horses in it'. Froissart gives a broadly similar description: 'Then the king caused a park to be made behind his host near a wood, and there was set all carts and carriages. And within the park were all their horses and into this park there was but one entry'. What we seem to have in these two descriptions is a large, hollow circle or square of wagons drawn up tightly together so that horses within could not escape. The carts might have been surrounded by wooden palings, but certainly there was only one gap between wagons that allowed access. It could be speculated that the main supplies of the army were in this park, along with the horses. Baker tells us only that Edward 'kept back the war horses with the supply train'.

These three accounts all go out of their way to mention the wagon park so it must have been important, though none of them give much detail. The only clues to its position are Froissart telling us it was in the rear near a wood and Baker saying it was kept back. This might position it near the dense wood that is known to have been just south of the manor of Crecy Grange. This was almost a kilometre behind Edward's windmill. In this position it would certainly have been well out of the way of the fighting – unless things went horribly wrong for the English. It would not, however, have been a very convenient place for supplies of food, drink or arrows. A one-kilometre run there and another back would have slowed down runners wanting to bring up any supplies from the wagon park to the fighting men.

The Italian chronicler, Villani, also mentions the wagon park, but in very different terms. According to Villani, who was presumably drawing on accounts from returning Italian mercenaries, the wagons formed part of the English defences. He goes into some detail about the way that padded cloth sacks or bags were hung over the sides of the wagons to make them impervious to incoming crossbow bolts. He also states that some archers and guns were positioned within the carts to shoot at the advancing French. The St Omer Chronicle mentions in passing that the English rear guard looked after the baggage.

It is worth recalling that just before the English army left England news was received of a victory won by Sir Thomas Dagworth at St Pol de Leon in Brittany on 9 June. Dagworth had been greatly outnumbered by a French force of cavalry and infantry, but had beaten off all attacks and even managed to capture three French knights. A key element in Dagworth's success had been his use of supply wagons as a form of *ad hoc* field defence. We don't know if the use of wagons in this way was a regular English tactic or if Dagworth had come up with the idea himself. Certainly Edward would have been aware of Dagworth's exploits and known that the tactic had been highly effective against the French system of attack.

The old brick monument that stands in the centre of Crecy village is thought to have been erected to the memory of Edward's grandmother, through whom he inherited Ponthieu. The English army would have marched past here on their way to take up position on the ridge above.

Although much about the wagon park must remain obscure, there is a scenario that does make sense of the information that we have. We have already seen that in the likely disposition of English forces, part of Crecy Ridge facing the French advance was held by the Black Prince with his men drawn up on a relatively narrow front. The longer northern section of the ridge was, however, held by Northampton with fewer men. Although Northampton was unlikely to face the full wrath of the French, he could be expected to face an attack of some description.

There was a need to strengthen Northampton's position. It may be that Edward decided to use Dagworth's tactic of using carts as part of a system of field defence. If the wagon park was used in this way, then Froissart's comment about it being beside a wood indicates where it was. Northampton's left wing rested on the village of Wadicourt. Although most farmland in this area was given over to grain crops, most houses had pig pens, orchards and vegetable patches. Wadicourt would be no exception so there would have been one or more orchards of fruit trees. Perhaps this is what Froissart meant.

As if to clinch the matter, the section of Northampton's line that might have been most vulnerable to a French mounted charge was the gentle slope that led up from the floor of Crecy Valley behind the small knoll in front of Wadicourt. This formed almost a little valley of its own and provided an easy way up to the ridge top. Any French force using the valley would emerge on to high ground beside Wadicourt and behind the left flank of the English army.

If anywhere needed a form of temporary defences, it was the section of ground at the head of this little valley and beside the orchards of Wadicourt. Positioned here, the wagon park could be described as being 'held back' or 'behind the host' while still being part of the English front line.

Villani's account reads rather as if the entire English army stood within the wagon park to receive the French attacks. Not only would this have made the inside of the park extremely cramped, but it does not square with the English sources, which state that the horses were in the park and the army drawn up outside it. Villani was, of course, drawing on the accounts of men who had seen things only from the French side. Perhaps some carts were included in other vulnerable parts of the English line as well as being used to form the park around the horses.

As we shall see, the Italian mercenaries were involved only in the earlier stages of the battle, when the French were attacking the division of the Prince of Wales. From their viewpoint in the Crecy Valley, looking up towards the Prince of Wales, they would have seen field defences – perhaps including carts – manned by infantry and archers on either side, with an open gap between them held by the Black Prince and his men-at-arms. Perhaps it is to this that Villani refers when he talks about a fortification of carts with an entrance around which the fighting raged.

The positioning of the guns is even more obscure, but again a plausible solution can be found. Villani says that the wagon park was defended by guns, but also that the initial French assault was greeted by gunfire. Other chroniclers do not mention the guns, nor do any of the letters written immediately after the event. As we shall see there may have been a good reason why the guns did not rate much of a mention, but that does not answer the question of where they were.

The question is made difficult only if it is thought that the English did not have many guns with them, three is a number often given. It may well be that there were only three medium calibre guns with the army – for reasons already mentioned it is unlikely that there were any really large bombards. But that is not to say that there were not quite a number of small poleguns. If the English did have a number of these small hand-held firearms then it might explain how guns could be reported in different parts of the field.

Of course, short of inventing a time-travel machine, we can never be entirely certain how the English army was drawn up for battle on the ridge north of Crecy. The scenario outlined here fits all the known facts, would have made good use of the technical merits of the weapons the English had and fits the topography of the ground that was fought over. However Edward drew up his army, he was certainly happy with the results. All he had to do now was to wait for the French.

XII

Crecy – Afternoon

It was mid-afternoon by the time King Philip's scouts Miles de Noyers, Henri le Moine, Olivier d'Aubigny and Count John of Hainault got to Crecy. They came riding up the road from Abbeville, almost certainly accompanied by an armed body of men and probably with a herald in attendance to identify the coats of arms of English knights. The first sight that the Frenchmen will have had of the English was as they forded the Maye, but it is clear that they rode on across the Vallée Maté to reach the top of the Rathuile Ridge from where they could survey the entire English army.

According to Froissart, the English 'saw them well and knew well how they were come thither to view them. They let them alone and made no move toward them, and let them return as they came.' Certainly, the four knights must have stayed on the Rathuile Ridge for quite a few minutes, for their report back to Philip was full and detailed. If Edward was happy to accept battle on his terms, he probably did not want to do anything that might dissuade the French from attacking.

One of the banners the four knights will have seen was the personal banner of King Edward. At this date a king such as Edward would have had two flags for use on campaign. The first was the royal banner, a large flag taller than it was wide that was embroidered with the royal arms. The banner was usually made of expensive, heavy silk, embroidered with silk and even with gold thread. It was usually stiffened by having a wooden pole running along its upper edge that held it out stiffly so that it could be seen clearly even on still days. The royal banner of England had, until recently, been a red field embroidered with three golden lions – the arms of England familiar today from football flags and the like. By the time of Crecy, however, Edward had quartered the three lions with the arms of France: golden lilies scattered on a blue background.

Being a large, heavy and expensive item, the banner was usually unfurled only when battle was imminent. It would remain fairly stationary throughout the action to mark the command post of the king. At Crecy it would remain standing close to the windmill on the top of the Crecy Ridge.

Two archers dressed as for the Crecy campaign. The man in the foreground is knocking his bow in preparation for action, while the man behind knocks an arrow. With thanks to the Medieval Combat Society, www.themcs.org

Commanders also had their own personal standard. A typical standard was a long, narrow flag about four times as long as it was tall. It tapered toward the fly end and ended in two rounded tips. The standard was made of cheaper materials than the banner and was habitually flown from a pole outside the owner's tent on campaign. In battle it was carried by a trusted knight who stayed as close as possible to the standard's owner at all times. So if the banner showed the command post or rallying point for the army as a whole, the standard showed where the commander actually was at any given time. This allowed men who needed the king's personal attention to find him by looking for the standard waving over the heads of the army.

Edward's standard was divided into two parts. Next to the staff was a square panel bearing the red cross on white; that is, the flag of St George. The tapering section of the standard was a blue stripe over a red stripe. Superimposed on to the two stripes was a gold lion wearing a crown and with one paw uplifted. There were also a number of gold crowns and sunbursts scattered around the lion. Finally, there was a white stripe running diagonally across the design on which were embroidered the words '*Dieu et mon droit*'. This motto, meaning 'God and my right' is today more familiar as the motto of the Order of the Garter, but its origin was as Edward's personal motto.

According to Baker, Edward also had a third flag, though it remained furled at this point. This was the dragon banner, which Edward ordered to be unfurled only when he saw the Oriflamme appear among the French ranks. This flag was neither Edward's banner nor his standard so it had no regular place in the heraldry or chivalry of the time. It is just possible that this was the last time that the ancient flag of pre-Norman England was seen on a battlefield. Traditionally, the dragon banner took the form of a metal dragon's head and forelegs behind which trailed a cylindrical golden banner, rather like a modern windsock. The flag had its origins in the Kingdom of Wessex, whose kings became the kings of a united England after the Viking wars. After the Norman conquest of 1066, the English dragon continued to be flown by English armies, though the royal family preferred their own heraldic device of the three lions. After Crecy it is not heard of again.

Having seen the English army drawn up in battle array and having noted that Edward's banner was unfurled, the four French knights turned and rode back over the Maye to return to Philip and report.

As they rode south toward Canchy they were rather surprised to come across the head of a column of troops. Le Bel says these mounted knights were less than a league from the English. At this date, the league was not a fixed distance, so le Bel might have meant anything between 2.5 and 5 kilometres. The returning scouts ordered the advancing knights to halt while they reported back to the king, telling them that the English army was only a short distance ahead.

The four knights then rode on to try to find the king. As they rode, they found themselves passing through a mass of soldiery. The Chemin de l'Armée was crowded with the various conrois of men-at-arms and units of infantry from the rear guard of the Count d'Alencon. There is no mention that they met d'Alencon himself, though he must have been hurrying forward to find the English. They will also have passed Doria and the Genoese crossbowmen as they formed the lead element of the Philip's division.

Further south the road became increasingly congested and the units, confused. These were the men who had marched cross-country from the Abbeville-Noyelles road. It is likely that each individual unit had held together well, but all sense of order of march had evaporated. Shouting to every unit they passed to halt and await orders, the four knights pushed on and eventually found Philip about four leagues from Crecy. King Philip at once halted and called together his entourage to hear the report. As the king's party halted, so did those coming up behind, though not without some confusion.

The meeting that followed proved to be crucial. It is reported at length by le Bel, who was probably told all about it by his patron Count John of Hainault who had been there. The story is repeated in Froissart, who adds a few details. To understand what happened at the meeting and its repercussions, it is necessary to appreciate the expectations of those involved. King Philip was still angry at the way he had been duped outside Paris and, as he saw it, betrayed by du Fay at Blanchetaque. He was determined to close with the English army and destroy it. He had already that day discounted the views of King John of Bohemia and openly declared that the English were a beaten and fleeing army. If he had been puzzled by the initial report that the English army was at Crecy, he probably thought that Edward had halted out of exhaustion and desperation.

The other senior French nobles were of like mind. Moreover, they were keen and eager to secure valuable prisoners to boost their own honour and to fill their coffers with ransom money. Neither they nor Philip were in any mood for delay.

Having seen the English army, however, the four knights were of the opinion that the English did not look like a defeated army, but more like one that was getting ready for a fight. Brought before the king and his nobles, they seem to have realised that what they had to say would not be welcome. Although they were all experienced and skilled soldiers, none of them was a nobleman of the first rank. According to Froissart, when Philip asked for their report, the four men all looked at each other and kept an embarrassed silence.

Finally, Philip turned directly to Henri le Moine and ordered him to speak up. 'Sir, I shall speak since it is your pleasure,' replied le Moine. Then he glanced around his three colleagues seeking to spread the blame, adding:

> … under the correction of my fellows. Sire, we have ridden and seen the behaviour of your enemies. Know you the truth, that they are drawn up in three divisions and are waiting for you. Sir, I will give you this advice, saving your displeasure. You and your army should rest here and stay for the night. By the time all of your army catches up with us it will be very late and will take time to get them all into good order for battle. Everyone will be tired and disorganised, while your enemies are fresh, rested and ready to meet you. Tomorrow there will be time to order your army at your leisure and advance on the enemy with more deliberation and with faith in God and St Denis. You will have more time to decide how to attack them. For, sir, it is surely true that they will wait for you.

There was a tense silence. Then Philip nodded and said he agreed. The army would halt for the night. He sent one of his Marshals riding back down the road towards King John of Bohemia carrying orders to get all the jumbled units sorted out during the hours of daylight that remained and then to camp for the night. The other Marshal rode forwards to look for d'Alencon an order him to pull his division back to where Philip was camped.

Meanwhile, events had been getting beyond Philip's control. When the four knights had come cantering back from Crecy they had ordered the men they passed to halt. The reaction of those men can be easily imagined. For eighteen days they had been stalking the English army. They had seen town after town go up in flames. They had seen swathes of countryside laid waste. They had got themselves all keyed up for a battle outside Paris that had never happened. Swarms of refugees had cursed the English and begged them to take revenge. They had hurried north from Paris. They had missed the English at Blanchetaque by hours. They had heard their commanders say how the English were as good as beaten. At last they had the English at their mercy, and now some tomfool knights had come galloping past ordering them to stop. Who were these knights anyway? Most of them weren't even French. What right did they have to push around the noble knighthood of France? Well, the last legitimate orders from a commander they recognised had been simple and clear: go to Crecy and fight the English. So now they were going to go to Crecy and they were going to fight the English.

While Philip and his nobles had been listening to le Moine's report, his army had continued its advance. Like the scouts before them, the leading conrois of knights will have caught their first sight of the English army as they splashed over the ford in the Maye. Common sense would have told them to get on to high ground quickly, so they will have cantered up to the Rathuile Ridge.

The militia infantry were no less keen to get into action. Froissart tells us that 'when they saw that they were near to their enemies, they took their weapons and shouted "Down with them! Let us slay them all."' As the leading knights had gone forward, so did the infantry. Some units wanted to hang back and await orders, halting in the road and causing confusion among those who wanted to push forward.

But the general trend was toward the Maye and the enemy. As before, each unit seems to have kept its cohesion more or less, but the congestion, hold ups and conflicting orders were beginning to cause confusion. One by one, French units crossed the Maye and climbed up on to Rathuile Ridge to stare across at the English drawn up on Crecy Ridge. Among the French was the herald who would later write the *Chronique de Flandre* and record the titles of the banners that he saw flapping lazily in the hot August air.

Baker tells us what this process looked like from the English position. 'The English troops stood drawn up in the field, while the threatening size of the French army was continually increased by new reinforcements'. Hour after hour passed as the knights, squires and militia continued to pile up on the high ground facing the English. By about 6.00 p.m. the entire ridge was a heaving mass of French soldiers. It must have been a daunting time for the English.

Edward was a skilled commander who knew his men well. To ease the tension at this difficult time, Edward sprang into action. Calling Northampton and Warwick to join him, Edward mounted a small horse and set off to ride around his army. The horse was similar to those ridden by the hobilars and other common soldiers who had brought horses with them. Edward was no doubt making the point that he was one with the soldiery at this point.

To further pass the time in useful activity, Edward decided to knight several of the esquires who had acquitted themselves well in the campaign so far. One chronicler says that fifty men were so honoured, as well as two knights being raised to the status of knight banneret. Receiving such a title in front of the assembled army and nobility of England was an immense honour. No doubt the ritual was carried out with as much pomp and heraldic show as could be mustered. Anything to waste time and keep the men occupied.

It seems that at this point Edward had not yet donned the heavier elements of his armour and was probably dressed only in his mail shirt and leggings. Bareheaded, Edward 'rode from rank to rank desiring each man to take heed that day to his right and his honour. He spoke it all so sweetly and with so cheerful a face and a merry laugh that all such as were discomfited took courage in the seeing and hearing of him.' So writes Froissart. Baker records that 'having inspected the men to make sure they would await on foot for the enemy attack, he commended all things to God and the Blessed Virgin'. Waiting for battle is a tense, difficult and stressful time for all concerned. Watching an enemy army gather not a kilometre away, increasing in strength as every minute passes must be indescribably difficult. No wonder Edward felt the need to do something to help his men.

At some point, the Count d'Alencon arrived on Rathuile Ridge. Like everyone else in the French army, he was keen to get at the English. As both the most senior commander and most senior nobleman present, he had the military and social clout to have his orders obeyed without question. Having taken in the situation, he went to work.

Over the years, the Count d'Alencon has come in for a lot of criticism for his actions on the afternoon of 26 August. In part, this is because his plan failed so spectacularly, but also because he was killed and so was unable to answer his critics. Whatever faults he may have had, d'Alencon was an experienced soldier and no fool. At the time of Crecy he was forty-nine years old and had first seen action twenty-two years earlier. He had fought at Cassel, taken part in the 1340 campaign and trained for war since birth.

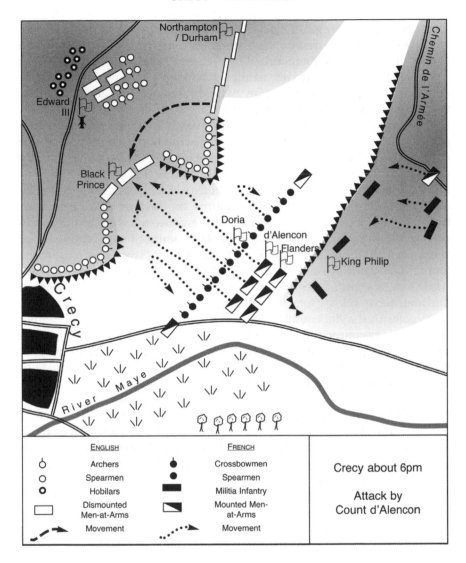

ENGLISH

♂	Archers
○	Spearmen
●	Hobilars
▭	Dismounted Men-at-Arms
➤	Movement

FRENCH

●	Crossbowmen
●	Spearmen
■	Militia Infantry
◥	Mounted Men-at-Arms
·····➤	Movement

Crecy about 6pm

Attack by
Count d'Alencon

Although he did not survive to record his actions that day, it is fairly clear what d'Alencon was doing on the Rathuile Ridge. The French army was arriving in dribs and drabs, without orders but full of fighting spirit. Most of the units that had arrived were from d'Alencon's rear guard, so he wasted little time in issuing orders and getting some sort of organisation imposed.

Given that d'Alencon was well versed in the standard French offensive tactics he would have tried to get the gathering troops positioned accordingly. He would soon have realised that the steep terraced bank that ran along the western edge of the Rathuile Ridge was impassable to formations of horsemen. This would make it an ideal location for the armoured infantry to draw up in their solid ranks to form an immovable anchor around which the mounted men-at-arms could manoeuvre. It was a position that was easy to defend against enemy cavalry, and was reasonably good should the English infantry try to advance. Certainly it was the best defensive infantry position on offer.

No doubt d'Alencon and his staff spent some time directing the militia and rural units into a defensive line along the crest of the terraced slope. But if the steep drop formed an ideal place for the infantry, it also made a cavalry charge over it impossible. There was simply no way that the French men-at-arms could surge forward from the Rathuile Ridge, cross the Crecy Valley and ride up to crash into the English army on the Crecy Ridge beyond. Instead, the only clear route of advance for a dense mass of mounted men was to ride along the north bank of the Maye, south of the Rathuile Ridge and form up in the southern end of the Crecy Valley. If they kept close to the foot of Rathuile Ridge they would be out of range of the English bowmen while they got themselves altered from a marching column and arrayed in the long lines necessary for a successful charge. But men-at-arms themselves were notoriously vulnerable to a charge while in the process of changing formation. D'Alencon would have wanted to avoid laying his men open to a surprise charge of English knights down from the ridge opposite. Almost certainly he kept his men-at-arms drawn up on top of the southern end of his ridge, screened by the infantry manning the defensive line.

D'Alencon will also have been studying the English army opposite. As ever in warfare, it is important to realise that a commander such as d'Alencon took his decisions based not on what the situation was, but on what he believed it to be. We already know that d'Alencon thought the English to be a spent force. What he could see on the battlefield would influence his decisions.

The Rathuile Ridge on which d'Alencon sat his horse was lower than the Crecy Ridge. He would have been unable to see beyond the crest of the ridge. We know that Edward was on the crest, near the windmill that later took his name, and that he had his division drawn up in reserve close to him. If Edward had placed his division behind him, they would have been largely invisible to d'Alencon who might therefore have concluded that the English army was even smaller than in fact it was. Such a move was not normal in medieval warfare, where the usual emphasis was on display and intimidation. We must assume that d'Alencon had a clear view of most of the English army and a reasonably accurate idea of its strength.

Of the front line that he would be attacking, d'Alencon would have seen the archers and infantry drawn up behind the more easily defended, terraced sections of the ridge. In the gap between these sections at the southern end of the ridge, d'Alencon will have seen a solid phalanx of knights and men-at-arms under the banner of Edward the Black Prince.

This knight of average means has dismounted to fight and so is probably English, although the differences in knightly equipment between England and France at this date were minimal. His helmet is of the very latest design being a dog-faced bascinet, a light but strong helmet with a moveable visor. Under the helmet he wears a mail coif that covers his skull and hangs down to give additional protection to shoulders and throat. Otherwise his equipment is typical for a knight of the 1340s. He wears a mail suit of armour that reaches to his wrists and to below the groin. Over this he wears a surcoat that is embroidered with his coat of arms, as repeated on his shield. His left hand is protected by the shield, which is now smaller than would have been usual a generation earlier. The right hand is encased in a mail mitten that has a leather face on the inside to allow the knight to grip his sword securely. The sword he wields is typical of the single-handed, slightly tapering blade that was the standard knightly weapon at this time. Both his upper arms and the forearm on this sword arm are protected by curved sheets of steel held in place by leather straps, the first pieces of plate armour to become widely available. There may be small plates strapped to his chest under the surcoat, a form of additional armour that was becoming affordable to an average knight by this date. His legs are encased in mail leggings that reach to his toes. The thighs have additional protection in the form of brigandine leggings – strips of metal secured between two layers of cloth and then strapped into position.

Behind, he would have seen the banner of King Edward himself. Further north d'Alencon will have seen units of archers, infantry and dismounted men-at-arms under the banner of Northampton and other more junior commanders. These men were drawn up at the top of the ridge where the slope up from the valley lacked the insurmountable terracing, but was not as gentle as that in front of the Black Prince.

Such a disposition of forces was not too far divorced from what d'Alencon would have done in a similar position. To his eye, the archers and the spearmen who guarded them were unarmoured rural levies. It was right that they should be put behind the best defensive positions. To the north, the more mixed units would have appeared to him to be made up of these same unarmoured men. The dismounted hobilars would have been taken for semi-armoured militia, while the men-at-arms would have been clearly distinguishable as such.

From Alencon's viewpoint, the most vulnerable section of the English ridge was that gentle slope up from the valley floor at the southern end of the ridge. The top of this slope was guarded by none other than the Prince of Wales himself, accompanied by the Earl of Warwick and a cluster of other famous men whose banners the Count's herald could identify. Quite rightly, the English king had put his best troops to protect his weakest point.

D'Alencon will not have been surprised to see the English knights on foot. Although he had never faced the English in a major battle – his only experience having been skirmishes in the 1340 campaign – he will have heard all about this strange new tactic from other Frenchmen and, possibly, from any visiting Scots. He will have known that the English preferred to receive an enemy attack on foot, though they liked to attack on horseback as they had done the previous year at Auberoche in Aquitaine. That Edward had his knights dismounted showed d'Alencon that the English were on the defensive.

D'Alencon and the other French commanders at Crecy will also have heard much about the English archers. At Morlaix in 1342 and at St Pol de Leon earlier in 1346 it had been the archers that had been instrumental in gaining the English victory. In both cases, the English in defensive positions had driven off mounted French charges. But both battles had been fairly small affairs compared to the imminent clash at Crecy.

Perhaps d'Alencon thought the longbow an overrated weapon. Certainly he had never seen the awesome power of an arrowstorm. In France there were archers in plenty, but on the field of battle they had largely been superseded by the crossbowmen. Hand-operated bows were seen as being rather old-fashioned and suitable only for hunting. However effective the English archers were – and the French can have been in no doubt that they were – there was a counter weapon of equally awesome power. It was for that weapon that d'Alencon and the French were waiting. At about 6.00 p.m. it arrived. The battle could begin.

XIII

Crecy – Evening

After giving his orders to his army to halt for the night, King Philip would have ordered his immediate entourage to start pitching camp and getting ready to cook dinner. It cannot have been long, however, before Philip began receiving messages telling him that all was not going to plan. The troops ahead of him on the line of march were pushing forward in confusion, while those behind were in an even greater muddle.

In fact, the movements and actions of King Philip in the crucial hour or so that followed are enigmatic. Our best source for the movements of the French high command is le Bel, whose patron John of Hainault was with the king throughout most of the day. His chronicle leaves King Philip somewhere near Marcheville having given the halt order at about 4.00 p.m. Philip is not mentioned again until late in the battle when, as we shall see, he takes a prominent part.

Baker likewise barely mentions King Philip's role in the battle itself. He says that Edward unfurled his dragon banner in response to seeing that King Philip had brought the Oriflamme with him, and implies that this took place before the French attack began. Writing just days after the battle, Richard Wynkeley also reports seeing Philip's banner before the fighting began. 'The adversary', writes Wynkeley, using his usual term for Philip, 'intending to attack the king personally stationed himself in the front line'. It should be remembered that it was impossible to recognise a man across the width of a battlefield, especially if his face were hidden by a helmet. What Wynkeley saw was Philip's banner.

The only definite statement of Philip's movements at this crucial time comes from Froissart who writes that when he learned of the chaos enveloping his army, Philip rode forward to try to take control of the situation but 'when the French king saw the Englishmen, his mood changed. He said to his Marshals "Begin the battle in the name of God and St Denis."'

This mounted knight is equipped in similar fashion to the dismounted knight. He has a similar dog-faced bascinet to protect his head, but elsewhere relies mainly on mail for defence. The plates on his right arm can be seen clearly here, as can the round metal plates, known as besagaws, that cover the gaps at elbow and shoulder can be seen. His horse is a charger (known as a roncin in France), a mid-price war horse that would have cost around £50 in 1346. This type of horse was bred and trained for battle. It was strong enough to carry its rider and his armour at a fast canter when charging, and for sustained periods at the trot when manoeuvring for tactical advantage on the battlefield. It was trained to ignore the noise and smells of battle by being daily subjected to clashing pans, waving banners and trays of blood brought from the kitchen. Such horses were expected not only to charge, but also to be nimble in close combat. They had to walk backwards, leap sideways, kick backwards and even bite on command. Another type of horse known as a destrier was larger, stronger and more thoroughly trained. It was correspondingly expensive at around £100. On campaign most knights took four horses with them. One would be the destrier or charger that was mounted only when battle seemed imminent. The second would be a palfrey or hackney costing around £10 for riding when combat was not expected. The other two were probably cheap horses, such as those ridden by hobilars, for carrying armour, spare clothes and – almost certainly – a servant. This man has discarded the cloth housing, as was becoming common by the 1340s, but keeps the high-cantled saddle that was designed to hug the man around the hips, bracing him into position when charging with a lance or to help him keep his seat if wounded.

One indirect clue comes from the movement of the Genoese mercenaries. As we have already seen, the usual position for such men was with the king's division and, by the time of Crecy, Philip had his own reasons for keeping a close eye on Doria. All the writers who talk about the start of the battle agree that the gathering French host facing the English delayed an attack until the Genoese crossbowmen arrived, and that they did so around 6.00 p.m.

What may have happened is that Philip began to settle down, sending out orders to halt and reorganise the army. When he learned of the growing confusion on the road, he remounted his horse and went forward. He took with him the Genoese. Although he had his doubts about the loyalty of these mercenaries when it came to facing the English, they did have one very strong advantage at this point. It was Philip who was paying them, so they could be relied upon to do what they were told without regard to prickly personal honour or pride. Perhaps Philip reasoned that the levelled crossbows of the Genoese would persuade any recalcitrant nobles to follow orders and fall back to the king's camp near Marcheville.

As Philip and the Genoese pushed their way forward, he would have found the chaos on the road worse than he had imagined. 'There is no man, unless he had been there on the road,' wrote Froissart, 'who could imagine or tell the truth of the evil order that was among the French army'. Le Bel agreed:

> None would pull back unless those in front came back first, and those in front refused to retreat as it was a shameful thing to do. So those in rear continued to advance. They still rode proudly ahead, one in front of the other without any order and so came within sight of the English. And now it was even more shameful to retreat.

Once Philip got to the Rathuile Ridge, however, everything changed. There he found d'Alencon and the rearguard in much better condition than the chaos on the road behind. Moreover, d'Alencon was eager to attack. He will have shown his elder brother the small numbers of Englishmen compared to the French army. And he would have wasted no time in pointing out the main features of the English defensive position.

The key feature that he must have highlighted was the smooth, gentle slope up from the valley to the Black Prince's position. A successful charge by mounted men-at-arms up that slope would punch through the thin line of dismounted English men-at-arms. Once that line was broken, the French could pour through to fan out on either side, as was their preferred tactic. It did not matter how effective the English archers had proved to be at St Pol or Morlaix; they did not wear armour and had few close-combat weapons. Once the armoured French horsemen got in among them they would be easy victims.

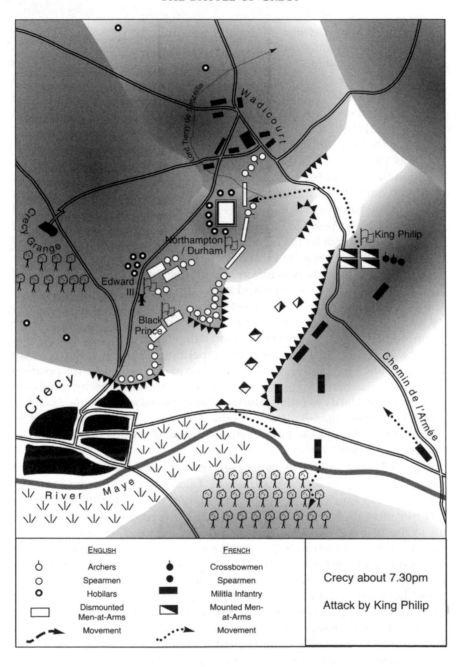

Crecy about 7.30pm

Attack by King Philip

It must be admitted that d'Alencon was quite correct. The awesome effectiveness of mounted, armoured men charging into unarmoured infantry had been proved time and again in preceding years. It would continue to be effective for some years to come. At Mauon in 1352 1000 English archers were ridden down and slaughtered by 140 French knights who charged into their flank, having managed to approach unseen through a small wood. If the French could get up on to the Crecy Ridge, the victory would be theirs. It would just be a matter of counting the English bodies.

It was probably at this point that Philip unfurled his banner and so declared that the battle was to begin. He would now have sent messengers galloping back down the line of march with new orders for all units to hasten to the battlefield as quickly as possible. Even more confusion and disorder will have resulted. That orders of some sort got to near the rear of the column is shown by the fact that King John of Bohemia was soon hurrying up towards Crecy as fast as he could. Equally, the road had become a swirling mass of soldiers as different units decided to do different things. At least some bodies of militia and a few conrois left the road altogether and proceeded to get hopelessly lost in the unfamiliar terrain.

On the English ridge, the sight of Philip's banner and the Oriflamme prompted Edward to unfurl his dragon banner and issue his final orders. Among these would have been the repetition of a key order already passed through the ranks earlier that day: no man was to leave his position in the defensive battle line for any reason at all. Most importantly, nobody was to run forwards to pillage the dead or try to take a prisoner from the wounded or bewildered. 'If we win the day', said Edward, 'there will be plenty of time for pillage, but if fortune turned against us there would be no point in taking booty.'

This order not to take prisoners was not an example of cold-blooded ruthlessness, it was simple good sense. Taking a noble prisoner was an easy way to gain riches through ransom, and many knights and others were keen to do so. But taking a prisoner involved leading the victim off to the rear and guarding him to prevent escape. If the prisoner was wounded, he would need to be carried away – a task for two or more men. Edward's army was outnumbered enough as it was without men sneaking off from the front line in search of riches.

To drive the point home, Edward announced that once victory was assured he would personally give the order for pillaging, robbing and prisoner-taking to begin. But if anyone started before that order was given he would be immediately hanged. Edward had already hanged men who had broken his order not to pillage monasteries, so the English knew that he meant business.

Back on the French side of the valley, Philip was issuing orders to Doria and the Genoese. He at once ran into trouble. According to the usual French tactical model, a charge by mounted men-at-arms on prepared defensive positions, such as those of the English, should be preceded by either an infantry attack or a crossbow assault. The firing of a sustained barrage of crossbows would thin out the ranks of the defenders, even those sheltering behind hedges or fences, and so disrupt their formation prior to the charge of heavy armoured cavalry.

Philip and d'Alencon would have wanted Doria and his men to advance along the gap between the River Maye and the Rathuile Ridge, then fan out into a wide line. They would remain there while the men-at-arms who had reached the field formed up behind them in case the English tried a mounted charge at this point. When all was ready, the Genoese would advance towards the English, spend some time shooting at the defenders, then step aside to make way for the devastating charge that was to be led by d'Alencon.

Doria was not happy with the plan. His men had been marching on and off since a little after dawn, and there had been no time for a proper meal. The Italian crossbowmen were undoubtedly the most heavily encumbered of all the infantry who fought at Crecy. As we have already seen, they wore armour that was impressively modern and complete by the standards of the day, and they had to carry their weapons and bolts as well. The men were tired, hungry and in need of a rest.

Even more important was the fact that they did not have their supply carts with them. These may have been lost in the confusion of the cross-country march, or they may have been left behind at the king's camp near Marcheville. After all, the Genoese had thought they were merely accompanying Philip to impose order on the French army and force the more foolhardy to pull back and make camp. They had not been expecting to fight a battle. Whatever the reason for the loss of the carts, it meant that the crossbowmen had neither their spare bolts nor, crucially, their pavises. It was these large, cumbersome wooden shields that protected the crossbowmen from incoming missiles while they reloaded their weapons.

Among the crossbowmen at Crecy would undoubtedly have been the survivors of the fighting at Caen. They will have reported to Doria on the English tactics and the effectiveness of the English longbow. No doubt the stories of the Caen battle had also been passed through the ranks. As professional soldiers, Doria and his men will have heard all about the English longbow and the arrowstorm. At Caen the Genoese had seen for themselves the range and killing power of the bow, and the dead they left behind would have left them in little doubt of its effectiveness. They were also aware that the fusillade unleashed on them at Caen had merely been during an intense skirmish, not an organised assault. Doria and his men had not seen an arrowstorm, but they must have had a good idea of what was coming. They did not want to advance without their protective pavises.

No doubt Doria once again deployed the arguments earlier advanced by Henry le Moine in favour of waiting until the following day. But neither Philip nor d'Alencon were in any mood to listen. Their blood was up, their enemy was at hand and they wanted a battle. D'Alencon did not mince his words. According to Froissart he ended the discussion by declaring 'A man is well at ease to be charged with such rascals as these, who are cowardly and fail us now when we most need them.'

Doria would have known that Philip and his nobles had a low opinion of him and his men after the events at St Vaast and Caen. The accusation of cowardice must have stung him, particularly coming from a man whose ancestors were still commoners when Doria's had been noblemen. He must have realised that his contract and payments were probably at risk. Doria turned away and went back to order his men.

The crossbowmen, accompanied by their infantry support, filed forward between the Rathuile Ridge and the Maye. They would have turned to their right, then deployed out into a long line facing the English army. Without their pavises the Genoese could not take up their usual formation. They probably formed up in about three or four lines, each with gaps in it through which to allow those behind to shoot. The armoured infantry most likely took station behind the crossbowmen, ready to push forward past their comrades if they were needed to form a defensive line.

It was usual practice to accompany infantry with conrois of mounted men-at-arms to guard their flanks against a sudden and overwhelming charge by enemy knights. It is most likely that d'Alencon put some mounted men on the flanks of the Genoese as they drew up. This may have been as much to keep the allies that he distrusted in their place as to protect them from the enemy. The bulk of the French men-at-arms who had arrived by this time were pushed forward behind the crossbowmen. They likewise turned right and began to form up in the gap between the foot of the Rathuile Ridge and the crossbowmen.

Getting these proud French *seigneurs* to submit to being organised into formation was no easy task. Each conrois was trained well enough to form up, charge, rally and re-form on its own, but now d'Alencon was trying to get dozens of different conrois and thousands of men to form up in ordered lines. No conrois wanted to be given a position other than in the front line, where their honour demanded they should be and where the chances of grabbing a valuable hostage from among the English would be greatest. It should be recalled that, so far as the French were concerned, they faced a beaten rabble whose ranks would collapse at the first charge. Nobody wanted to miss out. As soon as d'Alencon and his staff got one section of line sorted out and moved off to deal with another, those knights aggrieved at their station began to nudge forwards, causing the careful work to break down.

It was at this point, according to the *St Omer Chronicle*, that a poignant episode occurred. Count d'Alencon's standard bearer was an elderly knight named Jacques d'Estracelles who had fought skirmishes against the English. He had been riding back and forth trying to get the truculent knights into order. Either to be able to shout louder or to breathe more easily in the sultry air, d'Estracelles had removed his helmet. He now came trotting up to d'Alencon in concern. Gesturing to the badly formed lines he told the count that it would better to delay the attack.

D'Alencon was already angry and frustrated, now he turned on his friend. The count bellowed at d'Estracelles so that everyone could hear. He berated him for taking off his helmet in the face of the enemy, told him to pull himself together and not to be so frightened. 'Now put your helmet on and get ready to attack', he finished.

The tirade had been unwarranted, and d'Estracelles was not one to have either his courage or his honour insulted. He snapped his helmet back into position and glared at d'Alencon. 'I will follow orders,' he remarked, 'I will put my helmet on. But it won't be me who takes it off.' He rode off to take his position at the head of the front line with d'Alencon's banner in his hand and waited calmly for the orders to charge.

Suddenly, all eyes turned south to the wooded slopes of the hill beyond the Maye. A flight of crows was rising noisily into the air from their roost among the trees. Calling their raucous cries, the great black birds circled upward, then flew over the Maye to swirl around over the heads of the jostling French knights.

The reason for the birds' behaviour was soon obvious. Dense black clouds were piling up in the sky to the south. The day had been humid and sticky. Now an evening thunderstorm was sweeping in to clear the air. Quite how heavy the resulting rain was is open to debate. Froissart describes it as 'a great rain torn apart by a terrible thunder', while Villani records it as a short shower. It was, in any case, over quickly, for the thunderheads rolled on across the sky and the sunshine burst through once again.

The sudden rain cannot have cheered up the grumbling crossbowmen. According to some French chroniclers, it caused the Genoese real problems. The sudden drenching, it was said, caused the crossbow strings to get damp and so become unreliable. The story is generally thought to be a retrospective effort to put the blame for what followed on the foreign mercenaries and the weather. It is difficult to believe that the professional mercenaries did not have heavily waxed strings that could cope with a short shower, no matter how heavy it was. On the other hand it is impossible to discount the notion that the rain had some sort of effect.

If nothing else, the rain would have made the ground wet. It had been hot and dry for the previous six weeks, so the soil would have acquired a hard crust. Heavy rain falling on to such ground can run off quickly, which in the Crecy Valley would have meant it ran down to pool near the banks of the Maye, just where the crossbowmen were standing.

Up on Crecy Ridge, the English had been watching the proceedings. They had seen the slow gathering of the French units, seen the royal banner appear and then the advance of the mercenaries to screen the ordering into formation of the French men-at-arms ready for the charge. But if the Genoese crossbowmen were unhappy, the English king's gunners must have been distraught.

They would have got their guns into position early in the day, and then begun the laborious process of getting ready for action. First, they would have unloaded the one or two barrels of pre-mixed gunpowder from the wagon and rolled it forward. No doubt the different ingredients had shaken themselves out so that the barrel had to be tumbled or turned end over end several times to remix the different powders. The effectiveness of that particular batch of gunpowder would then have been proved by the test-firing of a small gun a few times with measured quantities of powder and missiles of known weight. The master gunner, Robert Aubyn, would then have worked out how much powder would be needed to throw a cannon ball down into the valley where the French would form up to attack. The correct quantity of powder would have been scooped into cloth bags and put ready next to the guns. No doubt the guns would all have been loaded with one charge and ball to be ready for instant firing. He and his men would then turn to the task of opening up fresh barrels of ingredients to mix new batches of gunpowder, each of which then needed to be proved for strength and efficiency.

All this time, the powder will have been exposed to the air, for once the airtight seal on the barrels was broken there was no way to prevent this. 26 September was a muggy day, with the air saturated with moisture. The master gunner would have known that, as the long hours passed by, his unstable powder was absorbing moisture from the air. What had been the proven strength of the powder that morning would now be incorrect, and the pre-packed measures, too small.

The gunners may been considering reproving the first batch when the disastrous shower of rain struck. Any powder and measures that could not be got under cover would have been ruined. It would take hours for them to dry out, and no time was available. The charges already in the guns were probably safe, though nobody could be certain, but all else was lost. Perhaps Aubyn detailed men to start mixing up a fresh batch. This would have involved dashing off to the wagon park to broach new barrels of ingredients and then get mixing again. Wherever the wagon park was, it was not close by. The process would take much time, so maybe Aubyn did not bother.

Whatever Aubyn and his men were doing as the rain cleared away, they were interrupted by a great, raucous shout from down the valley. It was the Genoese. As the shout died away, a deafening chorus of trumpets and cornets boomed out: 'with drums rolling and shouting the noise was like thunder to the English'. says Baker.

The more-experienced men on the English ridge will have known the shout for what it was. It was a tradition among mercenaries that would endure for at least another two centuries, to begin an action with a dramatic display intended to emphasise their professionalism and power, and so demoralise the amateur troops that they so often faced. The usual routine was to form up in a line, crouch down on the ground and then on a given signal for all the men to leap up and scream as loudly as possible. This was followed by deathly silence and absolute stillness. Then the mercenaries would step forward in unison a certain distance, again in absolute silence. Then they would crouch down again and repeat the performance.

It may sound faintly ridiculous today, but such a performance called for a degree of discipline and ability that was beyond the reach of most units of soldiers in the fourteenth century. Watching some 5,000 men go through this orchestrated routine in silence form a range of around 300 metres would be nerve-racking to farm-boys unused to such things.

To the English on their ridge, the Genoese display was no doubt impressive, but the men from the retinues were semi-professionals and even the arrayed men had been on campaign for some weeks. Froissart tells us: 'they stood still and moved not for all that' A second time the Genoese advanced and put on their display, and Froissart says: 'the Englishmen moved not a foot'. A third time, the Genoese marched forward, then leapt and screamed.

Now the Genoese did not advance again. They raised their crossbows to their shoulders and shot up the slope, into the glare of the sun as it slipped low into the western sky. The impact of the crossbow fire is open to dispute. Froissart says that 'they shot fiercely', but le Baker maintains: 'their crossbow bolts did not reach the English, but fell a way off.' We know of one English knight who is recorded some days later as being sick due to a crossbow bolt he received through his foot at Crecy, so at least some of the bolts reached the English.

Edward could not afford for the Genoese to continue their shooting. His defensive tactics depended entirely upon close co-operation between his archers and dismounted men-at-arms. If the crossbowmen stayed where they were and continued to shoot, they would find their range soon enough and casualties in the English army would mount. He needed to drive off the Genoese. He decided to loose the arrowstorm in its full intensity for the first time in the campaign.

The archers would have been using bodkin-head arrows. These arrows were designed to penetrate mail armour, and heavily armoured infantry almost invariably relied chiefly on mail. With the Genoese standing still while they bent to reload their weapons, the archers could be confident of their range. 'Then the English archers stepped forth one pace,' writes Froissart, 'and let fly their arrows all at once and so thickly that it seemed to snow.' Given the range over which they were shooting, probably between 150 and 200 metres, the English would have got their second arrows into the air before the first ones reached their targets. In all some six volleys probably followed each other in rapid succession. The Genoese and the French behind them had never seen anything like it.

The Genoese were in a long, straggling line across the front of the English army. This was not ideal for arrowstorm shooting, as some arrows would unavoidably fall in front or behind the crossbowmen, but even so, the sheer intensity of the shooting must have been breathtaking. Assuming Froissart's numbers to be roughly correct, some 2,000 archers could get their weapons to bear. This would mean that some 12,000 arrows struck the already dispirited Italians in less than a minute.

Bodkin arrows would have had difficulty penetrating the stout iron helmets and plate sheets which many of the Genoese wore, but would punch easily through the sections of mail. Many men would have been killed outright and others wounded by the steeply falling volleys of arrows. Those whose helmets or armour deflected the arrows would still have suffered. The sheer impact of an arrow strike was considerable, and could knock a man to the ground even when it did not penetrate his body.

As the arrowstorm struck the Genoese, the guns ranged alongside the men-at-arms belched fire and smoke with a thunderous roar. Cannon balls arced through the sky, smashing into the Genoese formation with startling results. Swords, lances and arrows can kill a man, but cannon balls can utterly destroy a human body, leaving nothing but bloody fragments scattered over the grass. Neither Frenchmen nor Genoese had expected to find themselves facing guns in open battle. The shock was enormous. Nobody was to know that the guns would not fire again due to the damp powder.

How many Genoese were killed or wounded we do not know, but the casualties were certainly considerable. Baker tells us: 'Much to the terror of the crossbowmen the English archers began to kill their enemies with arrows. They ended the hail of bolts with a rain of arrows.' Villani says that the English shot three arrows for every bolt the Italians could let fly. The Genoese were accustomed to shooting and receiving slow but steady and well-aimed volleys of bolts. The awesome deluge of thousands of missiles striking home in such a short period of time clearly shocked them. As the numbers of dead and wounded mounted, the Italians turned to fall back.

From their point of view, the retreat was justified. They had been employed to do a professional job, not to stand and be slaughtered. They had warned that without pavises and spare bolts they could achieve little, and had been proved right. It was time to call off the attack, wait for morning and try something new.

But from the point of view of King Philip, Count d'Alencon and the other French commanders things looked very different. The Genoese had abandoned St Vaast just before the English landed and they had fled Caen, leaving gallant Frenchmen to face the English alone. And now here they were falling back again, disobeying orders and leaving the fighting to the French once again. Were they cowards? Were they traitors?

To King Philip it did not matter. He had had enough. 'Slay these rascals', he shouted. 'They get in our way and trouble us without reason'. The men-at-arms who had been guarding the flanks of the Italians now turned on their comrades, hacking and cutting with their swords. The front ranks of the French men-at-arms, still jostling each other in their attempts to get into position, joined in. The Genoese fled as best they could. Some turned south to splash into the marshy Maye, others headed north up Crecy Valley. Within a few minutes the survivors were gone.

Now d'Alencon gave the order to charge. His conrois of mounted men-at-arms had been in something less than perfect order to start with. Having been involved in the skirmish with the Genoese, they were now even more disordered. Nevertheless, this was what the knights and nobles had trained for almost from birth. Proud, ill-disciplined and quarrelsome the French *seigneurs* may have been, but nobody ever doubted their courage or skill in battle. They had made France the leading military power of its day, and now they were going into action.

The mass of cavalry will have stretched at least 300 metres from one flank to the other. They would have been drawn up three or four ranks deep to give impetus to the charge, but still allow as many as possible to bring their weapons to bear on the enemy. Froissart tells us they were a mixed force of Frenchmen, Germans and Savoyards, as would be expected given the disordered way in which they reached the battlefield. Froissart also implies that there were two main formations, the second being led by the Count of Flanders. Presumably, this was a reserve force being held back to deliver a second charge either to exploit the success of the first or to help it overcome resistance if it were held up. This would have accorded well with established French practice.

Froissart tells us: 'Count d'Alencon advanced in regular order upon the English to fight with them … riding past the archers and came to the [Black] Prince's division where they fought valiantly for a long time.' Froissart, of course, was writing for the knights, and wanted to move on to this part of the action. Le Bel gives a clearer and more violent view of the Count's advance:

The arrows of the English were aimed with such great skill at the knights that their horses would not advance a step. Some leapt backward, stung to madness; some bucked dangerously; some turned their backs to the the enemy; others simply fell to the ground and their riders could do nothing about it.

Undoubtedly, the archers were using their broad-headed horse arrows at this point. Le Bel's description of some horses simply falling over is typical for horses that have lost a lot of blood from the types of serious but non-fatal wounds these arrows were intended to inflict. Baker tells us: 'The French line of battle was badly disordered by stumbling horses'.

The carnage of the arrowstorm was indeed frightful. Horses went wild, collapsed or bolted uncontrollably. Yet still the French came on. As the charging mass drew closer, the archers changed over to bodkin arrows, seeking to start killing rather than merely wounding and disabling. The bodkin was most effective at ranges under 100 metres, a distance that a charging horse can cover in 15 seconds. An archer might get off three arrows in that time, but the chances of stopping the thundering onslaught of a cavalry charge was very slight.

But then the archers were not trying to stop a charge of knights coming straight at them. As Froissart reminds us, the knights were riding past the archers. The bowmen were behind their field fortifications on top of the terracing where the knights could not get at them directly. The French were charging up the long, gentle slope towards the Black Prince and his men-at-arms. The arrows from the archers were plunging into the flanks of the French. Baker says: 'The archers did not meet the enemy head on, but shot at them from the sides.'

The effect of this shooting from the flanks was awful. Baker records: 'the pressure was so great that men in the middle of the French army were trampled and suffocated without a mark on them.' Clearly, the riders on the flanks were veering inward to get away from the deadly archery, crowding those in the centre of the mass. Later, riders in cavalry charges that came under similar flanking fire have recorded that their horses were lifted off the ground by the pressure of crowding.

Still the French came on. The lines of English men-at-arms waiting at the top of the slope stood steadily as the horsemen thundered up the slope towards them. They all knew that success in halting a cavalry charge such as this rested on every man standing resolutely in his place so that the formation looked like a solid wall of steel to the horses. If even a few men backed away or moved out of place the image of an impassable obstacle would be broken and the horses would not come to a halt. With thousands of big men on big horses bearing down on the English knights, it must have taken enormous courage simply to stand there and await the impact. But stand they did.

Baker describes the French as 'charging headlong into the English ranks in order to display their prowess', but then explains that 'when they attacked the armoured English, they were cut down with swords and spears.' The French charge was stopped in its tracks, but the attack was not yet over. The French had the advantage of height in the savage hand-to-hand combat that now began. And enough of them had got up to the

English lines that as soon as one Frenchman was killed, wounded or fell back through exhaustion another spurred forward to take his place. This was just what the French knights were skilled at.

It was at this point that Jacques d'Estracelles was brought down and killed. As he had predicted to Count d'Alencon just a few minutes earlier, it would not be he who took off his helmet.

The Black Prince was just sixteen years old at the time. This was his first major battle, and a terrifyingly brutal introduction to warfare it must have been. Baker, writing for an English patron and no doubt keen to record the event favourably, tells us:

> In this desperate battle Edward of Woodstock [the Black Prince was often called this as he had been born at Woodstock] displayed marvellous courage against the French in the front line. He ran horses through to fell the knights, crushed helmets, cut lances apart, avoided enemy blows. As he did this, he encouraged his men, defended himself and helped fallen friends to their feet. He set everyone an example.

Richard Wynkeley confirms that the Black Prince was in the thick of it, writing: 'the prince was in our front line'.

As the close combat with the Count d'Alencon's men reached a peak, the English knight Sir Thomas Norwich ran back from the struggling mass of men towards the windmill where King Edward's banner and standard were flapping lazily in the gentle summer's air. Froissart tells us that he had been sent by the Earl of Warwick, though this is not certain. His mission, however, was clear: he had come to ask the king to send forward the reserve.

'Sir,' gasped out Norwich, according to Froissart, 'The Earl of Warwick, Sir Reginald Cobham and others as are about the prince, your son, are fiercely fought and sore handled. They desire you that you and your division come to aid them for if the Frenchmen increase, as they will, your son and they have too much to do.'

Edward glanced forward towards the struggling mass of men. 'Is my son dead, or hurt or thrown to the ground?' he asked.

'Nay, sire,' said Norwich. 'But he is hard pushed and hath need of your aid.'

'Well', said the king, 'go back to those that sent you and tell them that they should not send to me again whatever may happen – so long as my son lives. And tell them that they must let the boy win his spurs this day. For, if God be pleased, I would have this battle and the honour thereof to be his.'

Sir Thomas hurried back to the fighting, reporting the king's words which, apparently, put fresh heart into everybody.

It seems a remarkably cool decision by King Edward to refuse aid to his son and heir at such a moment. Perhaps from his viewpoint things did not look too bad.

As the men of d'Alencon's formation tired, the Count of Flanders led his charge up the long slope. Much the same process as had been used before was repeated. Froissart uses identical wording. The mounted men surged up the hill, their ranks being thinned and disordered by the archers shooting in from the safety of their spurs of high ground on either flank. This time, the charging knights had to avoid the dead and wounded men and horses left behind by d'Alencon's charge. But, like their comrades, the men under Flanders' command burst past the archers' deadly arrowstorm to crash into the melee around the Black Prince's front line.

The arrival of the Count of Flanders and his second force of knights tipped the scales. The line of English men-at-arms began to give way and bend backwards, thinning dangerously. The young Black Prince was knocked to his knees by a blow that left him wounded and bleeding. He struggled back to his feet. According to the Bourgeois of Valenciennes, he was then knocked down again, this time by a French horse. Flanders saw the prince go down and shouted that he had been captured, and spurred his horse towards the prostrate prince.

Sir Richard FitzSimon, the Black Prince's standard bearer, was beside the young prince as he went down. In this moment of desperation, FitzSimon threw the standard down to cover the young man, then stepped forward to stand on it so that he both protected the prince and stopped the all-important standard being carried off. He was carrying one of the long, double-handed swords with which the English chose to fight when dismounted. With his first blow he hacked down the French knight who had knocked over the Black Prince. The Count of Flanders was next to die as he pushed forward to try to secure the Black Prince as a prisoner. Yet still the Frenchmen pushed forward in their eagerness to win the battle and seize a valuable prisoner. The Englishmen around FitzSimon were struck down until he alone was standing.

Suddenly, FitzSimon found Sir Thomas Daniel standing beside him, and other English knights were pushing forward. Fitzsimon must have been both delighted and surprised to see Sir Thomas for Daniel belonged not to the Prince's advance guard, but to Northampton's rear guard. It seems that Northampton had seen the prince's standard go down and, not being attacked himself, had sent a force of knights running on foot to help out. Daniel pulled the standard upright and with FitzSimon hauled the teenage prince to his feet.

The Black Prince was groggy, but conscious. With their leader back on his feet and his standard once more visible, the English recovered and pushed forward. The French seemed to lose heart at this turn of events. Those that were still on horseback turned around and cantered back down the slope to rally out of range of the archers. Those on foot also turned to make their way down the slope.

They were hotly pursued by the English men-at-arms. Le Bel records: 'The English lords who were on foot ran after them, striking them at their will, because they could not help themselves or their horses.' Villani agrees that the English charged forward at this point, but says that some of them were mounted.

As the English men-at-arms came down the slope, they were accompanied by various archers and Cornishmen who Froissart calls 'certain rascals' armed with long knives. They fell upon the wounded Frenchmen, slitting throats and stabbing between armour plates before beginning to strip the bodies.

King Edward was furious. His orders had been disobeyed and the English line was becoming dangerously disordered, while the vast masses of Frenchmen continued to gather in ever-increasing numbers on the Rathuile Ridge. It may have been at this point that the English suffered their worst casualties of the battle. Richard Wynkeley records an incident when a large number of Welshmen were killed 'because they foolishly exposed themselves to danger'. Edward's anger had the desired effect, for before long the Black Prince and his men were back up on the ridge where they had begun.

Philip was also where he had been when the attack had begun. He had lost a lot of men. All his Italian crossbowmen were gone, those that survived having fled the battlefield. Both of the counts who had commanded the men-at-arms, d'Alencon and Flanders, had been killed. The returning knights reported seeing Flanders go down in the struggle around the Black Prince's standard, but nobody knew what had happened to d'Alencon.

At this point, the narrative of the battle begins to break down. Up to now, Le Bel had told a reasonably consistent story that can be cross-checked with the other chronicles and accounts. But le Bel now abandons any attempt to produce a consecutive sequence of events. 'The misfortunes of the French lasted until midnight', he records, and then moves on to talk about what happened at that time. He thus skips over some five hours of action.

In their accounts Baker, Froissart and others record plenty of events, anecdotes and comments, but no attempt is made to put these into a coherent account of the battle. The truth is probably that the light was beginning to go by around 8.00 p.m., making it even more difficult than usual for any one person to get a clear idea of what was going on anywhere other than in his own immediate vicinity. Since Baker, Froissart and the others relied upon what men who had been at the battle told them, their accounts understandably become rather disjointed.

And as the daylight faded, so too did the discipline and order of the French army. The confusion and chaos on the roads leading up to Crecy has already been described. For those units that arrived in the afternoon, the situation was not too bad. D'Alencon and Philip quite clearly made a concerted effort to get order restored on the battlefield before they launched their first assault on the English. Infantry units were put into defensive positions on the Rathuile Ridge outside of the archery range of the English. Men-at-arms were kept held back ready to be formed up to attack and the Genoese were ordered forwards – albeit against their better judgement – to try to thin the English ranks with crossbow bolts.

But after this first attack the situation got rapidly worse. With every passing minute new units were splashing across the ford in the Maye to march up on to Rathuile Ridge or turn left along the river towards the sounds and sights of fighting. Their haphazard arrival and disordered state meant that the confusion that until now had been confined to the roads and back areas, began to spread to the battlefield itself.

Although it is difficult to get a detailed account of what was going on during these hours, the overall picture is clear enough and some of the anecdotes reveal rather more than might be supposed.

In his letter home written after the battle, Edward III refers to 'the small area where the first onslaught occurred'. By this he must mean the gentle slope up to the Prince of Wales' division. He then goes on to refer to 'fighting that took place elsewhere on the field'. Edward wrote his letter in French – then the accepted diplomatic and courtly language – and his phrasing is precise. He means that after this first attack, the battle spread to other parts of the same battlefield. The fighting did not move to other parts of the country, but remained in roughly the same place, although not in front of the Black Prince's division.

Edward also states: 'The enemy bore themselves nobly and often rallied'. A similar point is made by Michael Northburgh who wrote: 'The battle was very fierce and long drawn out because the enemy fought so well'. In a third letter, written within days of the battle, Richard Wynkeley, says much the same but adds some detail: 'the adversary was twice driven off, and a third time was defeated after he had gathered his men and the fighting had been fiercely renewed.'

The impression of three major attacks is also given by Baker. Immediately after describing the first assault on the Black Prince's division, he says: 'So the fearful face of war was displayed, during which time the French raised a general war cry three times', though he goes on to say 'the French charged fifteen times'. To a man such as Baker, writing for an audience of rural knights, the phrase 'general war cry' will have meant a formal crescendo of noise organised by the commander of the army – such as the cacophony of trumpets and drums that sounded before the Genoese advance.

The picture that emerges from these English sources is that the French launched three major, well-organised attacks on the English line on the evening of the main battle. The first of these was undoubtedly that thrown at the Prince of Wales and which came so close to success, and two more were to follow. In addition to this there were numerous other, less formal assaults that may well have added up to fifteen as Baker maintained.

We must now turn to a scattering of incidents and events to see if they can shed any light on the progress of the battle after the failure of the first attack.

Some attacks were certainly launched by French noblemen acting on their own initiative and leading their own contingents of men. The attack of Count Louis of Blois and the Duke of Lorraine is mentioned by Froissart, the *St Omer Chronicle* and others. The two men were brothers-in-law, which may account for the fact that they co-operated. More tellingly, Louis' brother was Charles of Blois who had fought the English at Morlaix in Brittany the previous year.

The two Blois brothers must have discussed the Morlaix conflict at some length over the winter. They would have realised that it was the unarmoured horses that made the French knights so horribly vulnerable to massed archery. They would have discussed ways to get around the problem, and it was some such solution that Louis of Blois and his brother-in-law tried to put into effect at Crecy.

The two nobles led their contingents of knights into the Crecy Valley, but they ignored the slope up which d'Alencon had charged and rode further north to where a section of steep terracing was manned by English infantry. There the Frenchmen dismounted. Leaving the horses in the hands of grooms, Blois and Lorraine led their men up the slope towards the steeper section of hill. As this slope would have been impassable to cavalry it had not been attacked before, so it was not guarded by armoured men-at-arms.

As the attack developed it came under an arrowstorm, presumably of bodkin arrows. Several men were killed or wounded, but the majority got through unscathed. By abandoning their horses, the knights had managed to reach the English lines in good order and in a formed body. Now the fighting turned into hand-to-hand combat where the armoured Frenchmen would have had the clear advantage.

Unfortunately for Blois and Lorraine, they simply did not have enough men with them to make a real difference. Froissart records: 'Louis of Blois and the Duke of Lorraine fought lustily under their banners, but at last they were closed in among a mass of Englishmen and Welshmen.' Blois was skewered by a Welsh spearman while he was trying to scramble up a sheer terraced wall; Lorraine was killed as he tried to draw his men back down the slope in good order. Although this attack failed, it was widely recorded and made a big impact. Within a few years, the dismounted advance by armoured knights would become the standard French tactic when faced by massed English archers.

What this event shows us about the conduct of the battle was the noblemen were now acting independently of the king. Not all acted as carefully as did Blois and Lorraine. Count John of Harcourt, Godfrey Harcourt's bother, led a mounted charge up to the ridge, though precisely where is unknown. With him rode his son, another John, and his brother-in-law Count John Aumale. The elder Harcourt and Aumale were both killed by armour-piercing arrows, while the younger Harcourt had his horse killed. He fell to the ground, being slightly wounded in the process. Picking himself up, the young man walked back to the French lines.

The actions of Charles, the newly elected King of the Romans, are a real mystery. Le Bel does not mention him at the battle at all, so presumably he arrived during the five hour period when le Bel records nothing. Baker says nothing of him either. Northburgh says: 'the nobleman called the emperor-elect barely escaped with his life, or so men say.' That little qualification 'or so men say' is interesting. This is the only time that Northburgh mentions anything that he cannot state as an absolute fact. Obviously, the fate of such an important man would be of interest, but just as clearly there was something odd behind the phrase.

Froissart, as ever, gives more detail and may get close to the reason for the confusion. 'Lord Charles of Bohemia', he writes, 'arrived on the field in good order. But when he saw that the fighting was going badly for his side he left quickly. I cannot tell you which way he went.'

It can only ever be speculation, but perhaps an English herald on Crecy Ridge saw the distinctive banner of Charles appear somewhere on the Rathuile Ridge, only for it to disappear soon afterward. Charles was not going to go around boasting how he cleverly fled the battle rather than throw his life away. Indeed, so far as we know, he never mentioned Crecy again, and nobody was going to be so tactless as to ask the Holy Roman Emperor what he had done that evening.

The picture that emerges from these incidents is of noblemen arriving on the field of battle individually and at intervals, then throwing themselves forward (or not in Charles' case) as soon as they got within sight of the English.

However, we know that King Philip was still on the battlefield because he did not leave until after dark. Was it King Philip who was ordering these numerous small-scale attacks against the English? It is possible. At some point, Philip had a stand-up row with one of his Marshals, Robert de Saint Venant. The cause of the argument is not recorded, but it ended with Philip angrily waving Saint Venant away and shouting after him: 'Very well then. I'll be my own marshal this day if you carry on like that.'

The role of the Marshal of France on the field of battle was to organise and direct the knights and men-at-arms. Presumably, the argument had been over the use of the men-at-arms. Perhaps either Philip or St Venant had been ordering the piecemeal attacks by conrois of men-at-arms as they arrived, and the other had objected. We shall never know.

We do know that at some point later in the evening King Philip led an organised assault on the English ridge. This, it must be assumed, was preceded by one of the two later general war cries recorded by Baker.

King Philip was almost certainly up on the Rathuile Ridge watching the progress of the battle taking place below him and at the same time issuing orders to units as they came across the ford behind him and to his left. If this is where Philip was we can reconstruct what he would have been seeing at around 7.00 p.m.

The first mighty attack had been shattered. The surviving men-at-arms had regrouped somewhere, perhaps at the southern end of the Rathuile Ridge, but were not up to organising a new attack. The units of men-at-arms who had come along since – such as those of Blois, Lorraine and Harcourt – had charged bravely but fruitlessly up the slope of the Crecy Ridge. Their bodies lay scattered across the slope facing King Philip. The survivors may have been milling around at the foot of the Rathuile Ridge. There they were out of range of the terrible English arrows, but unable to get up to the high ground because of the long terrace that lined the western face of the ridge.

Obviously, the piecemeal attacks were getting nowhere, and may have been the cause of the argument between the king and his Marshal. Philip would have realised that only an organised assault, such as that launched earlier by d'Alencon, stood a chance of success. He would have begun bringing the new arrivals up on to the ridge to keep them under his close control. That still left him with the problem of where to launch his attack.

The slope up to the Prince of Wales was now obstructed by hundreds of dead and wounded men and horses. In any case, the deadly flanking archers were still in place and the Prince of Wales' division had been reinforced. That place offered little prospects of success.

Looking straight in front of him, Philip will have seen the fairly gentle slope up from the valley to the English ridge north of the Black Prince's archers. This was good ground for cavalry and was held only relatively weakly by Northampton's division which was stretched thinly. Unfortunately for Philip, the steep terrace down into the valley that lay only metres in front of him made a descent by organised conrois of knights impossible. The only way to reach the base of the slope was to ride around the terrace and then up the valley. The English could not fail to spot the move and could be counted on to reinforce Northampton's position before the French charge could get going.

Further to the north, on the extreme right of his position, Philip would have sensed a better chance of victory. From his position on Rathuile Ridge, he would have seen the thin line of Northampton's division curling back from the ridge crest as it got closer to Wadicourt. At the far end of the English ridge was a small knoll edged by steep terracing. This may or may not have been manned by Englishmen. Most likely it was not, for it was an isolated position that could be approached easily by cavalry from the southwest. And just beyond the knoll was an opening to a small valley that cut south-westward in front of Wadicourt. Philip may well have had some local farmers with him to advise him on the lie of the land. Even if he did not, his own eyes would have told him that this small valley sloped up on to the Crecy Ridge, emerging on the far left of Northampton's thinly stretched division. Crucially, anyone advancing up that valley would be out of sight of King Edward, Northampton and the other senior English commanders as the knoll blocked their view.

Once again, Philip seems to have gone through the same thought process that he and d'Alencon had followed some hours earlier. Once they could get up on to the Crecy Ridge, the French mounted knights could sweep all before them, crushing the English army and winning a spectacular and bloody victory. But, just as before, they first had to get there.

That an attack of some kind took place here can be confirmed by the fact that after the battle the little valley became known locally as the Vallée de Marché à Carognes, which translates roughly as the Valley of the Carcass Market. This area was not at the time of Crecy a livestock farming area, nor has it been since, so it is unlikely that the name refers to any sort of outside agricultural event. The only time that a large number of animal carcasses would have been found hereabouts was after the Battle of Crecy when horse bodies were plentiful. Horses are big, heavy animals and moving their bodies around is an awkward and time-consuming job. After a battle, they tend to get buried where they fall. If the little valley was the scene of equine carnage it can only have been because a charge by mounted French knights came to grief there. We know that King Philip led an attack, but not where it took place. We know an attack took place in the little valley, but not who led it. It is probable that the two attacks were one and the same.

Philip would have calculated that the approach up to the ridge would be lightly defended. Not only was Northampton's division thinly dispersed when the battle began, but it had since been weakened further to reinforce the Black Prince. And if Philip and his mounted men moved quickly they could canter round to approach the valley before any of the English, running on foot, could get there to oppose them.

Froissart hints that this may have been the case. Writing of the Black Prince's division he says: 'the French king would fain have gone thither, but there was a great hedge of archers before him.' Perhaps the devastating effects of the archery also put Philip off a direct attack and pushed him towards the little valley. After all, he had achieved a brilliant success eighteen years earlier at Cassel by launching a flank attack. Perhaps he was trying to emulate that victory.

We should imagine Philip waiting on Rathuile Ridge until enough new conrois of mounted men-at-arms had gathered under his royal banner and the Oriflamme. Then he led them off, heading north along the Chemin de l'Armée. The column of knights would have ridden along the road, across the head of the Crecy Valley, then into the entrance of the little valley behind the knoll and up the gentle slope towards the English ridge. This would have been the movement that, seen from the English ridge, was described by Richard Wynkeley as 'A third time, the adversary having gathered his men, the fighting was fiercely renewed.'

Wynkeley gives us some details of the French charge that followed: 'The King of France was wounded in the face by an arrow and only just escaped alive. His standard bearer was killed in his sight, and his standard was torn to shreds.' Edward III writes only: 'they were defeated and our adversary [Philip] fled.'

Froissart, as so often, concentrates on an anecdote about a particularly brave deed by a noble knight. Having first related how the night before the battle King Philip had given Count John of Hainault a splendid black warhorse, Froissart explains that as the battle began Count John decided that he would rather ride his own trusted and dependable mount, so he gave the royal gift to his standard bearer Lord Thierry de Senzeille. Froissart continues:

> This horse took the bit between his teeth and carried Senzeille straight through all the ranks of the English. He would have wanted to return, but the horse fell into a great ditch and he was badly injured. His page had followed him and alighted from his horse to help Senzeille to his feet. The English did not leave their ranks to take them prisoner. The French knight could not go back the way he had come because of the English army. He escaped another way.

Froissart later tells us that Philip was forced to take a horse back from Hainault 'for his own horse had been slain by an arrow,' presumably during this attack.

The picture that seems to emerge from these disjointed anecdotes is that the charging French knights were met by an effective arrowstorm as they came up the valley. Large numbers of horses were killed – a sign of massed archery – and Philip was wounded while his standard bearer was killed. There is no mention of close combat by any writer, so presumably the French did not get to hand-to-hand terms with the English men-at-arms.

It is at first difficult to see why the French did not close with the English. The valley in question is 100 metres wide and 400 metres long, sloping gently up to the ridge summit. Its sides are shallow. They would not have been difficult for a body of horsemen to get up while keeping formation.

While it can only be guesswork, there is a scenario which fits the known facts. Northampton had sent men-at-arms to help the Black Prince. While these certainly came from his right wing which was closest to the Prince, he may have replaced them by moving knights down from his left wing.

This will have left the small valley to be guarded by archers and infantry, presumably under the command of trusted knights but without the support of a phalanx of armoured men-at-arms.

When Philip and his men entered the valley, the archers would have begun shooting down into them from the valley sides. As in the earlier attack against the Black Prince, this flanking fire would have caused the French column to pull in on itself as men on the sides of the column tried to get away. The direction of the French charge would, therefore, have been funnelled up the centre of the valley until something stopped them.

It is unlikely that ordinary infantry could have stood firm against a massed cavalry charge in the way that heavily armoured men-at-arms could do. It is, of course, possible that the arrowstorm alone proved enough to halt the attack and drive it back, but this had not been the case in the earlier attacks, nor at earlier battles such as Morlaix or St Pol de Leon. If, however, the wagon park was located at the top of the valley and was manned by lightly armed spearmen and infantry, this could have stopped the mounted charge. Without English knights being engaged in any heroics, Froissart would not have thought to mention these events.

Whatever happened, the French king's attack was halted and thrown back with heavy losses. Philip was now reduced to the same state as so many of his knights and nobles. He was wandering almost aimlessly around in the foot of the Crecy Valley trying to find his colleagues, rally his troops and vainly direct fresh attacks on the English.

The timing of Philip's attack is uncertain. We know that d'Alencon's attack took place around 6.00 p.m. and that some time had elapsed since then. Perhaps it was around 7.30 p.m. that Philip left the ridge to launch his doomed venture.

Certainly, Philip had gone by the time that King John of Bohemia arrived on the Rathuile Ridge for nobody mentions them meeting or even seeing each other. None of the contemporaries give a precise time for King John's arrival, but later Czech writers are adamant that it was at sunset, around 8.00 p.m.

Although almost blind, King John was an experienced and able commander. He asked his men to describe the scene before them, which they did. Appreciating the disaster unfolding and the massive casualties taken by the French, King John then asked a very human and understandable question: 'Where is the Lord Charles, my son?'

The Bohemian knights would have peered into the gathering gloom, but been unable to see the young man's banner. No doubt a quick discussion followed with the militia infantry who were still lining the terraced drop down into the valley. They would have revealed that Charles had been there, but had ridden off. 'Sir', the reply to the king's question came, 'we cannot tell. We think that he be fighting.'

Exactly what went through the mind of the grizzled old warrior king we have no way of knowing. He must have known that if his son had taken part in a mounted charge against the English, and his banner could not be seen, then he was most likely dead or wounded. On the other hand it was rapidly getting dark and his son might simply be out of sight somewhere. Whatever King John thought, Froissart records what happened next:

> The valiant King of Bohemia then said to his men 'Sirs, ye are my men, my companions and friends in this great adventure. I require you to bring me so far forward that I may strike one stroke with my sword on the enemy.' The knights said that they would do his commandment, and to this purpose they did not want to lose him in the crowds. They therefore tied the reins of their horses each to the other and set the king in the middle. Then they rode forward to set the king to accomplish his desire.

And so King John of Bohemia came down off the Rathuile Ridge into the gathering gloom of a summer's night and rode off into legend.

Meanwhile, King Philip was in despair. It was now dark and he had only sixty men with him. He could hear other French knights milling around the valley floor in the dark, and the occasional shout as some brave souls launched a charge up the slope. But he had no real idea what was going on and no chance of influencing events. He seems to have lost his nerve, shouting orders into the darkness and demanding action and knowledge from men incapable of providing either.

Eventually, Count John of Hainault grabbed the king's horse by the bridle and managed to get the king's attention. 'Sire, depart hence,' Hainault said. 'It is time to go. Don't throw your life away wilfully. If you have lost this battle, you will win another time.' Philip lapsed into silence, almost a daze, so Hainault rode off pulling the king's horse behind him.

The little cavalcade rode north, out of the northern end of the Crecy Valley – another indication that Philip had launched his charge at this northern end of the battlefield – and headed towards the Castle of Labroye. By the time they arrived, the group was reduced to Philip, Hainault, Charles de Montmorency and three others. The constable of the castle will have known that both the English and French armies were nearby and may even have had scouts out who reported back to him that a battle was taking place. He was certainly cautious when this small group of knights approached in dead of night.

'Who is it that calls here this time of night?' the officer demanded peering down to try to see if he recognised any coats of arms or faces.

'Open up at once,' Philip called out wearily. 'You see before you the Fortune of France.'

The commander recognised Philip's voice and had the gates opened. He must have been astonished to see his king riding in wounded in the

This nobleman wears the very latest, most expensive and most effective armour available. Only a handful of men on either side during the Crecy campaign could have aspired to this quality and design of armour. The bascinet helmet is of quality steel and most probably was manufactured in southern Germany. Under the helmet he wears a mail coif, which has a flared cape to give extra protection to his shoulders, neck and chest. His arms and legs are encased in plates of sheet steel, with mail being reduced to the role of protecting the less vulnerable parts and those areas that are needed to flex and twist in battle and which were difficult to protect with plates. He carries a two-handed sword with a long, heavy blade of the type favoured by the English when fighting dismounted. His shield is unusual in that it is of the style called bouché that was

to become standard for jousting later in the century. The square shape was designed to cover the entire side of the man from the neck down to the waist, below which the rider was screened by the fence that separated jousting knights. The notch at the top was designed to hold the lance which was braced into the right armpit, allowing the knight to aim his lance tip by moving his shield. Perhaps he is preparing to take part in one of the chivalrous incidents that interrupted the main action of the Crecy campaign, and other military adventures.

face and accompanied by only five knights. Food and drink was quickly brought forward, and presumably fresh horses, for Philip made it clear that he was not stopping, but would ride on toward Amiens. The castle commander asked what had happened. Philip glared at him. 'We were betrayed,' he said. It was midnight.

Back on the Crecy Ridge, the coming of darkness had at first brought little respite to the English. Groups of mounted French knights still made sporadic attacks, hoping to escape the arrowstorm by coming under cover of darkness. But by this time all cohesion had gone. The attacks were disorganised, badly executed and carried out by too few men to be successful. Gradually the attacks tailed off.

For the English, peering down into the valley and trying to decide what was going on, it was a tense time. They could hear the cries and groans of wounded men and horses, but they could also hear the clinking of armour and horse harnesses as mounted men moved about down on the valley floor. Voices drifted up as men called out to each other seeking comrades and friends. From further off the sounds of marching men could be heard as if thousands of infantry were manoeuvring around on the Rathuile Ridge.

The English had been fighting for hours. Attack after attack had been driven off. They were tired and weary. Baker describes the Black Prince 'and his men leaning on their lances and swords beside mounds of dead men, taking deep breaths and resting, awaiting a new onslaught'.

Torches were lit and thrown forward down the slope in the hope that their light would reveal what was going on. But to no avail. There were thousands of armed Frenchmen out there in the dark somewhere. But where? And what were they doing? If the solid ranks of militia swept forward now, could the exhausted English stop them? Nobody knew.

If the French army had possessed a better chain of command and been more disciplined some sort of attack might have been organised, and been successful. But King Philip had fled and the various units left behind had no orders and no way of knowing what they were meant to do. Le Bel describes the scene:

> The sorry remnant of the army – lords, knights and commoners – who were left behind withdrew like defeated men. They did not know where to go for it was dark and they did not know the local towns and villages and they were tired and hungry. They went off in small groups, not knowing if their friends and relatives were alive or dead.

It was this movement that the English heard as the sounds of marching men. Edward had the windmill by which he had had his command post set on fire. By the light of the blazing building the English could finally see that the valley in front of them was empty of moving French units, and that the ridge beyond was rapidly emptying. Edward allowed most of his army to fall back from their ranks to eat and sleep, but insisted they keep their armour on and weapons ready to hand. Scouts were posted to keep an eye out for any fresh French move.

Accompanied by his senior companions, King Edward marched forward to find his son. The two men embraced and Edward declared: 'Good son. God has saved you this day. You are my son and this day you have behaved well and nobly. Truly you are a worthy man to be a king.' The boy had won his spurs.

XIV

Crecy – The Second Day

As the chill light of dawn spread over Crecy on the morning of 27 September 1346, the English awoke to find themselves enveloped by a thick mist. The slope in front of them was littered with the bodies of French knights, while wounded horses hobbled about the scene. But even the valley floor was hidden from view. Of the wider scene the English could see nothing.

Edward was clearly nervous. He must have known that he had defeated the main force of men-at-arms, but he will also have seen the haphazard way in which the French army arrived on the battlefield. Even as dusk had closed in, fresh units had been appearing on the Rathuile Ridge. How many French men-at-arms were left he did not know, nor did he know where the tens of thousands of infantry had got to.

It was urgent that Edward should find out where King Philip and his army were and what they were doing. The English were still outnumbered and to move from their defensive position on Crecy Ridge would be very dangerous until they had some idea of what they were facing. Sending out lone riders or even small groups of scouts would be suicidal should they run in to the main French army. Instead, Edward dispatched the Earl of Northampton and Earl of Warwick with 500 men-at-arms and 2,000 archers to investigate. As Northampton and Warwick rode off into the swirling mist, Edward had his army stand to their posts. He wasn't taking any chances. Northampton and Warwick moved east, past the southern end of the now deserted Rathuile Ridge, then turned south to cross the River Maye and probe towards Abbeville. This was the direction from which the French army had come and, most likely, the way they would have retreated.

As they advanced, the English came across small groups of Frenchmen who had camped out in the fields the night before. They were now standing around leaderless and wondering what to do. Most fled when the saw the English, seeking safety in the mist, others stood to fight and were quickly killed. Charles, King of the Romans, had his camp attacked and fled westward as his men scattered. It took him until the following day to gather his force back together again.

The Battle of Crecy as recorded in a manuscript produced only a few years after the event. By the standards of the day this is a remarkably accurate representation. The contest between English archers and Genoese crossbowmen is highlighted in the foreground, while the hilly nature of the terrain is clearly shown. The flight of King Philip to the Castle of Labroye is shown in the left background. Only the fact that the English knights are shown mounted is incorrect.

Somewhere near Marcheville, Northampton and Warwick saw what they had dreaded. Looming up out of the mist was the head of a large column of French militia, marching steadily and determinedly north towards Crecy under fluttering banners. Guessing that Philip had rallied his troops and was now marching to continue the battle, Northampton deployed for battle. Quickly the English archers raced out to get into good shooting positions, then let fly a devastating arrowstorm.

The head of the French column collapsed under the deadly blows of the arrows, and its formation began to break up. That was the moment when Northampton unleashed his mounted men-at-arms to crash into the disorganised French infantry and tumble them into flight. It was a classic

charge of armoured horsemen smashing the enemy formation to fragments, then turning back to kill and wound as many as possible, harrying
the fleeing men so that there was no chance that the infantry could rally
and offer more opposition.

Unlike on the previous day, the English were on the Sunday free to take
prisoners. Eager hands raced to grab hold of the few knights and noblemen among the French. When the fleeing infantry had disappeared into
the mist, Northampton gave the signal to rally and brought his force back
to reform.

Meanwhile, the prisoners had been questioned and revealed that they
were the militia of Rouen. They had been left behind at Rouen to guard
the city by Philip when he had followed the English up the Seine twenty
days earlier. Then they had received the summons to march to Abbeville
to join the army that Philip was mustering. They had arrived at Abbeville
the previous day and been told that the king had gone on to Crecy. The
Rouen militia had been marching north, unaware that a battle had been
fought when they had run into Northampton. They had not realised the
strangers were English until the arrows began to fall.

A quick search of the battlefield revealed the body of the Archbishop
of Rouen among the dead. No sooner had Northampton digested this
news than a rider came galloping in with the news that a new and
much stronger column of Frenchmen was approaching. This body of men
included a force of men-at-arms riding under the banner of the Knights of
St John. Hurriedly, Northampton again drew his men up for battle. Again
the French were taken utterly by surprise. The arrowstorm did its work
of breaking up the enemy formation so that it could be burst apart by the
charging men-at-arms. This time Northampton allowed the pursuit to
continue for longer, adding to the death toll.

After they had rallied again, the English found that they had killed Sir
Jean de Nanteuil, Grand Prior of the Knights of St John and captured the
Archbishop of Sens and the Archdeacon of Paris. By this time the mist
was beginning to lift. Northampton took the risk of sending out smaller
parties of riders to scout the whole area. If these two powerful forces had
been on the move towards Crecy, who knew who else was on the move.
In the event, the English found no further large formations of Frenchmen,
only small, isolated units wandering about in search of news , leadership
or even a place that they recognised. A series of running fights developed
across the open countryside south of the River Maye.

Finally, around mid-morning, Northampton was satisfied that there was
no real danger from the dispersed, disorganised and leaderless French
troops that he was encountering. Calling off his men, he led them back
north to Crecy to report to King Edward. He estimated that his men had
killed something over 4,000 Frenchmen, though given the mist and disorganised nature of the mobile fighting it was impossible to be certain.

When he received the news, Edward stood down the army. Mass was celebrated to care for the souls of the soldiers, then the grim task of clearing up the carnage began. Edward sent Sir Reginald Cobham and Sir Richard Stafford, with three heralds, down into the valley. Their task was to collect up the shields and banners that would identify the important knights and noblemen who had been killed. A complete list was to be drawn up both so that the king would know the extent of his victory, and also so that it could be sent to the French heralds who would inform the bereaved families. The bodies of anyone particularly important were to be carried to one side so that they could be given individual burial. As ever Edward was being the perfect, chivalrous knight with this punctilious observation of good form.

It wasn't long before Sir Reginald was back to tell King Edward that the task they had been set was too great for just five men. So many noble Frenchmen had been killed that they could not hope to make a list by themselves. Edward came a little way down the hill to see the truth of the slaughter for himself. For the first time he began to understand the extent of what had happened the previous evening. He detailed Sir Thomas Holland and Sir Henry Percy to join in the task because both had lived abroad for a number of years and might recognise foreign coats of arms. Sir Olivier Ghistels of Flanders also joined in.

To speed things up, Edward also put to the task his personal household clerks who moved behind the knights and heralds with rolls of parchment scribbling down names and descriptions of arms. It was this that gave the Crecy Valley its modern name: Vallée des Clercs.

All that day the knights and clerks moved through the battlefield collecting the shields and making their lists. Following them came teams of soldiers whose task it was to strip the bodies. Anything useful or valuable was put to one side to be carted off as booty. Broken weapons, shields and saddles were thrown into great heaps, then set on fire. Meanwhile, great pits were being dug along the foot of the slope into which the bodies could be piled. The priests conducted funeral service after funeral service for the dead Frenchmen. Yesterday they had been enemies to be killed, today they were fellow Christians who deserved a decent burial.

One of the first important bodies to be identified was that of the blind King John of Bohemia. He was found beside his dead horse, along with the bodies of those of his knights who had tied their horses to his the night before. There they lay, all in a line, having died as they fought. Froissart later made it his business to try to find out what had happened, but other than vague stories from some Bohemians that their king had got within sword reach of the English front line he could discover nothing. None of the English had had any idea that they had killed him until his body had been found. His death had been as heroic as his life, and soon legends swirled around Europe of how he had met his death fighting gallantly in the gathering gloom of the Crecy twilight.

As soon as he heard the news, the Black Prince came to see the body. He ordered that it should be taken to Edward's own tent to be stripped and washed in warm water. It was then redressed in clothes fit for a king and put aside to await a message from the dead king's relatives or followers. Meanwhile, the young prince picked up King John's standard from where it had fallen. The flag was torn and muddy, but its design was clear enough: A black field scattered all over with ostrich feathers embroidered in silver bullion thread.

Edward the Black Prince would later adopt the standard for his own. His son, later Richard II, would carry a similar flag until he inherited the throne. The design would vary somewhat for a few generations, but eventually settled down to become three ostrich feathers tied at the base on a field of black. It remains the standard of the Prince of Wales to this day.

The bodies and arms of other nobles were being found with startling regularity: the gold lilies and silver circles of Count d'Alencon were found, as were the horizontal strips of red and gold belonging to the Count de Grandpré, the two gold bars on red of Count John de Harcourt, the black and silver stripes of Count Anseau de Vaudémont, the two golden fish on red of Count Étienne de Montbeliard, the black lion on gold of Count Louis of Flanders, the silver lion on gold of Count John de Roucy and the diagonal wavy silver stripes on blue of Louis Count de Sancerre – the list seemed endless. Count Guy de St Pol was dead, so was Baron Enguerrand de Coucy, William de Croi Chanel, Count John d'Auxerre, Louis of Blois, Count Peter of Rozmberk, and Duke Raoul of Lorraine.

When the battered shield carrying a red flower on a gold field was pulled aside it revealed the wounded, but still breathing, Sir Jean de Créquy. Thinking he had a good chance of living, the English spared his life and hauled him off to their camp. He did, indeed, recover and returned home having paid a ransom.

The banner of King James of Majorca was found broken and trampled in the mud beside the body of a knight so badly wounded that nobody could recognise him. In his letter home, Richard Wynkeley said that 'the king of Majorca is slain (according to common report)', while Edward III was less cautious and claimed him as dead for certain. In fact, King James had escaped alive and wasted very little time in bidding a firm goodbye to King Philip before riding south to his own lands as fast as a horse could carry him.

In all, the English knights and heralds found the arms of 1,542 knights entitled to carry their own coats of arms into battle. We know that the list of these men and their heraldic devices was drawn up and circulated, though it has not survived.

How many other Frenchmen were killed is a controversial subject. If 1,542 knights bearing their own arms had been killed in the repeated cavalry charges, there would also have been a fair number of esquires other men-at-arms – perhaps another 500 or more. Richard Wynkeley contents himself with the vague but evocative phrase: 'The flower of the whole knighthood of France has been killed.' As for casualties among those who were not men-at-arms, Michael Northburgh simply says that 'many commoners and footsoldiers' were killed. The main body of the French militia and other infantry was not engaged on the Saturday, though there are mentions in French chronicles of their involvement early in the day. Certainly, the Genoese crossbowmen suffered badly, first from the English archers and then from the French men-at-arms. Perhaps somewhere between 2,000 and 3,000 infantry were killed on the Saturday, plus those killed by Northampton's expedition the following day. In all the French lost around 9,000 men.

The English losses were extremely light. Le Bel states that the English army lost less than 300 men. Richard Wynkeley records that only two knights and one esquire were killed on the battlefield, though a great many were wounded and some of these probably died of infections and other causes in the days that followed. The scale of the victory was astonishing.

St Paul's Cathedral, London, as it stood in 1346. The news of Crecy was read out to the public from the steps of the cross that stood in the churchyard to the north of the cathedral.

XV

The Siege of Calais

On the Monday, two days after the battle, Edward moved his army off north from Crecy to get away from the smell and mess of the battlefield. The Bishop of Durham looked after the body of the King of Bohemia until it was collected by King Charles of the Romans for transport back to Prague. The bodies of the other noblemen were taken to the nearby Abbey of Montreuil and a message sent to the French that a three-day truce would be observed so that they could be collected.

On 1 September Edward faced up to the changed situation in which he found himself. He no longer had to worry about any sort of pursuit by Philip nor, in all likelihood, to any sort of opposition at all from a French field army. He could march where he liked and do what he liked.

As ever, things were not so simple as they might appear. The English were short of almost every sort of supply that could be imagined. Without the fear of a French army on their track, they could now spare the time to attack towns and castles. Knowing this, most garrisons chose to surrender as soon as a force of Englishmen appeared. As a result, the immediate food problem was soon solved. But the army was still short of arrows, horse-shoes and other military necessities. Many men were wounded, needing care and rest.

On 2 September Edward and his army reached Boulogne. He demanded the prompt surrender of the town, but the garrison rightly guessed that Edward lacked serious siege equipment and refused. Edward moved on to the port of Wissant, which was captured. Edward stayed there long enough to write his letter home announcing the great victory, and to ask for reinforcements and supplies to be sent to him. Wissant was then burned, and by 4 September the army was outside the gates of Calais.

The city of Calais was one of the largest and most prosperous ports in northern France. That was enough to make it a tempting target for attack, but its position was strategic, both militarily and economically. If Edward had control of Calais and Dover, he would be able to secure a tight grip on any shipping moving between the North Sea and the English Channel.

Timber defences and bulwarks built by a besieging army to protect its forces during the siege of a town. This illustration comes from half a century after the siege of Calais, but apart from the greater number of guns those used by Edward in 1346 would have been similar.

Not only that but the port was ideally placed to handle English exports to the continent, easing the intractable and complex issues about customs and taxation that had bedevilled English government for decades.

The failure of any important noblemen or significant sections of the population to join Edward's cause since he landed at St Vaast had by now convinced the English king that he was not going to get the French to accept him as their rightful king. Instead, he was now looking for a very practical and solid gain from his campaign. He decided that Calais would be his. The English began to build their siege works on 5 September.

King Philip, meanwhile, was still reeling from the disaster that had befallen him. Dawn the day after the battle had found him on the north bank of the Authie River some twenty kilometres east of Labroye. He paused at Doullens long enough to make sure that it was safe to ride over open country in daylight, grabbed a quick meal and then set out for Amiens.

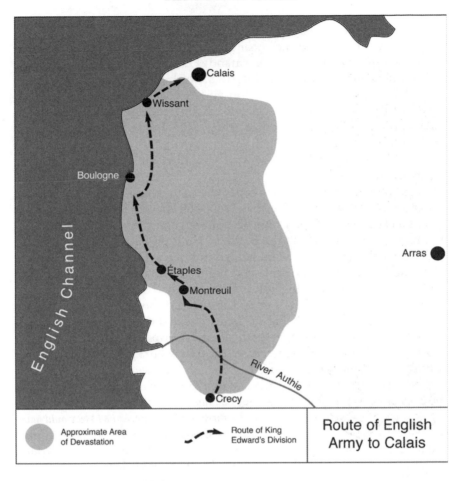

Route of English Army to Calais

Approximate Area of Devastation · Route of King Edward's Division

Over the days that followed, the true extent of the catastrophe gradually became clear to Philip. At first he hoped that his army had merely become disorganised and dispersed. But as the hours, then days dragged by he was forced to admit that huge numbers of his chivalry lay dead at Crecy, while most of the militias and infantry units had simply gone home after being left without orders and pursued by the English. He vented some of his vengeful fury by executing some of the Genoese crossbowmen on accusations of treason. He then sacked his remaining Marshal, Charles de Montmorency, who promptly rode off home in disgust.

Count John of Hainault, who had dragged Philip off the battlefield, asked permission to take his men home in case Edward invaded. Philip agreed, then watched as King Charles of the Romans also rode away with his men, taking the body of King John home for burial. King James of Majorca had already gone. Philip was left almost alone.

On 7 September he left Amiens and rode south disconsolately toward his palace at Pont St Maxence near Paris. There he at last got some good news. His son, Duke John of Normandy, had left the war in Aquitaine to local noblemen and marched north with the bulk of his army. Philip roused himself from his depression and began issuing new orders for northern France to be put in a state of defence. Messengers were sent to Calais ordering the garrison commander, Sir John de Vienne, to hold out until Philip marched to his relief.

Far to the north another ally was rallying to Philip's cause, though very much for reasons of his own. King David Bruce of Scotland had been urged several times by Philip to repay the many years of assistance given his cause by the French now that France itself was under attack. King David had delayed taking action, his nobles having seen at first hand what an arrowstorm could do at the Battle of Halidon Hill in 1333. But when he heard that King Edward had landed in France, David thought that the time had come for a large-scale and highly profitable raid into northern England. With Edward in France with England's main army the field would be open to the Scots – or so King David thought. In fact, Edward had recognised the threat that the Scots might strike when his back was turned. He had mustered men for the French campaign only from counties south of the Trent. North of that river, the men were told to stand ready for service should the Scots invade.

It was the end of August before David was ready. The Scots poured over the border near Berwick, bypassing that heavily fortified town and marching south across Northumberland, looting systematically as they went. By early October they were outside the city of Durham. King David occupied the luxurious hunting lodge of the absent Bishop of Durham at Bearpark, a few kilometres west of the city, while his army laid siege.

Raiding parties were sent out to range over County Durham, and it was one of these that ran into an advancing English army at Merrington soon after dawn on 17 October. Sir William Douglas, leader of the small Scottish force, at first thought he was up against some local arrayed men, but as the light improved realised that some 4,000 men were marching around his flank. Hurriedly mounting up and galloping north, Douglas lost half his men in the pursuit before he got away.

Galloping into the courtyard at Bearpark, Douglas ran up the steps and burst into the main hall just as King David was sitting down to lunch. With commendable speed, David sent out gallopers to pull his army out of the siege lines and recall the other raiding parties, telling them all to congregate on a ridge west of Durham city which blocked the road along which the English would need to advance to reach the city.

Led by Sir Ralph Neville, the English moved fast and reached the key ridge first. It was with some satisfaction that Neville found himself standing beside the famous Neville's Cross, a tall stone monument put up as an act of religious devotion by an ancestor of his. It was a good omen. Neville had with him about 800 men-at-arms, 5,000 archers and 2,000 infantry. He put his archers and infantry in three divisions on the ridge facing north towards Bearpark, and split up his men-at-arms so that they were in position to plug any gaps that occurred in the front line.

David had around 10,000 men by the time the battle began, some 2,000 of them men-at-arms and the rest spearmen wearing varying degrees of armour. The Scots drew up on a ridge parallel to and about 700 metres north of that occupied by the English. At around noon, David ordered his men to advance.

The Scots came on in their traditional dense infantry formations fronted by shields and bristling with spears. As they came on, the right wing found their path impeded by a steep ravine that caused them to break up their formation to cross. It took some while to get back into formation, by which time the centre under King David had come under a withering arrowstorm.

The Scots were not hampered by having vulnerable horses, but nonetheless they took casualties as they advanced. The clash between the infantry formations when it came was harsh and hard fought. When the reformed Scottish right wing came in to the fray, the English began to fall back. Neville sent in his men-at-arms to restore the balance. He then realised that the Scottish left wing, led by Robert Stewart, was hanging back. This gave the English the opportunity to move their right wing on to the flank of King David's formation.

The move proved crucial. Once they realised that they were being attacked on two sides, the Scots began to fall back. The withdrawal turned to a rout as the Scottish formation collapsed. King David took to his heels, but was brought to the ground by an obscure northern esquire named John Coupland. In the undignified wrestling match that followed, Coupland lost two teeth to a punch from David's mailed fist, but he managed to subdue the king and made certain of the capture by sitting on him.

The fleeing Scots were saved from a worse defeat by the onset of nightfall, which brought an end to the English pursuit. Stewart rallied the troops and led them back into Scotland in relatively good order. King David was sent south in triumph as a prisoner for King Edward. Young Coupland, needless to say, was rich for life.

Edward received the news of the Battle of Neville's Cross in his camp outside Calais. The defences of the city were strong and extensive and it had soon become clear that the English were not going to capture it by assault. Blockade and starvation were the only weapons that offered Edward the chance of success.

Inside Calais, Sir John de Vienne did some quick calculations. He believed that, given the losses at Crecy, Philip was unlikely to be able to mount a relief before spring. And there was not enough food inside Calais to see everyone through the winter. He therefore ordered the poorest citizens to be thrown out. These unfortunate people were understandably reluctant to be put at the mercy of the English king and had to be forced out of the gates at sword point.

In similar situations, besiegers have pushed evacuees back at sword point, leaving them to starve in the no man's land between the lines in order to impress on those within the city walls the ruthlessness of the besiegers. Commanders inclined to clemency allowed the evacuees through, though not before they have been stripped of anything valuable.

But Edward as ever wanted to boost his fame and his reputation for chivalry. He had the cowering Calesians brought before him, then conducted them to tables groaning with food and drink. After they had eaten their fill, Edward gave each person three silver pennies and sent them on their way. As le Bel wrote: 'This must be recorded as the act of a very noble nature.'

By this time, the English had built a wooden town outside Calais in which they lived. Queen Philippa travelled over from England to be with Edward, and did much to raise morale in the army. Siege lines stopped any supplies reaching Calais by land, though occasional ships slipped past the English fleet to carry food in by sea. Mounted patrols ranged far and wide both to strip the country of anything useful and to keep an eye open for any French forces that might be about. The towns of Guines and Marque both went up in flames. In November the castle at Hammes, a vital outwork of Calais, fell to the English. Then bad weather closed in and halted all military activity, though the slow, grinding process of starvation continued.

When the spring came, Philip was first distracted by a campaign against the Flemings around Arras. Having pushed the enemy back to Flanders, he finally marched to the relief of Calais. The French banners appeared on the hills of Sangatte on 20 July. Trumpets and drums were sounded in Calais to welcome their liberators. The English, warned of Philip's approach by their scouts, mustered for battle. In the event Philip pitched camp to study the situation. There was no battle that day.

Edward had not let his men lie idle over the winter. His camp was fortified and he had broken down all the bridges and causeways over the marshes except one. Effectively, that meant that to approach the English, the French must either cross a single bridge or march along the sand dunes; either route would restrict them to a narrow frontage where they would be vulnerable to the type of arrowstorm that had done so much damage at Crecy. After a few days probing the defences, Philip decided to try diplomacy.

He sent forward heralds with a long, convoluted message that raked over all the old ground of the quarrels of the past and ended by challenging the English to battle in open country thus 'allowing God to give victory to whom He chose'. The form of words was important for it carried echoes of trial by combat and put the onus on God. In effect Philip was proclaiming that he was so confident that he was in the right that he was willing to put the matter to God, while implying that Edward could only win by unfair means of which God would disapprove. It was a clever message designed to goad Edward into folly, or at least to appeal to neutral rulers elsewhere in Europe.

Edward was not to be fooled. After repudiating Philip's version of earlier quarrels and events, Edward said 'Tell him then from me that I have been here for nearly a year, openly and to his knowledge, and that he could have come sooner had he wanted to do so. If he will not come by one way, he can come by another.'

On 27 July two cardinals arrived, one of them the same Cardinal Etienne Aubert who had tried to mediate between Edward and Philip after the capture of Caen. This time the churchmen suggested a conference to be held between noblemen representing the rival kings, perhaps hoping that this might take the personal antagonism out of the situation. Edward agreed, sending the Earl of Northampton, the Earl of Derby and Sir Walter Mauny. Philip sent the Duke of Bourbon, Count John of Hainault an and Sir Geoffrey de Chargny.

For three days the noblemen and cardinals went over all the same arguments as before. They got nowhere for the simple reason that both sides thought they could win more by fighting than by negotiation. The conference broke up on 1 August.

The next day Philip struck camp and marched away from Calais. Edward wasted little time in sending out his mounted knights and hobilars to harry the French, forcing them to abandon several cartloads of food and drink, as well as several dozen tents and pavilions. The scene was set for the final act of the Crecy Campaign. Realising that it was only a matter of time before starvation killed them all, the citizens of Calais demanded that Sir John de Vienne surrender, getting the best terms that he could. Vienne climbed to the walls and waved a flag to indicate that he wanted to talk.

Edward sent forward the Earl of Northampton, Sir Thomas Holland, Sir Reginald Cobham and Sir Walter Mauny to conduct surrender talks. Vienne's offer was simple:

> My lords, you are most noble knights and know that the King of France, whom we regard as our sovereign has sent us here to protect this town and fortress. We have done our best, but now our help has failed us. We must die of hunger if the noble king, your lord, does not take pity on us. Beg him, therefore, that in the name of Pity he may show mercy to us and allow us to go in peace so that he may have the town, the fortress and all the wealth we possess.

Edward's answer, shouted up to the walls by Sir Walter Mauny, was uncompromising:

Sir Jean, we know the mind of our sovereign. It is not his intention that you should go in peace. You must all submit yourselves entirely to his will, to be killed or ransomed as he chooses. It is not surprising that he should be so angry seeing that you have caused him so much trouble and cost him so many men and so much money.

By the conventions of war of the time, Edward was quite within his rights. Vienne knew this, but decided to try one last emotional plea before he gave in. 'It is too hard a thing for us to consent to what you request,' he shouted, 'We would rather endure greater torments than man has ever suffered than allow the smallest child in this town to suffer the same fate as the soldiers. Humbly beg the king, therefore, to receive us with mercy as prisoners, but to spare our lives.'

The four English knights rode back to Edward and passed on the message. Exactly what followed next it is not easy to tell. We have the official version that was put out by King Edward afterwards, but there is a suspicion that this is more in the way of political posturing than reality.

According to le Bel and Froissart, drawing on Edward's version of events. Edward rejected out of hand the pleas for mercy. He insisted that the defenders and citizens of Calais must come out unarmed and unconditionally. It was Sir Walter Mauny, the only non-Englishman present, who dared face up to the king's anger and tell him to his face that this was unrealistic. He pointed out that the soldiers had only been following orders, while the citizens had simply happened to be in the wrong place. The English knights then joined in and gradually won over Edward.

The king was still, however, determined to make his point. He now said that he would spare the lives of everyone in Calais, except for six men. These men should be chosen by the Calesians themselves. They must come out of the city before any others wearing nothing but their shirts and with a hangman's rope around their necks.

When this message was delivered back to Vienne, he in turn passed it on to the town council of Calais. There was a stunned silence, then shouts of protest and some weeping. After a while the richest man in Calais, Eustache de Saint-Pierre stood up. 'It would be a great shame,' he said, 'if we all die of hunger if anyone can prevent it. I have sure and certain faith in the Lord our God that he will forgive me my sins. I am therefore ready to be the first of the six and accept what King Edward will do.' Soon five others agreed to join Saint-Pierre and the terms of surrender were agreed.

On 3 August the gates of Calais swung open and out marched the six burghers, members of the council. As agreed they came barefoot, dressed only in their shirts and with ropes about their necks. They were met by the Earl of Northampton who led them to an open field where the English army was drawn up and Edward sat on a throne placed on a platform.

Saint-Pierre knelt in front of Edward and held out the keys to the town and castle of Calais. 'Noble king,' he said, 'We bring you the keys and yield them to your pleasure. We have done this in order that you see fit to spare the rest of the citizens who have suffered so much. Have pity upon us.'

Sir Walter Mauny stepped forward to ask Edward to spare the lives of the six citizens, Edward refused. He called over a member of his personal guard. 'Cut off their heads,' he ordered pointing at the Frenchmen. Northampton and Derby now added their voices to the pleas for mercy, but Edward was unmoved.

Then Queen Philippa stepped forward and knelt down in the mud beside Saint-Pierre. 'Noble lord,' she said to her husband, 'I beseech you on my knees for love of Our Lady's son to have mercy on these men.' Edward glared at her, and she burst into tears. Edward shifted uneasily in his seat. 'My lady, I wish that you had not been here, but you have made your request so tenderly that I have not the heart to refuse you. And though I do so unwillingly, nevertheless take these men. I give them to you.'

Philippa then led the six men away to a tent where they were presented with six suits of expensive clothes and six purses containing gold coins. The fact that such things were ready and waiting does not seem to have struck anybody as being at all unusual.

The mighty city of Calais was the only concrete gain that Edward got from the Crecy Campaign. Philip absolutely refused to make peace on any terms that Edward would have found remotely acceptable. The war dragged on. Indeed, interspersed by periods of peace, the conflict dragged on until 1451 – earning the protracted period of struggle its popular name of the Hundred Years War. Calais itself would remain English until 1553, giving England's monarchs a vital springboard for continental campaigns and securing control of the Straits of Dover. And yet the impact and effects of Crecy proved to be far more wide ranging and important than the fate of a town, however important.

Of most immediate importance in France was the horrific death toll among the nobility and knightly classes. Never before had so many important men been killed in so short a time. Quite apart from the emotional trauma that struck so many families, there were practical matters to sort out. For months the legal courts were paralysed sorting out the often complex details of inheritances and feudal dues that inevitably followed the death of a landholder.

These events were followed by a political crisis of the first order. Philip tried to shift the blame on to the Duke of Burgundy, who had been running many aspects of the government of France for the previous few years, and his three assistants. If the tax money had been raised properly, Philip argued, he would have had more time to muster and organise his army. So Burgundy was expelled from court and his assistants thrown into prison. In their place, Philip brought in three abbots of rich and powerful monasteries to run things. The churchmen overhauled state finances and administration. Having done their job, they were in turn dismissed by Philip who then turned to his son and heir, Duke John of Normandy.

All these changes in government failed to address, or even recognise, the real problems. First, Philip had been defeated and been forced to flee ignominiously into the night. Second, the knights and nobles had been defeated utterly and completely by a bunch of commoners armed with bows. The blow to the prestige of the king, and his family, led to decades of internal turmoil as regional nobles and councils refused to recognise central authority unless forced to do so. National fragmentation and mutual suspicion more than once led to civil war.

The loss of prestige by the knightly class was even more dramatic and long-lasting. Nearly every contemporary continental writer lays the chief blame for defeat at Crecy on the pride, ambition and stupidity of the knights. They were blamed for pushing forward instead of halting. They were blamed for attacking a strong defensive position. Above all they were blamed for losing. Considering that so many of these men had died fighting for their country this seems a bit harsh. It is undeniable, however, that warfare was changing and with it the ability of the knights to dominate the battlefield. If the knights could no longer win wars and

A Victorian engraving of Edward III shows him as a warrior king, an image he did much to foster during his lifetime.

so guarantee the safety and peace of the realm, their social and political status was brought into question.

The nobility responded at first by denying that they were to blame for anything. Later they realised that the importance of their old role was gone for good. Instead, they collectively moved to a new justification for their role as the social and political elite. It began to be said that the business of government and war were too important to be left to a bunch of amateurs. The city militias were downgraded in importance and the feudal levy of troops abandoned. Even those proud knights who had not enough money to afford armour were stripped of their position.

Instead, France moved towards a system in which the mass of the population, be they rural peasants or city merchants, were viewed as being the economic basis of the kingdom and of society. Their job was to provide the money and resources that could then be used by the professional rulers and administrators. These men were, naturally, the nobles and knightly classes. It was their task to run the government, to provide leadership in warfare and to hire such specialists – be they mercenaries or accountants – that were needed. As the men doing all the work of government, it naturally followed, the nobles should not pay taxes.

From the point of view of the nobles the new ideas and systems did make some sense. They would eventually allow France to mobilise her far superior reserves of wealth and manpower to defeat England and, in due course, to become one of the most powerful kingdoms in the world.

Time would show, however, that this system led inevitably to an increasingly rigid and stratified society. The nobles came to despise the farmers who produced food and the merchants who produced money. The lower classes were there to be taxed and to have good done to them for the benefit of the state. The nobles increasingly saw their own role as that of the enlightened superiors who knew better what was right for the kingdom, and indeed for the people within it, than did the people themselves.

The whole system came crashing down in the French Revolution of the 1780s, but the habits of thought have persisted. The wise and noble administrators who work in the corridors of power at the European Union believe that they know better than the common herd what is good and proper. And like the French nobles they do not pay the same taxes as do the humble folk whose labours support the whole edifice.

In England there was no such crisis of despair and defeat. Indeed, the most immediate effect was an upsurge of support for King Edward and his wars. The Parliament willingly approved new taxes to fund the siege of Calais and the long years of war that followed. Volunteers flocked to the banners of retinue leaders, eager to serve their most chivalrous king and to get a share of the plunder.

The most immediate effect of the Crecy campaign on England was to convince Edward and his knights that they actually could defeat the much larger, more prosperous and more powerful kingdom of France. What had begun as a routine dispute over feudal rights and duties very quickly became a national struggle to assert the dignity of their outraged king. With this goal in mind, and a belief in ultimate victory, the English carried on with the war with such determination and perseverance that it became the Hundred Years War.

Not needing to cope with the blow of catastrophic defeat, the English nobility and knightly classes were not faced with the need to find an urgent answer to the question of what their role in society should be, given the new technological face of war. That is not to say that they were not themselves confronted by the need to change, merely that they had more time to do it and could do so in a more benign atmosphere.

Even before Crecy the English knights and nobles had been moving in a different social direction than their French counterparts. They were rather more in the way of what we might call team leaders. In the years after Crecy the process accelerated. Gradually, the status of knight became divorced from its purely military role and more closely allied to social status. It was a status to which anybody might aspire, given the right conditions. Merchants and successful yeomen farmers could within a generation or two find their families sporting a coat of arms and even, given a bit more time, a title. It was a system that lacked the orderly logic of the French model and one that often suffered from confusion and inefficiency, but it was flexible enough to weather the storms of the economic, social and industrial upheavals that the centuries brought.

It is easy to overstate the importance of a single event. After all the changes in military hardware, tactics and strategy that took place in the fourteenth century were happening anyway. What the Battle of Crecy did was to force everyone to sit up and take notice. As so often it was a single event that brought into sharp focus the diffuse and complex changes in society. The Battle of Crecy changed everything.

Epilogue

King Edward III returned home from the siege of Calais as a national hero. The prestige he won at Crecy gave him the power to rule England and Aquitaine pretty much as he liked, while retaining the support and loyalty of his people. When the Black Death struck in 1349 he was able to get society and government back on track remarkably quickly. In 1360 he concluded the Treaty of Bretigny with France. This restored to him almost all his ancestral lands in France, though he was still denied the royal title that he claimed. As he grew older, however, Edward's firm grip on affairs of state began to slacken and his fourth son, John of Gaunt, became the effective head of government after about 1366. Increasingly, Edward gave himself over to social fun, often in the arms of his mistress Alice Perrers, whose ability to get her hands on royal funds became legendary. He died in 1377.

If anything, Edward the Black Prince was even more popular after Crecy than his father. As the dashing young hero of the hour, the prince had neither the responsibilities of his father nor the history of plot and intrigue that clung to the king. The Battle of Poitiers in 1356 cemented his reputation as the foremost military man of his generation, something his later victories in France and Spain only enhanced. In 1361 he married Joan, 'the Fair Maid of Kent', whom he had known since childhood. In 1362 he was created Prince of Aquitaine by his father and sent to govern that southern duchy. In 1368 he began to suffer from a mysterious disease that seems to have been some sort of progressive degeneration of the nervous system. In 1371 he gave up the rule of Aquitaine and the following year retired from public life altogether. He died in 1376, leaving his infant son Richard as heir to Edward III.

The Earl of Northampton, William de Bohun, returned to England to be put in charge of negotiating the ransom for King David of Scotland. He later saw further service in France where he again acquitted himself well. He died in 1360 at the age of fifty, leaving his titles and estates to his son Humphrey.

Thomas Beauchamp, Earl of Warwick, continued his impressive military career in the years that followed, retaining his position as Constable of England until his death in 1369. He fought at the Battle of Poitiers in 1356, contributing much to the English victory by pushing some of his archers forward into a supposedly impassable marsh to shoot into the French from their right flank. He was succeeded by his son, another Thomas.

Henry Grosmont, the Earl of Derby, who had become the Earl of Lancaster in 1345, became Lord High Steward and turned more to diplomatic and government roles. In 1354 he produced a remarkable religious and philosophical work entitled *Livre de Seyntz Medicines*. This book focussed on seven wounds that he claimed to have received during his military career, but which were in fact allegories of the seven deadly sins. He died in 1361 leaving two daughters as the heirs to his vast estates and immense wealth. One daughter married John of Gaunt, son of Edward III, bringing the Lancaster title into the royal family where it remains.

Godfrey de Harcourt realised during the siege of Calais that Edward was not going to restore him to his family titles and estates by becoming King of France and that neither would Philip be induced to do him any favours while he, Godfrey, remained in the English camp. In 1347 he returned to France to be reconciled with Philip, though he never regained his full estates from that suspicious monarch.

The one-eyed Sir Thomas Holland earned a fortune from the ransom he got for the Count d'Eu, captured at Caen. He continued with his active military career, mostly in Brittany. In due course he won his court case and married Joan, 'the Fair Maid of Kent', who later married the Black Prince. Through her he became Earl of Kent, a title that passed to his son, another Thomas, on his death in 1360.

Sir John Chandos, who was a junior knight in the English army at Crecy, later rose to senior rank and was one of the sources drawn on by Froissart. He fought at Poitiers in 1356 and later moved to Brittany where he was so successful that he effectively won the war for the pro-English Montfort faction. He was killed during a confused night skirmish in 1369, and was much mourned by knights and noblemen on both sides of the continuing Hundred Years War. Froissart wrote:

> I have heard him at the time regretted by renowned knights in France; for they said it was a great pity he was slain, and that, if he could have been taken prisoner, he was so wise and full of devices, he would have found some means of establishing a peace between France and England.

Sir Walter Mauny, sometimes called Baron Manny, abandoned his native Hainault after the Crecy Campaign and moved to England. He was given extensive estates by Edward III in return for his much-valued services as a diplomat and negotiator with various continental powers. He is now better known as the founder of the monastery in London that at the time of the Reformation became the Charterhouse, a charitable institution that still cares for the elderly and runs a school.

King Philip VI of France never recovered fully from his defeat at Crecy. His attempts to shift the blame for defeat on to others failed and his reputation was ruined. The local regions of France refused to approve new taxes, bringing the royal government to the brink of bankruptcy by 1349. He died in 1350, leaving his throne to his son John, Duke of Normandy.

John, Duke of Normandy, became King John II of France in 1350. Six years later he lost the Battle of Poitiers to the Black Prince and was captured on the field. In 1360 he was freed after agreeing to pay a massive ransom, one of the highest ever secured during the Middle Ages. When he proved unable to keep up the agreed scale of payments he voluntarily returned to England, where he died in 1364. he was followed on the throne of France by his son King Charles V.

Ottone Doria returned to Genoa after Crecy. He remained a leader of mercenaries and even returned to French employment a few years later. The date of his death is not recorded with any real certainty. The Doria family remained active in Genoese affairs for centuries, one branch moving to Brazil in the sixteenth century.

Carlo Grimaldi returned to Monaco after the Crecy Campaign. His family still rule as Princes of Monaco.

Charles, King of the Romans, became the Holy Roman Emperor Charles IV in 1355. He abandoned the pretensions of the Empire to be the political embodiment of Christendom and instead focussed on creating a modern and powerful state in central Europe. He spent lavishly on the arts and on his native Bohemia. He issued the famous Golden Bull which laid down in minute detail the ceremonies and procedures for electing a new Emperor – and which was to remain in force to the demise of the Empire in 1806. He died in 1378, and was followed as Emperor by his son Sigismund.

King James of Majorca returned home to Majorca to defend his much-reduced realm against King Pedro of Aragon. Pedro struck in 1349, killing James and driving his son into exile.

The Count d'Eu, the Constable of France captured at Caen, had trouble raising the ransom demanded for him. He came to some arrangement with King Edward, the precise details of which have not survived. Whatever deal he struck, it proved a bad one. On his return to France he was executed for treason.

Bibliography

Of the medieval writers mentioned in the text, the *Chronicles* of Jean Froissart are the most widely available to modern readers. They have been published in a number of editions and translations. These include a translation by Penguin Classics and another by the University of Michigan Library. Even six centuries on, the book is lively, exciting and thrilling.

The *Chronicle* of Jean le Bel is less widely available, though in 1966 the Folio Society of London produced a history of the Hundred Years War that reproduced lengthy sections of le Bel's work, including his complete account of the Crecy campaign. This book can sometimes be found in second-hand shops or on internet auction sites. A complete modern reprint of le Bel's works (so far available only in French) was published in 2001 by Elibron. The other contemporary letters and chronicles are rarely available outside specialist libraries and collections.

Of the modern works on the Hundred Years Wars, it would be unfair to pick out some that are better than others, for every reader has his or her own tastes and preferences. I will make an exception for the impressively exhaustive tome on medieval archery written by Robert Hardy and Matthew Strickland entitled *The Great Warbow* and published by Sutton Publishing. The various booklets published by Osprey are easily accessible to a casual reader and the books by W.M. Ormrod reveal much about the social and economic history of the reign of King Edward III. Spellmount, the publishers of this book, have produced a number of good books on other aspects of medieval warfare.

Index